The Politics of Sexual Harassment

Sexual harassment, in particular in the workplace, is a controversial topic which often makes headline news. What accounts for the cross-national variation in laws, employer policies, and implementation of policies dealing with sexual harassment in the workplace? Why was the United States at the forefront of policy and legal solutions, and how did this affect politicization of sexual harassment in the European Union and its member states? Exploring the way sexual harassment has become a global issue, Kathrin Zippel draws on theories of comparative feminist policy, gender and welfare state regimes, and social movements to explore the distinct paths that the United States, the European Union, and its member states, specifically Germany, have embarked on to address the issue. This comparison provides invaluable insights into the role of transnational movements against sexual harassment as well as into future efforts to implement the European Union Directive of 2002. It also illustrates what policy-makers and employers in the United States can learn from the European Union and its member states' alternative paths to gender equality.

KATHRIN S. ZIPPEL is Assistant Professor of Sociology at Northeastern University, Boston. She is also a Visiting Assistant Professor in the Committee on Degrees in Social Studies at Harvard University and an Affiliate at the Minda de Gunzburg, Center for European Studies at Harvard University.

The Politics of Sexual Harassment

A Comparative Study of the United States, the European Union, and Germany

Kathrin S. Zippel

CAMBRIDGE
UNIVERSITY PRESS

CAMBRIDGE UNIVERSITY PRESS
Cambridge, New York, Melbourne, Madrid, Cape Town, Singapore, São Paulo

Cambridge University Press
The Edinburgh Building, Cambridge CB2 2RU, UK

Published in the United States of America by Cambridge University Press,
New York

www.cambridge.org
Information on this title: www.cambridge.org/9780521609944

First published 2006

Printed in the United Kingdom at the University Press, Cambridge

A catalogue record for this book is available from the British Library

ISBN-13 978-0-521-84716-2 hardback
ISBN-10 0-521-84716-8 hardback
ISBN-13 978-0-521-60994-4 paperback
ISBN-10 0-521-60994-1 paperback

Contents

Tables

Preface

When I interviewed a German employee in the Human Resources department of a US – German corporation about workplace policies against sexual harassment, she said that her company did not have one: "Sexual harassment is a cultural problem in the United States, but we don't have that here . . . We are in Germany, and the Americans are in America." She expressed a belief shared by many in Germany and Europe: *Europeans do not have a problem with "sexual harassment" – it's an American problem.* Are Americans simply more puritanical and litigious than Europeans, who are more relaxed and sophisticated in sexual matters, as they would like to think? Have feminists gone too far in the United States, or are employers in Europe fifteen years behind?

The European perspective is surprisingly similar to the accounts found in some mainstream US news magazines, which have blamed feminists for exaggerating an insignificant problem and for bringing *political* and then *sexual correctness* to campuses and workplaces in the United States. Yet, no one today will dismiss the potential political significance of allegations of sexual harassment. In 1998, the Supreme Court called President Bill Clinton into court over allegations of sexual harassment made by a former public employee. Clinton explains in his autobiography that when he considered hunting down Osama Bin Laden, advisors suggested it could be interpreted as deflection from the Paula Jones lawsuit and the Monica Lewinsky affair (Clinton 2004: 799).

When we try to explain differences in European and American approaches to sexual harassment, it is tempting to look for individual and cultural explanations. Are US women just oversensitive to sexual harassment, while women in Europe do not mind sexual jokes or remarks about them, and instead enjoy physical contact or pornographic images in the workplace? Are East German women just more self-confident, more accustomed to working with men, and capable of telling a man off, so sexual harassment is not so great a problem for them? Although these are intriguing questions, this book is not about how individuals experience sexual harassment in different national contexts. Though I have heard and read hundreds of accounts of sexual harassment on both sides of the Atlantic, I did not compare individual victims' or perpetrators' stories. Rather, the book explores the *politics* of sexual harassment, focusing on the institutional responses of courts and state agencies to this problem through policy and legal measures. In addition, the book examines the politics of sexual harassment at the workplace level by looking at the introduction of employers' policies, as well as challenges to their practices, including sexual harassment prevention efforts. Specifically, I ask whether feminists can take credit or be blamed for the transformation in workplace cultures and employer practices that we have witnessed in the United States and are beginning to see in Europe.

I take a political sociological approach, asking how governments, state agencies, and employers have responded to sexual harassment by comparing the emergence and implementation of laws and policies. As a German who has spent significant time in the United States, Germany, Great Britain, Italy, and Greece, I am aware of striking differences between sexual cultures in the United States and Europe. But my study, which uses an institutional political approach, is about the processes by which activists, workers, employers, (civil rights) attorneys, state bureaucrats, and judges have redefined these workplace cultures and norms because of the heightened awareness of the problem of sexual harassment, by which I mean unwanted attention of a sexual nature or the involuntary eroticization of working relationships.

The politics of sexual harassment in the United States or Europe cannot be sufficiently explained by individuals' attitudes or national, cultural norms toward sexuality in the workplace which are not uniform. Instead, over time on both continents there have been changes in awareness along with contention around what constitutes sexual harassment. In the United States, definitions of sexual harassment remain controversial and are debated in the workplace and in courts. Hence, any assertion about an "American" culture also disregards diversity and change within the United States. Europeans will argue that there is no "homogeneous" European sexual culture; in fact, opponents of the European Union law used the cultural diversity argument for several years in an attempt to keep sexual harassment beyond the reach of the European Union.

Certainly, there are differences in national gender, sexual, and cultural norms about what is and is not appropriate in displaying nudity, pornography, and sexuality in the media and in public spaces in general. Cultural practices vary too – for example, how people greet each other with hugs, kisses, or handshakes. These cultural differences, however, do not explain different laws and policies against sexual harassment. Focusing on these differences in socio-sexual culture in fact obscures how much consensus there is about sexual harassment and how dramatic the changes in awareness about the problem have been. For example, Americans and Europeans agree that, in principle, supervisors should not be allowed to demand sexual favors from their subordinates. No one on either side of the Atlantic thinks coworkers or supervisors should feel free to physically approach anyone, for example, by grabbing a breast or buttock.

Less consensus exists about the idea of a "hostile work environment." What if a supervisor does not attach threats or offer favors to his sexual requests, but just keeps asking a subordinate for a date, telling her sexual jokes, and complimenting her hair, body, and clothes? What if the perpetrator is not someone in an organizational position of power? Are colleagues who make sexual jokes and remarks or distribute emails with pornographic jokes sexually harassing an individual woman even if she is not a "target"? These discussions focus, however, on "borderline" scenarios, without taking the context into account and frequently without considering the harm done to victims.

Surprisingly there is vast common ground in thinking about victims of sexual harassment. Europeans and Americans have shared the attitudes that victims are either innocent victims of men's sexual advances or (morally) loose women who "ask for it" by the way they dress or talk. There is also a modern, cross-culturally consistent version which sees women as hypersensitive, not cool enough to laugh about jokes and remarks, or not confident enough to "just say no" if a man makes a move. These strategies, which attempt to explain why an incident might be unfortunate but is not really sexual harassment, have been identified by feminists as "victim-blaming strategies."

Legal concepts of sexual harassment in both the European Union and the United States begin with the victims' perspective and focus on the harm caused by harassment rather than on the intentions of the perpetrators. They thus question common cultural assumptions that women always enjoy heterosexual "flirtation" or seduction. They draw attention to the fact that sexual harassment can be intimidating, hostile, degrading, humiliating, offensive, and, not incidentally, even discriminatory. These definitions allow for "cultural" standards to determine what constitutes, for example, an intimidating environment. They also allow for individual variation of perceptions; while some women might feel flattered if a man like Arnold Schwarzenegger puts his arms around them and grabs them, others will not. The perspective of victims might also depend on their job security. For example, in Eastern European countries, under state socialism unemployment officially did not exist because work was guaranteed as a citizen's right. East German women could feel more empowered to respond to jokes than US Latina workers who risk not being able to continue their job the next day if they do not comply with the sexual demands of their bosses. Depending on a woman's status in the workplace, sexual harassment might be perceived as more or less threatening. A woman's status can be different depending on her race/ethnicity, age, years of seniority, immigration status, protection under collective bargaining agreements, gender conformity, sexual identity, and, perhaps, how easily she could be replaced by a more compliant worker.

This study is about social movements that have challenged these cultures of everyday behavior and employer practices. Feminists have argued that sexual harassment is an expression of male abuse of power over women and have questioned workplace cultures where eroticism is a taken-for-granted part of the workplace. They have argued that these workplace cultures hierarchically construct jobs, gender, and (hetero) sexuality simultaneously without regard to the consent of those involved. Underlying the struggles over the power to define what does and does not constitute sexual harassment in the workplace are feminists' demands for equal recognition, sexual self-determination, and economic rights for women. Lawmakers have been deciding how exactly sexual harassment should be addressed: as a women's rights issue, an issue of violence and/or sexuality, an issue of workplace discrimination, or other workers' rights protections involving health and safety. The grounds upon which sexual harassment is considered to cause harm are important because, as sociologists of law have pointed out, laws and (employer) policies themselves shape the meanings, shared beliefs, and interpretations of a controversial subject such as sexual harassment.

This book tells the stories of those actors who have tried to politicize sexual harassment and to demand that employers, unions, courts, and legislatures should address the issue. These stories are linked in interesting ways, and tell us about how transnational movements have the potential to reshape politics in national contexts. Because all twenty-five European Union member states have to adopt or reform laws against sexual and gender harassment by October 2005, this book addresses questions facing feminists, policy-makers, and other advocates of sexual harassment policies. How can we use laws to achieve change? The European Union has also required its member states to adopt laws against harassment based on race, ethnicity, sexual orientation, disability, religion or belief, and age. Simultaneously, discussions about bullying, "mobbing," and moral harassment target a wide range of demeaning and abusive behaviors at work. By broadening harassment to all workers, independent of their gender, these countries have "mainstreamed" concerns about sexual harassment. Hence, an important question is the relationship between these constructions and sexual harassment.

This research also highlights the challenges facing the movement against sexual harassment in the United States. Professor Anita Hill's testimony did not hinder the Senate from confirming Clarence Thomas as a Supreme Court judge. However, the hearings did widen awareness of sexual harassment and did mobilize a broad movement. While the legal revolution has been celebrated as a feminist success story, there have been several indicators that the pendulum is swinging back in recent years. Those who enter workplaces in the United States today do not remember Anita Hill and most likely associate sexual harassment with Paula Jones's allegations against Clinton and the testimony by Monica Lewinsky. Political backlash delegitimizes victims of sexual harassment and discredits allegations against high-profile public officials; Arnold Schwarzenegger was elected governor of California in 2003 despite the allegations of sixteen women. Complaints to the Equal Employment Opportunity Commission have dropped since 1998. Legal scholars agree that the 1998 Supreme Court decisions have made it more difficult for victims to win sexual harassment cases in the court because they are now obliged to use internal workplace procedures first. Though the Supreme Court expanded the scope of employer liability for sexual harassment by supervisors in *Faragher v. City of Boca Raton* and *Burlington Industries Inc. v. Ellerth*, the court ruled that employers can limit their liability with antisexual harassment policies. In this situation, the European policy approaches – to define sexual harassment as a violation of dignity, as well as to combine sexual and gender harassment with "mobbing," moral harassment, and bullying of all workers – can prompt US advocates to reexamine their approaches.

If I had photographed this research process, I would have an album many times thicker than this book with the pictures of the many people who were willing to be interviewed, who shared their stories with me, who confronted me, who engaged me in discussions about this complex issue, and who helped me conduct this research and write this book. I am in debt to these many women and some men who have dedicated themselves to standing up against, resisting, and challenging various abuses of power.

The album would also be filled with the many places that I worked on the book. My friends and family made my travels in Europe possible and enjoyable. I wish especially to thank Bärbel Zippel, Sonja, Katharina, Moritz, and Hans-Jörg Seidenspinner, Jeanette Oellers and Manfred

Zippel, and Dagmar Jung. In addition, Dr. Barbara Degen opened her house to a stranger, let me sleep on her couch, and graciously let me use her personal archive in Bonn, for which I am deeply grateful. This project has moved me – along with boxes upon boxes of material – several times across the Atlantic. In fact, the issue of sexual harassment insinuated itself in the very application process that first brought me to the United States. In an interview for a study-abroad fellowship, a committee asked me about the phenomenon of political and sexual correctness in the aftermath of the Senate hearings of Anita Hill and Clarence Thomas. Their interest was likely not purely academic; one of the members of the committee was himself a sexual harasser. Upon my arrival in the United States in the fall of 1992, I was surprised to find a high level of mobilization around sexual harassment among feminists in US universities; they were already pushing for revisions of existing policies, while German university campuses seemed to lack awareness of the issue entirely. Because of the complexity of the issue it has not ceased to interest me.

I want to thank the Scholarship Development Fund of the Provost of Northeastern University, which provided generous support for my finishing this project by offering faculty release time and funding for editorial and research assistance. In addition, I want to thank Professor Panos Kazakos at the University of Athens in the newly founded European Integration and Politics project, where I was a visiting fellow in 2003. The DAAD fellowship at the American Institute for Contemporary German Studies in Washington D.C. generously provided me summer funding in 2001. The post-doctoral fellowship at the European Union Center of New York at Columbia University allowed me to learn and teach about the European Union, while a dissertation student fellowship from the European Union Center at the University of Wisconsin-Madison supported the very early phases of this research project. Finally, the exchange program fellowship of the University of Wisconsin-Madison and the European University Institute provided me with the necessary European-wide exchange of ideas in Florence, Italy.

I am in debt to my many mentors, colleagues, students, and friends who have seen this book through various stages and have relentlessly helped me to improve it. They include Dirk Ahlgrim, Amber Ault, Susanne Baer, Mark Bell, Chris Bobel, Phyllis Brashler, Lisa Brush, Mia Cahill, Patricia Craig, Myra Marx Ferree, Laura Frader, Phillip Gorski, Katja Guenther, Kieran Healy, Adrienne Heritier, Deborah Kaufman, Maureen Kelleher, Tom Koenig, Greta Krippner, Sandy Levitsky, Patricia Y. Martin, Marianne McPherson, Mark Pollack, Pamela Oliver, Ann Orloff, Ilona Ostner, Susan Ostrander, Rachel Power,

Gordana Rabrenovic, Silke Roth, Abigail Saguy, Virginia Sapiro, Brian Steensland, Maria Stratigaki, Verta Taylor, Polymeris Voglis, Erik Wright, and Jonathan Zeitlin. I want to extend special thanks to Kimberly Morgan, who has read many versions of this manuscript and provided me with critical and crucial feedback. I also am eternally grateful for the careful editorial help of Alison Anderson, Vivienne Church, Michael Kaufman, and Deborah Howell-Ardila. Many thanks to Dirk Ahlgrim, designer and photographer, for his unfailing support, humor, and for the exceptional book cover that he both envisioned and created.

Thanks also to two anonymous reviewers for their timely and very insightful, constructive criticism. Sarah Caro at Cambridge University Press was the best editor a first-time author could ever hope for.

I dedicate this book to my mother, Bärbel Zippel, for her continuous support of all my endeavors.

Abbreviations

9 to 5	National Association of Working Women
AASC	Alliance Against Sexual Coercion
ACLU	American Civil Liberties Union
AFL-CIO	American Federation of Labor and Congress of Industrial Organizations
AFSCME	American Federation of State, County, and Municipal Employees
ArbG	Arbeitsgericht (Labor Court)
ASF	Arbeitsgemeinschaft Sozialdemokratischer Frauen (Association of Social Democratic Women)
AVFT	Association Européenne Contre les Violences Faites aux Femmes au Travail (European Organization against Violence against Women at Work), Paris
AZO	Arbeitszeitordnung (Regulation of Hours of Work)
BAG	Bundesarbeitsgericht (Highest Federal Labor Court)
BBG	Bundesbeamtengesetz (Federal Law for Civil Servants)
BDA	Bundesvereinigung der Deutschen Arbeitgeberverbände (Federal German Employers' Association)
BetrVG	Betriebsverfassungsgesetz (Works Council Constitution Act)
BGB	Bürgerliches Gesetzbuch (Civil Code)
BpersVG	Bundespersonalvertretungsgesetz (Federal Law on Employees' Representation)
BT-Ds	Bundestags-Drucksache (Document of the Federal Parliament)
BverfG	Bundesverfassungsgericht (Constitutional Court)
BverwG	Bundesverwaltungsgericht (Highest Court of Administration)
CDU	Christlich Demokratische Union (Christian Democratic Union)

CEEP	European Centre for Enterprise with Public Participation
CLUW	Coalition of Labor Union Women
CSU	Christliche Soziale Union (Christian Social Union)
DAG	Deutsche Angestellten-Gewerkschaft (Union of German Employees)
DBB	Deutscher Beamtenbund (German Association of Civil Servants)
DFR	Deutscher Frauenring (German Ring of Women's Organizations)
DG	Directorate General
DGB	Deutscher Gewerkschaftsbund (German Confederation of Trade Unions)
EC	European Community
ECJ	European Court of Justice
EEC	European Economic Community
EEOC	Equal Employment Opportunity Commission
EP	European Parliament
ERA	Equal Rights Amendment
ETUC	European Trade Union Confederation
EU	European Union
EWL	European Women's Lobby
FDP	Freie Demokratische Partei (Free Democratic Party)
FR	Frankfurter Rundschau
GewO	Gewerbeordnung (Regulations for Commerce)
GleiBG	Gleichberechtigungsgesetz (Equality Law)
IG Metall	Industrie Gewerkschaft Metall (Union of Automobile Workers and Machinists)
ILO	International Labor Organization
JarbSchG	Jugendarbeitsschutzgesetz (Law on the Labor Protection of Youth)
KSchG	Kündigungsschutzgesetz (Law on the Protection against Dismissals)
LAG	Landesarbeitsgericht (Higher Labor Court)
MdB	Mitglied des Bundestags (Member of the Bundestag)
NLRB	National Labor Relations Board
NOW-LDF	National Organization for Women's Educational and Legal Defense Fund
NOW	National Organization for Women
NWLC	National Women's Law Center
OECD	Organization for Economic Co-operation and Development

ÖTV	Gewerkschaft Öffentliche Dienste, Transport und Verkehr (Union for Public Services, Transportation and Traffic)
OJ	Official Journal of the European Communities
PPE	Peoples Party of Europe
RNGS	Research Network on Gender Politics and the State
SPD	Sozialdemokratische Partei Deutschlands (Social Democratic Party of Germany)
StGB	Strafgesetzbuch (Penal Code)
TAN	transnational advocacy network
TEU	Treaty of European Union (Maastricht Treaty)
UAW	United Auto Workers
UNICE	Union of Industrial and Employers' Confederation of Europe
U.S.M.S.P.B.	US Merit Systems Protection Board
VAWA	Violence Against Women Act
VG	Verwaltungsgericht (Administrative Court)
WLDF	Women's Legal Defense Fund
WOW	Women Office Workers
WWU	Working Women United

1 Sexual harassment and gender equality

Sexual harassment serves as a vivid example of heated struggles over sexuality, power, and gender equality on both sides of the Atlantic because it fuses the issues of violence against women, sexuality, and workplace equality. Several notable, high-profile cases in the United States raised public awareness of the problem of unwanted sexual attention in workplaces and brought the term "sexual harassment" into living rooms throughout the world during the 1990s.

Although Europeans were often skeptical about the relevance of the issue to their lives, surveys report that about the same percentage of women in the European Union[1] (EU) member states and in the United States have experienced sexual harassment at work. There have been several notorious scandals involving European men accused of harassment. The British Crown has been in the news twice regarding allegations of sexual harassment among the staff. Most recently, Elaine Day, forty-five years old, a former personal assistant who worked for Prince Charles's household for four years, resigned and filed a sexual harassment and unfair dismissal suit, testifying that her dismissal was a retaliation for her complaint of "inappropriate touching" by the Prince's assistant private secretary Paul Kefford. She said that she felt threatened by Kefford and that he had sexually harassed two other staff members (al Yafai 2004).

An American woman who had worked for many years on the staff of the United Nations High Commission for Refugees filed a sexual harassment complaint against the High Commissioner, Ruud Lubbers, in 2004, alleging that he groped her after a meeting in his office. Lubbers, who was Dutch Prime Minister between 1982 and 1994, argued that

---

[1] The EU is the supranational organization of twenty-five member states in Europe. I use European Community (EC) for policies and institutions prior to the Maastricht Treaty, the Treaty on the European Union, which went into effect in 1993. This study covers the events leading to the adoption of the 2002 European Directive defining sexual harassment; the ten nations that joined in spring 2004 are not considered.

the woman had misconstrued a "friendly gesture." UN Secretary General Kofi Annan publicly dismissed the complaint, announcing that it was unsustainable in court, despite the fact that an internal investigation recommended that "appropriate action" be taken (*BBC* 18 May 2004). One year later, in the context of the UN being under fire for corruption and sexual abuse by peacekeepers, this confidential UN report was leaked to the press and Lubbers resigned (*BBC* 20 February 2005).[2]

Sexual harassment has also been a problem in Germany. In 1983, a group of women staffers accused a male parliamentarian, Klaus Hecker, of the newly founded West German Green party, of groping their breasts. East German politician Heinz Eggert resigned as Saxony's Minister for Internal Affairs in the aftermath of harassment accusations by male staff members in 1995. Complaints by women students brought male professors of the University of Stuttgart in Hohenheim, Fulda, Berlin, Hannover, and Konstanz to court. Nonetheless, under current German laws, the women did not receive compensation, and the sanctions imposed on the men ranged from excusing them from their teaching obligations, to encouraging early retirement, to reducing their salary by 10 percent for one year. Punitive damages do not exist in German law. In the late 1990s, three young policewomen could no longer endure the sexual harassment and other hostilities they encountered as women in the police force and committed suicide. Their supervisors, the media, and judges, however, called their experiences not discrimination but "mobbing," which is a gender-neutral term for systematic workplace hostility of a long duration, in Germany described as "psychoterror at work."

The weak laws against sexual harassment in the European Union mean that women who file complaints risk becoming the accused themselves. In France, for example, several victims of sexual harassment who sought justice in court not only lost their cases but found themselves facing defamation libel suits from the men they accused. In these defamation cases, judges imposed severe penalties, including fines of €15,000 and several months of probationary prison terms (AVFT 2004).

---

[2] The UN is not the only organization that has promoted laws against sexual harassment while having to deal with issues of sexual harassment within its own organizations. The UN has specifically addressed sexual harassment, first in the document "Nairobi: Forward Looking Strategies for the Advancement of Women," which was adopted at the Third World Conference on Women held in Nairobi, Kenya, in July 1985, diffusing the concept of sexual harassment worldwide.

Yet, the increasing visibility of women in the workplace and the public's heightened sensitivity to violence against women have brought nation-states and supranational organizations to struggle over definitions of sexual harassment and the construction of regulations for everyday workplace interactions. This book explores the approaches to sexual harassment that have emerged in the United States and the EU, as well as in one EU member state, the Federal Republic of Germany.[3] These countries have varied in timing, policies, implementation, and enforcement. The United States has been a forerunner in this policy area. Since the mid-1980s, US courts and state agencies have addressed the issue within the framework of equal opportunities for women. Case law developments, enforcement and implementation mechanisms have created an environment in which many employers have adopted workplace policies against sexual harassment, following the advice of consultants in order to minimize the risk of expensive lawsuits.

In Europe, sexual harassment is often defined differently. The EU defines sexual harassment as a violation of the dignity of workers; unions and employers have addressed it in the context of conflicts among workers and abuses of power in general. Most EU member states have done little to combat sexual harassment in the workplace. Despite some legal reforms in the early 1990s, implementation and enforcement mechanisms so far have been less effective than in the United States. Employers ignore the problem, prevention efforts are rare, and victims' legal redress is weak.

This study compares the politics of sexual harassment at two levels: first, by examining how legal and governmental institutions respond to women's concerns, and then, how implementation and enforcement challenge politics at the workplace level. The United States has been at the forefront of sexual harassment policy development because of its common law legal system and civil rights legislation. The second-wave women's movement politicized sexual harassment with the goal of creating women-friendly workplaces and promoting gender equality. The courts have been exceptionally hospitable to holding employers responsible in the name of protecting women's equal opportunities at work. Nonetheless, feminist[4] notions have been able to enter the

---

[3] "Germany" refers to the Federal Republic of Germany after unification in 1990. Prior to 1990, East Germany did not have specific policy measures against sexual harassment.

[4] "Feminism" is a highly debated, politically charged concept, especially in cross-cultural studies. Feminist comparative researchers have identified several core ideas of feminism across Western post-industrialized democracies (Mazur 2002: 3). By feminist interpretation of sexual harassment, this book refers to views that locate the causes of sexual harassment in gender inequality and an abuse of power.

development of case law through attorney arguments, expert witnesses, and amicus briefs. As a result, US law defines sexual harassment as sex discrimination, from a victim-centered, subjective perspective.

Through the transatlantic diffusion of policy ideas, the EU translated the US model into a "European version" that defines sexual harassment as the violation of a worker's dignity. Since the early 1990s, it has slowly increased pressure on member states to take the issue more seriously. The transnational diffusion of ideas by the women's and labor movements and the increasing influence of the EU itself resulted in similar timing among member states.

While diffusion helps explain why European countries increasingly take sexual harassment seriously, it does not sufficiently explain how ideas actually get translated into policies and employer responses.[5] The United States, the EU, and its member states have embarked on different institutional routes or paths to change laws and change workplace policies and practices. Sexual harassment law was created in the United States following a path characterized as the "legal–regulatory route," by which courts expanded preexisting anti-discrimination laws. By contrast, in 1994 German legislators passed a new labor law, the Federal Employee Protection law, defining sexual harassment as violation of dignity.[6] In this "statutory–corporatist route," workers' rights, not issues of minorities, served as the analogy. The EU path was a "bureaucratic, expert-driven" route, in which administrative elites and elected officials decided policies. These distinct paths both facilitated and constrained feminists and other gender-minded actors in their drive to combat sexual harassment.

These paths also had an effect on the implementation of laws and their enforcement. The US legal–regulatory route prefers legal enforcement mechanisms over state regulation: harassed individuals are expected to file complaints to hold employers responsible. The German statutory–corporatist path gives flexibility to workplace organizations to devise policies, assuming that employers and unions can handle their own issues, preferably by collective agreements among employers and unions. Feminist concepts are easy to ignore in this process, since organized women's interests have no formal place in negotiations. The EU has promoted a combined approach, asking member states to strengthen

---

[5] Ulrike Liebert (2003) argues, for example, that member states' perception of the EU also influenced the ways they translated EU gender equality laws into national laws.

[6] Before the 1994 German Federal law, several German *Länder* (states) had already passed laws for the public sector through the same statutory route; however, they were largely ignored (see Chapter 4).

individual legal rights and relying on corporatism to implement sexual harassment laws.

These routes have advantages and disadvantages for changing employer practices and gender culture in the workplace. In the United States there is a *politics of fear* centered on sexual harassment; employers and male employees are told to be afraid of women's lawsuits. In Germany there exists a *politics as usual* that allows employers to ignore both sexual harassment and the law that requires them to protect women from it. However, neither approach accomplishes feminists' ultimate objective of gender equality in the workplace.

The Politics of Sexual Harassment is the story of the diffusion across two continents of a feminist concept, named by a grassroots movement, developed by legal scholars in the United States in the mid-1970s, and implemented in workplace organizations on two continents. The book looks at gender politics in the context of a globalization that has facilitated the transnational exchange of ideas and politicized concepts, expert knowledge, and policy and legal models among social movement actors and policy-makers. Drawing on theories of comparative feminist policy, gender and welfare regimes, and social movements, it examines how feminist actors have shaped these processes at the national and supranational levels, and in the workplace. Through transnational networks among unions, academics, the media, and policy-makers, the concept of sexual harassment traveled from the United States to the EU and its member states. The resulting nationally specific politics – legal reforms and workplace changes – have been profoundly shaped by the different routes.

To explain the history of sexual harassment policies it is important to look at the complex relationship between social movements and institutions. This relationship has been of critical interest in current comparative studies of public policies and social movements. To study the emergence and implementation of sexual harassment laws is to draw on (feminist) theories of political institutions and social movements.

We know surprisingly little about the origins of policy measures against sexual harassment. Despite the public attention it has garnered and the struggles of workplaces to handle it, there has been little sociological and political science research on sexual harassment. A vast literature on sexual harassment exists in social psychology, education, human resources management, and legal research in the United States, but there is astonishingly little comparative work on its cross-national politicization. Scholars of feminist political science and political sociology rarely consider sexual harassment when examining gender relations and the state. Only a handful of studies have investigated government responses and legal developments in the United States and EU member states. Most comparative studies have focused on legal reforms, implicitly using the United States as a model from which the EU member states deviate.[7]

The politics of sexual harassment in the United States, EU, and Germany offers intriguing insights into feminist politics and the role of states and international institutions in shaping gender relations. Sexual harassment policies are a prime example of how state policies reach into the everyday worlds of millions of workers. The issue is fascinating because it connects problems of violence against women and sexuality with gender inequality at work. These issues have been handled by very different sets of actors and institutional arrangements depending on whether sexual harassment is considered a health and safety issue or women's right to sexual self-determination. This distinction allows us to look at how gender ideologies – specifically notions of gender equality and sexuality – intersect with political and legal traditions to shape understandings of sexual harassment and emerging policies.

By systematically considering transnational as well as national contexts, this study also improves current conceptualizations of gender politics in feminist scholarship and policy studies.[8] In particular, because the EU has been a major force in putting sexual harassment on the agenda of its member states, sexual harassment policies are an excellent case through which to examine emerging gender politics in the EU. This comparison provides useful insights into how state, legal, and employer policy approaches and practices might indeed promote or hinder gender equality. These insights are important for European policy-makers, lawyers, and human resource professionals in their efforts to implement the 2002 EU policy directive in the member states, and for US policy-makers and employers in their assessments of alternative paths to gender equality. The study of the politics of sexual harassment thus contributes to scholarship on public policy, comparative public policy, institutions, and social movements.

Sexual harassment also provides a compelling area for investigating broader questions about the origins, adoption, and implementation of

---

[7] Most studies compare the United States to EU member states (Bernstein 1994), including Sweden (Elman 1996, 2000), Austria (Cahill 2001), and France (Saguy 2003). Only two studies compare two EU member states – Spain and the Netherlands (Roggeband and Verloo 1999) and Spain and France (Mazur 2002). In the few studies that examine specific countries, Spain (Valiente 1998) and France (Mazur 1994, 1996, 2002) have attracted most attention. Two German studies compare the United States to Germany (Baer 1995; Kuhlmann 1996).

[8] See Jackie Smith (2004) and Sidney Tarrow (2005) for a useful discussion of transnational movements.

policies ostensibly designed to create more gender equality in the work-place. Exploring cross-national variation in the new field of gender-specific policy, this book addresses two main questions: What explains differences in approaches to sexual harassment in terms of the timing and nature of the laws? What are the consequences for actual imple-mentation of these policies in the workplace? One aim is to compare policy formation in different national and supranational contexts in order to identify the critical factors that explain its origins. The second aim is to identify criteria for how policy approaches vary in the work-place. These criteria help us to evaluate how states, legislators, courts, and employers deal with this controversial issue.

This introductory chapter first discusses the significance of the politics of sexual harassment as a contemporary site of struggle over gender and organizational norms, sexuality, power, and gender equality, as well as the historical emergence of sexual harassment as a social problem. It further outlines the empirical puzzle of cross-national differences in approaches to sexual harassment. Drawing on the gender and welfare state literature and theories of feminist policy and social movements, it develops a comparative framework, focused on feminist involvement in policy formation, to examine the evolution of sexual harassment policies. The main actors and stakeholders in the politics of sexual harassment are identified, along with the institutional, political, legal, and cultural factors that shape the creation of national laws and regulations. Finally, comparative criteria to map out the cross-national variations in policy approaches to sexual harassment are proposed.

Why compare sexual harassment politics?

The politics of sexual harassment is the outcome of social and political processes in which ideologies of gender equality and sexuality are nego-tiated. Comparing the evolution of sexual harassment policy in the United States, the EU, and Germany identifies qualitative differences between policies and policy-making processes in historical, social, in-stitutional, and cultural contexts (Ragin 1994; Steinmetz 2004). These cases are not "independent"; the United States has influenced develop-ments in Europe and the EU has been a catalyst for policy in member states. Therefore, it is instructive to understand how the United States has affected the politicization of sexual harassment in the EU.

Germany and the United States are both advanced industrialized countries with democratic political systems and federal structures, but their political, institutional, and legal structures differ significantly. Specifically, their systems of workplace regulation, their women's movements and gender politics have markedly different histories (Buechler 1990; Ferree 1987, 1995b; Ferree and Roth 1998; Mushaben 2001, 1989; Moeller 1993; von Wahl 1999). Comparing the paths the two countries and the EU took to deal with sexual harassment allows us to examine the role women's movements played in the emergence of policies and to identify the complexity and conjunctural character of factors that produce policy trajectories and outcomes. Theda Skocpol (1984) calls this comparative strategy "highlighting difference," similar to Charles Tilly's (1984) notion of "individualizing" comparisons.

Sexual harassment is a particularly interesting policy field for several reasons. We can trace its evolution from a "radical"[9] feminist concern in a grassroots movement, to its formal acknowledgment as a "social problem," to its diffusion across the Atlantic and its translation into laws and practices in different cultural, legal, and political contexts. How this issue has been handled provides clues about the status of women in the workforce and their ability to effect legal and political change. The contentious debates over laws and policies are the locus of broader challenges and changes in gender and sexual norms – women's equality and socio-sexual workplace relations. Not surprisingly, the debates triggered by high-profile cases have taken place in politics, courts, the military, church, unions, workplaces, and educational institutions.

Some critics view sexual harassment laws as the quintessence of what is wrong with feminism. Mainstream media have contributed to this by blaming feminists for what they call *sexual correctness* (Zippel 1996). The plight of victims is seen as less newsworthy and exciting than that of men who become the victim of "false" accusations by vengeful women. Based on American media, Europeans have portrayed the issue as a "war of the sexes," and depicted feminists as moralist, anti-sex crusaders (*SittenwächterInnen* and *TugendblockwärtInnen*) seeking to sanitize the workplace from cherished flirtation and eroticism by reintroducing Victorian standards (Möller 1999; Saguy 2003; Baer 1996; Hauserman 1999). The German media, in particular, found more problems with American sexual correctness than with sexual harassment per se.

European media have been highly critical of what they perceive as the American preoccupation with sexuality, or "American excesses" in the 1990s. Reports of million-dollar punitive damage settlements fuel this perception. Skeptical European feminists, employers, and lawmakers have been reluctant to prohibit flirtation or consensual relations in the

---

[9] Radical feminists focused on violence and sexual exploitation as a primary source of women's oppression in patriarchal societies (Lorber 2001: 78).

workplace. Employers in the United States have justified these policies as prohibitions against the so-called "sexual favoritism," outlined in Equal Employment Opportunity Commission (EEOC) guidelines. Neither German nor EU sexual harassment laws include this notion. Instead, German advocates have insisted that neither the state nor employers should limit women's freedom to engage in voluntary intimate relationships at work. Spanish and French policy-makers have explicitly rejected broad US notions, and asserted that Mediterranean cultural values include flirtation and seduction as normal interactions between women and men in the workplace (Valiente 1998; Saguy 2003, Jenson and Sineau 1995).

Drawing on Europe's tradition of workers' rights and international human rights documents, EU member states are creating an alternative "European way" to address sexual and nonsexual forms of harassment in the broader context of "violations against workers' dignity."[10] Campaigns for fairness in the workplace and against violations of dignity of all workers tend to emphasize the *exclusionary* aspects of harassing practices, such as bullying, mobbing, and moral harassment. For example, when male coworkers in the police and other male-dominated occupations use sexual or nonsexual harassment to create an exclusionary, hostile environment for women, the problem is regarded as one not of *inappropriate sexual conduct* but of *exclusionary* practices against an individual.

Mobbing, a concept introduced by a Swedish doctor, Heinz Leymann, is known in Germany as "psychoterror at work," describing a conflict-laden communication among colleagues or between superiors and employees. It is a process by which one or more persons systematically, over a long period, attack someone directly or indirectly with the goal of marginalizing and getting rid of him or her (Holzbecher and Meschkutat 1999; Meschkutat, Stackelbeck and Langenhoff 2002). Similarly, Marie-France Hirigoyen, a French psychiatrist, coined the term "moral harassment" to capture emotional abuse including insults against individuals at work.

Neither notion locates the root in (gender) inequality, instead the focus is on the harm done. Hence, these European concepts apply to any worker. By contrast, US employees' rights to "privacy" in the workplace

---

[10] Several countries have already introduced laws. Sweden was the first EU country to have an Ordinance on Victimization at Work in 1993. Belgium and France passed laws against "moral harassment" in 2002. German, Spanish, and United Kingdom labor courts have increasingly recognized bullying, mobbing, and harassment (Bernstein 1994; Friedman and Whitman 2003).

are very weak, and anti-harassment law applies only to groups protected by civil rights legislation, such as women and racial and ethnic minorities. Does preventing exclusionary practices as "violations of the dignity of workers" jeopardize the feminist vision of a gender-specific concept of sexual harassment as some feminists have worried (Baer 1995, 1996, 2004; Carter 1992; DeSacco 1996; Ehrenreich 1999; Samuels 2003)? Or can the United States learn from EU member states to create inclusionary workplaces safeguarding the human dignity of all workers?

To follow the diffusion of the phenomenon of "sexual harassment" across different countries provides the opportunity to trace the influence of transnational social movements and international organizations. For instance, once feminists in the United States had named the concept, women in Europe did not have to reinvent it. Surprisingly, European women had their first success in passing measures against sexual harassment not in their home countries but in the EU (Collins 1996; Gregory 1995). With the EU measures in hand to legitimate their demands, feminist activists, women in trade unions, and state administrators brought the issue to national agendas. In this process, member states translated the concept of harassment into their own languages using nationally specific concepts.

Sexual harassment offers a unique opportunity to compare the relationship among social movements, states, and supranational organizations. Most studies of political issues focus exclusively on policy-making, or on mobilization of protest outside institutions; this study brings these together by examining the role feminists, both within and outside institutions, played in changing and adopting laws (Katzenstein 1998). The issue of sexual harassment in the EU arose simultaneously with the creation of (gender) equality offices and networks among various gender-minded actors, who became a driving force to create this new policy issue. Furthermore, the equality offices were part of a transnational network through which they could draw on important resources. Thus, the comparative study of sexual harassment provides an interesting means to study the relationship between insiders and outsiders in policy and legal change, and how gender equality bodies use transnational resources.

Because sexual harassment challenges gender workplace culture, it raises important questions about the role of the state and the law in cultural change. Should laws follow and reflect changes in public awareness of social problems, or are laws suitable tools to create and change awareness? The statutory path required a slower process of consensus building among political elites than the US legal–regulatory path where judges decided that civil rights law would be applicable to sexual harassment. But EU member states were reluctant to pass laws against sexual harassment, partly because feminists, unions, employers, and parties on the left and right have, for different reasons, been highly critical of the use of laws and courts to handle the issue. They have shared the belief that cultural change is the appropriate solution. Using law to regulate and constrain everyday behavior has also been contested in the United States. Some US feminists feared co-optation of their goals, and hence were critical of laws and bureaucratic procedures (Baker 2001).

As a workplace issue, sexual harassment provides a fascinating look at women's power to challenge gender inequalities. Beyond symbolic laws and "toothless paper tigers," effective implementation and enforcement are crucial here, as in other areas of anti-discrimination legislation (Cockburn 1991). What role can feminist actors play in shaping policies and gender culture in the workplace? Legal systems and workplace regulation not only construct roles for state agencies but also shape the ways collective actors, in particular women's organizations and unions, can initiate policy changes and participate in their implementation. The routes countries embark on to address workplace sexual harassment reflect these institutional arrangements that shape gender relations with important implications for the empowerment of women.

The emergence of sexual harassment as a social problem

The term "sexual harassment" is relatively new, originating only in the 1970s, but the experience has been an intrinsic part of women's experiences in the workplace at least since the beginning of industrialization at the turn of the twentieth century (Degen 1991; Segrave 1994). In Europe and the United States, employers, unions, and officials occasionally became concerned with socio-sexual workplace relations. The fact that domestic workers were frequently sexually exploited by their employers was well known, but it was considered less an injustice to women than a moral question, and women were blamed when they became pregnant (Segrave 1994: 23). For German trade unions these incidents became a vehicle to criticize the general exploitive nature of workplace relations, using the image of employers demanding sexual favors from innocent young women (Schmitt 1995; Degen 1991).

Women's entry into male-dominated work environments resulted in gender conflict. In 1891 Germany passed a law to hold employers responsible for upholding morals and appropriate behavior, the Gewerbeordnung zum Schutz von Sitte und Anstand (trading regulation on the protection of morals and propriety).[11] Yet German factory inspectors' reports in the early twentieth century pointed to widespread "*unsittliche Vorkommnisse* (immoral incidents) perpetrated by masters or male colleagues in the district's mills" (Canning 1996: 309).

After World War II, East German women recruited en masse into factory jobs frequently encountered sexual teasing and hostility on the shop floor. Donna Harsch documents incidents in East German factories: "Classic harassment, such as ridicule, lewd remarks, and sexual advances, was also rampant. Undeterred by any of this, one tough, self-confident woman did well in a series of male-dominated occupations. She conceded, 'it's open season on women in a men's factory'" (Harsch forthcoming: 51). The system of labor relations under socialism presumably meant that these women did not fear dismissal. Nonetheless, supervisors and party officials were in a position to offer better working conditions if women complied with their sexual demands or threaten retaliation if they would not.

Women's resistance to sexual harassment is not a new phenomenon (Bacchi and Jose 1994). Sexual exploitation in the workplace led to strikes by both female and male workers in the early twentieth century (Segrave 1994; Baker 2001; Degen 1991). After World War II, in both the United States and West Germany, individual women complained to their employers or to shop stewards and a few tried to take employers to court, sometimes with the help of their parents or husbands. But in practice women had little redress. Many were reluctant to talk or file complaints out of embarrassment or shame. Employers and shop stewards often did not take reports seriously, and women encountered ridicule, disbelief, or denial if they attempted to expose the unwanted behavior. Finally, sexual harassment frequently held worse consequences for the women than for the men who harassed them, since the women were transferred or dismissed (MacKinnon 1979; Holzbecher et al. 1990).

Challenging sexual harassment and employer practices through legal means was taxing because laws did not explicitly prohibit sexual harassment in the workplace and applying employment, labor, penal, and civil laws proved difficult.[12] Women bringing cases under employment laws on sex discrimination, contract law, or worker or unemployment

---

[11] Article 2 of §120b of the Gewerbeordnung Novellierung 1891.

[12] According to Holzbecher et al. (1990), there were altogether forty-three German laws regulating the rights of the person confronted with sexual harassment, prohibiting a harasser from continuing the job, rights of works councils, civil servants, and specific sexual offenses.

compensation faced the obstacle that sexual harassment was considered "private" behavior, irrelevant to workplace regulation and beyond the responsibility of employers (MacKinnon 1979; Plogstedt and Bode 1984). Even judges who found that it had occurred were reluctant to rule that employers were liable, because it was seen as a personal or private issue.[13] Unemployment benefits were refused to women who left work following incidents of harassment, because the decision to quit was viewed as a personal and voluntary choice (Farley 1978; Bertelsmann 1987).

On both sides of the Atlantic, a range of criminal and civil laws have been applied, including laws against rape, sexual assault, battery, sexual coercion, intrusion, and other offenses (Rubenstein 1987; Holzbecher et al. 1990; Baer 1995). US state tort law on intentional infliction of emotional distress has been applied to sexual harassment (see Cahill 2001). As for rape, legal remedies have been difficult to apply because of the gender biases of laws and courts (Smart 1995; Goy 1996).[14] Courts have used restrictive, inconsistent interpretations of what behavior and circumstances can be regulated by civil laws (see Holzbecher et al. 1990). Enforcement even of relatively strict West German laws prohibiting the exploitation of minors was difficult because of narrow definitions of "sexual" behavior. In 1981, the highest court decided that "demanding that a minor undress does not necessarily constitute a sexual act."[15]

Finally, there was a strong reluctance to consider the seriousness of sexual harassment and the economic and psychological harm it caused (Degen 1991). It was viewed as a *Kavaliersdelikt* (harmless crime) that did not require harsh punishment. Employers, unions, courts, and many women confronted with sexual harassment felt that men should not lose their jobs over an occasional *Ausrutscher* (slip). Until organized groups of feminists began to draw attention to the issue as an injustice

---

[13] For example, a US District Court judge in 1975 in *Corne v. Bausch & Lomb, Inc.* argued, "Mr. Price's conduct appears to be nothing more than a personal proclivity, peculiarity or mannerism. By his alleged sexual advance, Mr. Price was satisfying a personal urge. Certainly no employer policy is here involved, rather than the company being benefited in any way by the conduct of Price, it is obvious it can only be damaged by the very nature of the acts complained of" (cited in Stein 1999: 40).

[14] For example, because workplace sexual harassment most often happens without witnesses, proof beyond reasonable doubt is difficult, especially if a woman's credibility is undermined by gender stereotypes. Furthermore, assigning responsibility to victims rather than perpetrators has been a persistent cultural pattern (Brownmiller 1975). In court, judges and lawyers refer to women's sexually open attitudes and attire to account for men's inappropriate sexual overtures.

[15] BGH July 1, 1981, 3 StR 151/81, NJW 1981: 2204

and a social problem, it was considered largely a private matter, and employer and court reactions to complaints reflected this view.

Feminist demands

In the late 1970s and early 1980s, feminists of the second-wave women's movement argued that broad cultural, social, legal, and political changes were necessary, and the first books specifically on sexual harassment appeared in Canada, the United States, the United Kingdom, and Germany (see, for example, Brodsky 1976; Backhouse and Cohen 1981; Farley 1978; MacKinnon 1979; Plogstedt and Bode 1984; Wise and Stanley 1987). These feminists considered sexual harassment to be foremost a "gendered" problem, an abuse of power by men who held higher status than women as men and as supervisors.

Feminists argued that men who harassed women harmed women's dignity and integrity by offending, humiliating, and demeaning not only individual women but women in general (Brownmiller 1975; MacKinnon 1979; Baker 2001; Plogstedt and Bode 1984). By framing the problem as a form of sexual exploitation, they mobilized support from the anti-violence movements on both sides of the Atlantic. They insisted that sexual harassment was not a matter of "sexual desire" or "flirtation gone wrong," but an expression of male power over women (Farley 1978; MacKinnon 1979; Backhouse and Cohen 1981: 36ff; Plogstedt and Degen 1992: 17; Sadrozinski 1993: 32ff). These women used the analysis they had developed for other forms of sexual violence. For example, the first German Union Association (DGB) brochure on sexual harassment called it "mini-rape" (Plogstedt and Bertelsmann 1987: 7).

In addition, feminists argued that workplace sexual harassment did not occur accidentally but resulted from women's lower status and unequal pay. They clearly framed sexual harassment as a gendered problem that women faced as workers simply because they were women. This notion of "frame" refers to the ways in which social movements theorists examine how activists interpreted problems in ways to attract resources or allies (Snow et al. 1986; Snow and Benford 1992; Snow 2004). For example, by using the notion of abuse of supervisory power, activists' frame of sexual harassment resonated with both unions and employers and successfully linked abuse of men's power over women to supervisors' (hierarchical) power over women.

Feminists also framed sexual harassment as a problem with economic consequences: feminist legal scholar Catharine MacKinnon (1979) drew on feminist sociological theories to argue that sexual harassment is discrimination because it affects the economic rights of women as a group. Women not only suffer emotionally but risk job loss if they do not want to have sex with their supervisors, and might quit their jobs when they cannot endure belittling, demeaning, and other hostile actions by their colleagues.

Here feminists drew the important connection between sexual harassment as a workplace/discrimination issue and as an issue of violence/sexuality, linking economic to sexual rights. MacKinnon (1979) most prominently argued that demands for sexual favors can be a condition of hiring, promotion, or other economic advantages, and the menace of working environments hostile to women can compromise access to male-dominated, better-paid jobs. Basically, sexual harassment constitutes sex discrimination because of its unequal treatment of women and men at work (Baker 2001).

Second-wave feminists made a broader argument about the harm to *all women* caused by sexual harassment as a form of sexism. Rosemary Pringle (1988), for example, argued that women in female occupations, such as secretaries and nurses, faced gendered job expectations. Women have been expected to be (sexually) pleasing to men; for example, men have believed that receptionists and secretaries should smile, have "attractive" looks, and dress in a "feminine" manner, meaning with short skirts and low-cut blouses. Men suppose that women enjoy flirtation with any man at any time, a belief that also persists in court rooms (Fitzgerald 2004). Feminists argued that this cultural assumption reflected a privilege and sense of entitlement of men to eroticize and sexualize any woman through flirting, telling sexual jokes, and touching. In the worst-case scenario, supervisors felt they had the right to demand that women engage in sexual activities as part of their job. This analysis showed that sexual harassment is a problem where gender and sexuality intersect and therefore constitutes unequal gender relations: these gender-specific, normative, cultural expectations of women workers construct gender in the workplace in a way that, more generally speaking, reinscribes masculinity and femininity as mutually exclusive, heteronormative principles of social organization. Hence this form of institutionalized sexism contributes to inequality of women and men in the workplace by perpetuating unequal gender relations (Acker 1990; Gutek 1985; Hearn and Parkin 2001; Martin 2003). For example, Jennifer Pierce (1995) showed how sexual harassment contributes to gendered normative expectations of both women paralegals and women litigators that maintain sex segregation in law firms.

Based on this analysis, feminists demanded that supervisors, employers, and unions recognize the serious harm done to individual women and to women in general. They demanded that instead of punishing women who filed complaints, employers and courts should hold men who harassed responsible for their actions. Educational campaigns should raise awareness of the issue and enable women to speak out against sexual harassment.

Legal activism was one feminist strategy among many. The West German women in the Green party did not pursue their case in court, but called on party leadership to address sexual harassment in an effort to signal broader problems of sexism within the party. US pioneers such as the Boston-based Alliance Against Sexual Coercion (AASC) advocated a broad range of collective legal and extra-legal actions. They demanded committees for women's issues at work. They involved the media. Some advocated protest activities including demonstrations in front of harassers' homes and the workplace to use public shame strategies.

Feminists who demanded new policy measures argued that existing legal remedies were insufficient to allow women to challenge employers in court. For example, in the early 1980s Sibylle Plogstedt, a feminist sociologist and journalist, called on West Germany to adopt a broad, effective anti-discrimination law to promote women's equality at work that should encompass sexual harassment (Plogstedt and Bode 1984). US feminists also hoped that declaring sexual harassment illegal would change public awareness and employer practices, and stop men from harassing women.

Based on a feminist critique of patriarchal law (see Pateman 1988; MacKinnon 1983), however, feminists on both sides of the Atlantic were also ambivalent or skeptical about legal and state intervention. Fearing that engagement with the state would lead to co-optation of their goals, US feminist organizations did not advocate new laws because of their distrust in the ability of state and legal systems to apply and enforce the law in fair ways. Members of an advocacy organization feared that "married middle-class white women, if harassed by a man with less societal status, will probably receive benefits, while a poor Third World or lesbian woman, particularly if harassed by a 'respectable' man, may find compensation under this new law difficult to obtain" (Hooven and Klein 1978: 28, cited in Baker 2001: 133). Feminist historian Linda Gordon warned that "governments and institutions are more likely to act against accused men who are themselves members of vulnerable social groups – racial minorities, and leftists, for example (1981: 714)." The basic assumption is that (employer) organizations, states, and courts cannot promote (gender) equality because they are inherently patri- archal, hierarchical structures. Libertarians have been concerned about courts' and employers' micromanagement of social interactions and relations in the workplace.

In Germany, feminists have been skeptical about trusting employers to act on their behalf, based on the German history of state–employer relations in particular. Similarly, Green party and leftist political forces expressed reluctance to bring back regulations that were reminiscent of traditional German, paternalistic labor regulations. They were concerned about the German state bestowing employers with control over employees in general, and over what they interpreted as the "private" sphere of employees in particular. In the German context this apprehension is rooted in experiences with employers' powers based on paternalistic *Betriebsordnung* (work rules) during the Nazi period, and in experiences after World War II, when the East German secret police extended its power into the labor force through police informants at work, including demanding that supervisors report on employees.[16]

Hence, on both sides of the Atlantic, feminists have been concerned over the use of legal and policy regulations to deal with sexual harassment, discussions that continue today. How did the United States and the EU respond to individual and collective women's demands to take sexual harassment seriously? Have sexual harassment laws served as instruments for challenging gender and sexual norms in the workplace?

What explains state responsiveness to sexual harassment?

Feminists mobilized in several countries with different levels of success in politicizing sexual harassment and effecting legal reforms. There was a significant lag time in state and court responses to individual and collective women's actions. While case law on sexual harassment developed in Canada, Australia, the United States, and the United Kingdom from the late 1970, most EU member states took action by adopting laws only in the early 1990s, following the measures of the European Community and the US Senate hearings of Clarence Thomas. Spain adopted a law against sexual harassment in 1989 in anticipation of the EU measures, followed by Sweden in 1991, Austria, Belgium, and France in 1992, Germany in 1994, and Finland in 1995 (see Table 1.1).

---

[16] Thanks to Susanne Baer who pointed out the historical experience under Nazi rule (communication February 2005).

Table 1.1. *Laws against sexual harassment and/or relevant court decisions*

	Sex equality law	Sexual harassment law	Court decision
United States	1964	(EEOC) 1980	1987
European Community/ European Union	1976	1990/2002	
Austria	1979	1992	
Belgium	1978	1992	
Denmark	1978		1989
Finland	1986	1995	
France	1983	1992*	
Germany	1980	1994	1986
Ireland	1977	1998	1985
Italy	1991	1996*	
Luxembourg	1981	2000	
Netherlands	1983	1994	
Portugal	1989		
Spain	1980	1989	
Sweden	1979	1991	
United Kingdom	1975	1995	1986

* Criminal, penal code.

The laws adopted in the 1990s not only define sexual harassment in different ways but provide different means to hold perpetrators and employers responsible, from civil to labor to criminal law. Laws can provide access to courts to demand remedies and compensation from perpetrators or employers, for example, by applying tort and other civil laws. Criminal laws can sanction and penalize perpetrators. Labor laws can define employer liabilities and make them responsible to prohibit harassment, to adopt internal policies and workplace procedures, to take adequate action on complaints, or to prevent harassment from occurring. Laws vary greatly in the sanctions they attach to violations.

How "feminist" are sexual harassment policies?

Sexual harassment policies reflect competing and conflicting understandings of gender equality, sexuality, and gender relations and vary in the degree to which they reflect feminist analysis. Laws can define sexual harassment from the perspective of victims or perpetrators or aim at some objective viewpoint. The United States and the EU defined sexual harassment subjectively as "unwanted" behavior, reflecting feminist demands that harassment be considered from the viewpoint of the person who experiences it, not the intentions or motivations of perpe-trators. Germany used an objective viewpoint, "recognizably rejected behavior" (Baer 1995) (see Table 1.2).

How can we "measure" how feminist these policies are? Much of feminist policy analysis has been concerned with this question (Bacchi 1999). Amy Mazur defines feminist policy success in the following way: "Policy is considered a feminist success . . . if women's interests are represented in both substantive and descriptive ways"

Table 1.2. *Legal definitions of sexual harassment*

Equal Employment Opportunity Commission (1980) Guideline (United States)

Unwelcome sexual advances, requests for sexual favors, and other verbal or physical conduct of a sexual nature constitute sexual harassment when
(Quid pro Quo)
1 Submission to such a conduct is made either explicitly or implicitly a term or condition of an individual's employment
2 Submission to or rejection of such conduct by an individual is used as a basis for employment decisions affecting such individual, or
(Hostile Environment)
3 Such conduct has the purpose or effect of unreasonably interfering with an individual's work performance or creating an intimidating, hostile, or offensive working environment.

2002 Directive on Equal Treatment Directive (European Union) (2002/73/EC of 23 September 2002)

– harassment: where an unwanted conduct related to the sex of a person occurs with the purpose or effect of violating the dignity of a person, and of creating an intimidating, hostile, degrading, humiliating or offensive environment,
– sexual harassment: where any form of unwanted verbal, non-verbal or physical conduct of a sexual nature occurs, with the purpose or effect of violating the dignity of a person, in particular when creating an intimidating, hostile, degrading, humiliating or offensive environment.
Harassment and sexual harassment within the meaning of this Directive shall be deemed to be discrimination on the grounds of sex and therefore prohibited.

1994 Federal Employee Protection Law (Germany)

Article 10, Law for the protection of employees against sexual harassment in the workplace (employee protection law) defines
Sexual harassment is every intentional, sexually determinate behavior, which offends the dignity of employees in the workplace. This includes

1 Sexual acts and behaviors, that are illegal under other criminal law and,
2 Other acts or demands to these, sexual physical touching, remarks with sexual contents, as well as the showing or visible display of pornographic materials, if they are recognizably rejected by the person affected.

(2002: 38). She suggests a useful criterion for examining whether policies are indeed "gendered in a feminist way": assessing "whether policy content formally acknowledges the gendered nature of the social problems and designs solutions that attempt to redress gender-based inequalities" (2002: 38). This analysis helps us distinguish *gender-specific* and *gender-neutral* laws by noting whether *gender power* is taken into account.

Laws vary, for instance, as to whether they treat sexual harassment as a gender-specific injustice that happens to women as women, based on sex. The notion of violation of dignity is not gender-specific and can encompass violations, for example, of health and safety regulations or criminal and penal codes. When laws apply gender-neutral concepts they can ignore gender differences in perceptions and reactions to sexual harassment. Laws also vary as to when sexual harassment is illegal. The US concept of *quid pro quo* describes a situation in which a supervisor offers favors or threatens reprisals around sexual favors from a subordinate. Under the US concept of *hostile environment* not only supervisors but coworkers can create a humiliating atmosphere.

Laws and policies also vary in stressing *protection* or *empowerment* of individuals or collective actors. Carol Smart (1995) pointed out that demanding laws against violence against women always risks reinforcing gender stereotypes and notions of women's specific vulnerabilities, a risk that is also related to the century-long feminist theoretical political strategy debate: Should women demand specific protections and therefore possibly reinforce gender differences or demand to be treated the same as men? Because West German gender politics have stood for a *gender difference* approach while the United States has embarked on a *gender sameness* approach, the question will be how sexual harassment approaches fit into these categories (Ferree 1987; Scott 1988). The postwar West German difference approach meant, for example, that social and public policies considered women foremost wives and mothers, dependants of men. By contrast, the US approach, rooted in race analogy, has focused on equal treatment of women and men, an idea that gender differences should not count when it comes to equal access in the public sphere. The question, hence, is what should sexual harassment policies look like if they were to protect women from harassment while at the the same time ensuring gender equality, for example as equal access to the labor market in general, and access to male-dominated, better-paying jobs (Orloff 1993)?

Historical examples show that policies restricted rather than allowed women access to male-dominated workplaces and hence increased sex segregation. When the German state made employers responsible for upholding morals and appropriate behavior in the workplace in the nine-teenth century, the solution was to separate women and men. The 1891 *Gewerbeordnung* suggested segregating women and men if the nature of the company allowed it and the employer could not otherwise assure good morals and appropriate behavior. Instead of assuming that sexual harassment policies enhance gender equality we need to identify how feminist demands have been translated into laws and regulations and preventive efforts such as awareness programs. In short, these criteria help us measure how "feminist" sexual harassment laws are.

Alternative explanations for cross-national variation in policy approaches

What explains the differences in timing and nature of sexual harassment policies in the United States and in EU member states? Can differences in the cultures of sexuality, occurrences of sexual harassment, or numbers of working women explain why governments and courts have been more responsive to feminist demands in the United States than in most EU member states? We might think that transatlantic differences in cultural norms around sexuality would account for the variations. It is tempting to see policies in US workplaces as a result of American prudishness, which European employers supposedly do not share because of their allegedly greater sophistication in dealing with sexuality in the workplace.

But positioning US and European cultures as opposites ignores not only how similar they are but also the diversity within both. Despite national and cultural differences in awareness and interpretation of sexual harassment, there is a broad consensus that unwanted sexual advances in the workplace, especially physical forms, are a serious prob-lem for women. There is consensus that employers should not demand sex in exchange for jobs or better working conditions. There has been more debate about whether harassment by coworkers should be illegal. Finally, there is heated debate about what physical behavior is sexual and under what circumstances looks, jokes with sexual connotations, and sexual remarks constitute sexual harassment.

These debates indicate that cultural norms of everyday interactions between women and men have been challenged and begun to shift on both sides of the Atlantic. Cultural attitudes towards gender equality in general have been changing in post-industrial society, particularly in the public sphere and workplaces (Inglehart and Norris 2003). The politi-cization of sexual harassment coincided with what Duggan and Hunter (1995) called the "sex wars," cultural and political battles over sexual violence, "date rape," pornography, and recognition of nonheterosexual groups. Feminists challenged notions of women's (assumed) consent to masculinist visions of gender and sexual relations. Anti-rape movements demanded recognition that "No means no!" An anti-feminist backlash misappropriated the label of sexual correctness to downplay, simplify, trivialize, and ridicule these critiques (Faludi 1991). European media picked up these voices. German media instrumentalized the US critique to "modernize" anti-feminist debates (Möller 1999). For example, the rules at Antioch College, Ohio in the 1990s that students must actively ensure consent in sexual encounters were ridiculed as "anti-sex" and as reintroducing Victorianism. The same criticism was applied to workplace sexual harassment, and conservatives and libertarians alike called for the rescue of free speech.

During the 1990s the American public heard much about how allegations of sexual harassment could threaten men's careers. The German public learned about sexual harassment as the quintessence of sexual correctness through the eyes of the accused in American books and movies. David Mamet's play *Oleanna* (1992), in which a (feminist) woman student threatens to accuse a male assistant professor of rape, leading to the end of his academic career, was staged in Germany. The film *Disclosure*, based on the best-selling book by Michael Crichton, was a box-office hit in Germany. *Disclosure* is the story of a man sexually harassed by his female boss, who then accuses him of sexual harassment (a rather unusual situation, since surveys suggest that a small percentage of men report experiences of sexual harassment, and men not women are most often the perpetrators (Holzbecher et al. 1990; Timmerman and Bajema 1999; U.S.M.S.P.B. 1981, 1988, 1995; Welsh 1999). Thus in neither country has popular culture and public opinion been unified in support of strong laws to protect women, whereas concerns of how these laws could be applied against men have created fears and resistance, as well as worries that businesses would be overburdened by the costs and responsibilities of prohibiting and preventing sexual harassment from occurring.

In short, both the notion of sexual harassment and how to solve the problem have been the focus of controversies on both sides of the Atlantic. National cultures of sexuality do not sufficiently explain these different legal and policy outcomes.

Are women more often harassed in the United States than in Europe? Studies have consistently shown that women experience sexual harassment in Europe no less than in the United States (European Commission 1999; Rubenstein 1987; ILO 1992; Husbands 1992; Hodges 1996). About 42 percent of women and 14 percent of men in the US federal workforce reported experiencing some form of sexual harassment (U.S.M.S.P.B. 1981, 1988, 1995). Surveys of eleven EU member states between 1987 and 1997 show that sexual harassment is common (European Commission 1999; Zippel 1999a, 1999b). Summarizing these results, Timmerman and Bajema (1999) found that 30–50 percent of employed women reported experiencing some form of sexual harassment in the workplace. Surveys show that sexual harassment is a pervasive problem on both continents; government responsiveness cannot merely be the result of differences in how often it happens.

Does women's participation in the labor market explain the differences in state responsiveness? Countries with the highest labor force participation of women were not the earliest to adopt policies, and Spain, with low labor market participation of women, was the first EU member state to pass a law. In both the United States and EU member states, increasing numbers of women have entered employment since the 1960s (see Table 1.3). This growth did not automatically result in a strong "women's voice" to challenge the gender culture in workplaces. Labor markets continue to be characterized by persistent gender inequalities, including sex segregation, glass ceilings, marginal or part-time work arrangements, and often higher unemployment for women.

Table 1.3. *Labor force participation of women and men in 1960 and 1990 (percentage)*

	Labor force participation				Female share of labor force	
	1960		1990			
	Male	Female	Male	Female	1960	1990
Australia	97.2	34.1	86.1	62.3	25.1	41.3
Canada	91.1	33.7	84.9	68.2	26.6	44.5
Denmark	99.5	43.5	89.6	78.4	30.9	46.1
Finland	91.4	65.6	80.6	72.9	43.7	47.1
France	94.6	46.6	75.2	56.6	33.3	42.9
Germany	94.4	49.2	80.7	56.6	37.3	40.7
Italy	95.3	39.6	78.1	44.5	30.7	36.8
Netherlands	97.8	26.2	79.6	53.0	21.5	39.2
Norway	92.2	36.3	84.5	71.2	28.2	44.9
Sweden	98.5	50.1	85.3	81.1	33.6	48.0
United Kingdom	99.1	46.1	86.4	65.1	32.7	42.8
United States	90.5	42.6	85.2	68.1	32.5	44.9

Patterns in the timing and form of sexual harassment policies also provide more puzzles than answers when we look into the literature on the origins and evolution of social and public policies, EU compliance studies, and the gender and welfare regime. Why was the United States the forerunner on sexual harassment policies despite its reputation for minimal interference in workers' rights? Why would Sweden, a leader in gender equality, resemble Spain and France in resisting the EU guidelines to consider a "hostile environment" created by coworkers as sexual harassment, while Germany, a notorious laggard, adopted such a law in 1994?

Based on mainstream studies of welfare states, we would expect policies against sexual harassment to be developed earlier in Germany than in the United States, because workers' rights are depicted as stronger and more firmly institutionalized in Europe in general. Yet the United States was in the forefront of policy-making in this field. Gendered welfare regime studies cannot explain these differences sufficiently either (Hobson 2003; Lewis 1992, 1997; Orloff 1993; Ostner and Lewis 1995; Sainsbury 1994, 1996).

According to the influential typology of gendered welfare states introduced by Jane Lewis (1992) to consider gender dimensions of social risks, we would expect that countries pursuing a "dual-breadwinner model" would adopt protective policies early because their cultural and political frames support married women's employment. Countries wedded to the male-breadwinner model would be laggards, since their policies view women primarily as wives dependent on their husbands' earnings and do little to encourage equal access to the labor market.

Yet two strong male-breadwinner countries, the United Kingdom and Spain, were ahead of Sweden and Finland, dual-breadwinner countries. Austria and Germany, strong male-breadwinner countries, adopted broad policies against harassment from coworkers, while France, a moderate male-breadwinner country, was similar to Sweden in its narrow approach prohibiting only harassment by supervisors. By focusing primarily on women as care givers, this theory does not capture states' commitment to recognize women's rights as individuals. As several critiques have pointed out, they fail to explain (welfare) state interventions or noninterventions to ensure women's rights in sexuality, anti-discrimination, and anti-violence (Weldon 2002; Elman 1996; Brush 2002, 2003). Lynne Haney (1996) makes a compelling argument that states should be considered potentially fragmented rather than homogenous entities in pursuing "gender interests."

Sexual harassment provides a test for theories of "women-friendly" states because it is an issue of both workplace regulations and violence against women. The key question both academics and activists have asked is: Do states have the potential to be women-friendly as Helga Hernes (1987) put it? Can states intervene and improve gender equality in gender relations (Connell 1987, 1990; Franzway, Court and Connell 1989)? Sexual harassment policies require these gendered or gender-sensitive welfare states theories to expand and investigate comparatively states' commitments to physical and emotional integrity and women's sexual self-determination. By contrast with social or political rights, for example, body rights are concerned with the rights around one's body. They include sexual harassment, rape, sexual assault, physical and emotional violence against women, reproductive politics, prostitution, trafficking, as well as rights based on gender identity and sexual orientation. Rather than being solely monetary redistribution, these politics of recognition, as Nancy Fraser (1997) would characterize these politics around gender, race, class, ethnicity, and the body, are also about (sexual) self-determination of women and equality of respect, status, etc., all certainly intersecting with economic rights. But these body politics challenge our assumptions about which (welfare) states have been progressive based on their provisions for working women and mothers. As Julia O'Connor, Ann Orloff, and Sheila Shaver (1999) point out, the United States and other countries, considered liberal welfare states, have been surprisingly progressive regarding workplace anti-discrimination policies and abortion regulations, because of strong liberal, legal concepts of personhood that have defined the civil and political status of (gendered) individuals. Hence, sexual harassment allows us to investigate states' willingness/capacity to intervene on behalf of women concerning dynamics of gender power, sexuality, and male dominance in the workplace.

Generally speaking, the politics of sexual harassment reveal deficiencies in theoretical traditions that deal with movements, states, and policies. On the one hand, traditional policy studies have been concerned primarily with institutional politics or labor. In these theories, social movements appear primarily as interest groups or, in recent theories, as advocacy coalitions (Sabatier 1999). On the other hand, social movement theories have been most concerned about what determines whether these movements emerge as nontraditional forms of politics. Yet, women working within state agencies were intimately involved in developing the politics of sexual harassment, and movements were funded by these newly institutionalized (gender) equality agencies.

How do we explain movements' success or failure to affect policies and/or changes within states and/or through courts? Researchers have begun to look at how movements affect public policies and at the interaction of movements and states. For example, some researchers have analyzed how movements can contribute to the very formulation of social problems (Weeks et al. 1986; Rochon 1998). An emerging scholarship has investigated the relationship between social movements and states (Quadagno 1992; Clemens 1993; Burstein 1991, 1999).

Overall, the frameworks these researchers suggest have limited power to explain the differences between the United States and the EU because the paths for policy change have been so different. While they do point to several national-level factors, including party politics, etc. that can explain cross-national variation within the EU, they do not explain the similarity of the timing among the EU member states. Neither numbers of women in the labor force, nor the prevalence of sexual harassment experiences, nor theories of welfare states or the gender-sensitive breadwinner model explain the timing of sexual harassment policies in EU member states.

Paths to laws against sexual harassment

The argument advanced here is that the differences in timing depended on the paths countries embarked on. Liberal, Anglo-Saxon countries which took the "legal path" were first to respond. US courts began to recognize sexual harassment as sex discrimination in the late 1970s, followed by Australia (1984) and Canada (1980, 1989). A tribunal court in Northern Ireland (1983) and courts in other parts of the United Kingdom (1985, 1986) and Ireland (1985) applied sex discrimination laws to grant women the right to hold employers responsible (Hodges 1996; European Commission 1996). The pioneering role of the United States was due to the exceptional openness of the legal system and traditions of individual legal rights. The civil rights and women's movements used these features of the system to their advantage (McCann 1994; Burstein 1991, 1998). In the process of changing laws through the courts, judges not only took note of victims' experiences but listened to feminist attorneys, experts, and victim advocates.

Success came more slowly in countries which took the "statutory" route. The EU passed nonbinding measures in 1990 and a binding directive in 2002. By the mid-1990s, most member states had adopted new laws or amended existing ones (see Table 1.1). Parliamentary reforms required the consensus of the parties, a slow process in which feminist demands were watered down.

Preexisting laws and legal systems

The path of legal change through the courts depends on national legal cultures and systems. Countries with traditions of individual rights and anti-discrimination legislation clearly spearheaded legal attention (Husbands 1992; Hodges 1996). The most pronounced difference is that between the legal systems of the United States and Anglo-Saxon countries, based on *common law*, and "continental traditions based on *constitutional and civil law*" (Glendon, Gordon, and Osakwe 1994). The US system has "both statutory law and judicial interpretation of statutory and non-statutory law" (Cahill 2001: 12). Attorneys can propose analogies with other cases; judges must base their judgment not only on interpretation of law but also on precedent. In contrast, in continental traditions the judge's role is to interpret the law; judgments need not take into account previous decisions, so winning a case does not necessarily affect future rulings. Not surprisingly, litigation is not part of the German women's movement repertoire.

An important question, then, is how legal and parliamentary paths themselves shape sexual harassment policies. As MacKinnon (2002) asks, which legal process is more effective, common or civil law legislation? Common law traditions offer opportunities to effect legal change by supporting individual cases with the potential to set precedent. In countries with a civil law tradition, movements must convince legislators to enact reforms, so laws emerge through consensus among state agencies and political parties. As we will see, these processes shaped feminist strategies and ways of framing sexual harassment in the United States and in the EU member states.

Legal systems and traditions correlate with the timing and paths of policy adoption, and also shape social movement repertoires, but they are not a sufficient explanation of US, EU, and German activists' strategies. Although much EU sex equality law has come through European Court of Justice (ECJ) rulings, sexual harassment activists did not use litigation as a strategy for expanding existing anti-discrimination laws. German labor law shares certain characteristics with common law litigation, in flexibility and internal dynamics (Baer 1995); unions have successfully used litigation to expand strike laws. But West German feminists have not perceived labor courts as an opportunity to promote gender equality and sexual harassment law, despite their apparent potential. A few sexual harassment cases have made it to German labor courts, but judges have been reluctant to play an active role in shaping its jurisprudence, in striking contrast to highly political interventions in the gender-neutral issue of mobbing.[17]

These legal paths for change would not have been possible without preexisting laws against discrimination. Courts in countries which had laws against sex discrimination in the workplace based on individual rights were the first to recognize sexual harassment as sex discrimination. Such laws allowed attorneys and legal scholars, most prominently MacKinnon, to make the case that sexual harassment is a gender-specific issue that should be considered sex discrimination under the Civil Rights Act of 1964. Australia, Canada, the United Kingdom, Ireland, and the United States, countries with a strong tradition of individual rights in common law litigation, were in the forefront in developing laws through the courts. State agencies and women's movements in these countries played an important role helping courts recognize sexual harassment as sex discrimination, and they have consistently pursued a liberal, anti-discrimination approach of equal treatment in hiring, firing, and working conditions, focused on understandings of gender sameness in the workplace (O'Connor, Orloff, and Shaver 1999; Mazur 2002).

Diffusion of sexual harassment from North America to the EU

While legal systems explain the different paths and hence the difference in timing between the United States and the EU, the similarity among EU member states in their timing of adoption of sexual harassment laws (with the exception of the United Kingdom) points to common influences. The diffusion of US ideas and policy models played an important role on the continent. The increasingly important role of the European integration process helped spread these ideas, not only through EU measures but also through transnational advocacy networks. These are the roles of *transnational expertise* and *international institutions* in diffusing policies.

The concept of sexual harassment has quickly been diffused by transnational women's movements, international organizations and

---

[17] The highest labor court in Thuringia defined mobbing as a legal issue in 2001, ruling in favor of a man who sued his employer because the harassing actions of a manager had driven him to attempt suicide (Landesarbeitsgericht Thuringia, 10 April 2001, 6 Sa 403/00). Well aware that this ruling would set a precedent and bring public attention, the court stated its constitutional responsibility to take action because legislators had not done so. It set out clear guidelines for consequent rulings and held the employer responsible for preventing mobbing.

institutions, and the media. This international exchange of ideas, frames, discourses, knowledge, experiences, practices, and strategies is not a new phenomenon, as Nitza Berkovitch's (2002) historical analysis of women's rights, women's suffrage, prostitution, and labor laws shows. There have been various connections and links between women's activism around the globe (Naples and Desai 2002). Nor is the diffusion of social movements and public policies limited to the international women's movement. Social movement scholars have long pointed out that movements do not work in isolation but influence and learn from each other in various ways (Soule 2004). This exchange occurs between movements and across borders.

At the heart of these diffusion processes is the recognition of the power of ideas in galvanizing social movements and inspiring policies to combat social problems. The spread and exchange of ideas and expertise occur through direct and indirect ties between activists and policy-makers, which the EU, as a supranational institution, has actively furthered in its member states and beyond. Social movement researchers have argued that the media are crucial in the diffusion of ideas (McAdam and Rucht 1993); they also agree that networks are crucial mechanisms for exchange of information and can influence policy-making (Sabatier 1999; Heclo 1974; Keck and Sikkink 1998; Stone 1988, 1997; Risse-Kappen 1995).

For Keck and Sikkink (1998), nongovernmental organizations and experts work to communicate ideas and are oriented toward persuasion. Keck and Sikkink developed the useful concept of transnational advocacy networks (TANs) to examine the diffusion of the concept of violence against women. These networks include not only grassroots social movement activists but also governments, bureaucrats, experts, and academics.[18] Social movement activists, women in unions, and policy-makers in Europe borrowed the notion of "sexual harassment" from the United States. Feminists engaged in sexual harassment politics were particularly apt to use transnational forums to draw on and create transnational expertise and alternative discourses, including legal and policy definitions.

The process of finding a European solution to sexual harassment involved TANs of activists, unions, experts, and policy-makers. The

---

[18] "Epistemic communities" limits networks to experts rather than embracing activists as TANs do. This is because Ernst Haas and Paul Haas, who coined the term "epistemic communities," consider that only experts have the scientific credentials to influence policy-making, which in human rights issues for example is less "consensual knowledge" than, say, in environmental issues.

EU, as a supranational institution, also played an important role by creating a TAN on gender equality that acted as a catalyst for developing equal treatment laws in many member states. Some single-issue organizations found sympathetic allies in the emerging women's policy machinery in the EU. Advocates in member states were able to overcome resistance once the EU legitimized this "new policy area" and they could argue that their governments needed to comply with EU measures. Even though the EU recommendations and resolutions are relatively weak, "soft-law" policy tools, most EU governments took legislative action during the 1990s.

This development was spurred by EU influence in member states. The EU actively created transnational expertise that helped "Europeanize" sexual harassment, which was particularly important because some member states saw the issue as an "American import." By soliciting not only EU but also government and union funding, experts began to create transnational expertise that provided policy models for the national and local levels. For policy-making processes experts play an important role, because policy-makers and/or judges use their knowledge in legal and legislative processes (Stryker 1989, 1994). How German local- and national-level actors reacted presents a specific example of how member states drew on these EU measures.

Explaining qualitative differences between approaches to sexual harassment

Legal systems explain the timing of legal reforms in the United States and the EU, and common factors of diffusion explain the similar timing among EU member states. But how can we account for the differences in sexual harassment policy approaches in the United States and EU member states? We need a more fine-grained, contextual analysis of the paths through which the politics emerged and of the opportunities for feminists to shape policy approaches. This comparison reveals to what degree feminist concepts were translated into laws in the United States and the EU, and why transnational expertise was crucial for national-level advocates in the EU.

Feminist policy studies and welfare state theories fall short of explaining the differences in the evolution of sexual harassment approaches because they usually consider policy adoption only through parliaments–a model that fits neither the US nor the EU path. The factors they consider include parties or coalitions in power, labor strength, public opinion, state–society relations, political culture, and state structures (centralized or federal). Feminist studies have "gendered" these factors to include women's participation, for example, by examining percentages of women in government, state bureaucracy, and parliament. Some of these factors are useful to explain the German passage of sexual harassment, but they are less relevant for reforms through the courts or government representatives in the EU.

Influence of women's movements

These cases have in common the influence of second-wave feminist movements in the politicization of sexual harassment at the national and EU levels, though these movements were different, ranging from a US national-level movement against violence and discrimination at work, to a TAN in the EU, to a decentralized autonomous, feminist movement in West Germany. Feminists have been blamed for negative effects of sexual harassment policies and credited for bringing the issue onto the agenda, changing public awareness, and effecting legal decisions and policy changes (Weeks et al. 1986; Hodges 1996; Rubenstein 1987). When we compare policy outcomes, it is apparent that feminists had different levels of success. We need, therefore, to examine how these actors were involved in the initiation, adoption, and implementation of laws, and how their roles were circumscribed by the institutional arrangements with which they interacted.

Considering that sexual harassment policies emerged through such different paths, it is apparent that proponents for change encountered various *institutional arrangements:* in the United States primarily with the legal system, in Germany with the parliamentary system and industrial relations, and in the EU its supranational institutional structures. Social movement and collective action theorists examine the political and institutional context for mobilization with the concept of political opportunity structures. The basic idea is that movements' capacity to mobilize is shaped by opportunities and constraints in a political–institutional setting (see, for example, McAdam and Rucht 1993; Tarrow 1994; Kriesi et al. 1995). This concept has recently been modified to consider how movements themselves shape political opportunity structures. As in the movement against sexual harassment, political opportunity structures can constrain how movements form and mobilize. But movements themselves can change the institutional arrangements they might protest against (McAdam, Tarrow, and Tilly 2001). In addition, the European integration process and US politics changed the specific national–institutional setting and reconfigured the political opportunity structures for the EU member states (Roggeband and Verloo 1999; Imig and Tarrow 2001; Marks and McAdam 1998).

Generally speaking, combining feminist policy and social movement approaches helps identify the institutional context in which sexual harassment politics emerged. Strategies to politicize the issue were circumscribed by particular institutional arrangements, most importantly the legal and industrial relations systems, but also more recently established state agencies for (gender) equality, including anti-discrimination agencies and women's policy machineries.

Social movements can influence policy-making in various ways. Movements have an important ability to circulate and create new ways of thinking about issues. Feminist policy studies, particularly those of the Research Network on Gender Politics and the State (RNGS), have suggested a useful way to study the impact of women's movements and state machineries on feminist policy outcomes (Mazur 2002). They advocate examining how these actors were able to insert feminist frames and discourses into the policy debates they attempted to influence such as job training (Mazur 2001), abortion politics (Stetson 2001), and prostitution (Outshoorn 2004). This introduction of interpretive frames is crucial because much of the political struggle in new policy fields concerns defining concepts and determining which existing laws can be applied (see Stone 1988, 1997). Activists gave specific meanings to sexual harassment when they created the term. Defining the phenomenon radically changed interpretation of everyday behavior: behavior previously considered private became politicized and redefined as injustice done to women.

When social movements "frame" issues, they interpret the problem to attract resources or allies. We call these struggles over meaning and interpretive frameworks "discursive politics." Social movements engage in these struggles by conceptualizing a problem in new ways and creating alternative discourses (Eyerman and Jamison 1991; Fraser 1997; Gamson 1992; Jenson 1987; Katzenstein 1998; Stone 1988, 1997). When activists seek to establish sexual harassment as a legitimate field of policy intervention, they frame the issue in ways that resonate with particular gender ideologies, cultural and legal traditions, and national or supranational debates. Movements use frames strategically to convince employers, courts, and states to take the issue seriously. They have different discursive opportunities (Ferree 2003; Koopmans and Olzak 2004) – what Ferree (2003) defines as institutional anchors that connect institutional contexts to the cultural frames movements use. For example, US feminists used the frame sex discrimination, which allowed them to draw on the 1964 Civil Rights Act. In the German parliament, legislators used the European Community definition of violation of dignity.

But as Ferree (2003) argues, "radical" movement activists also choose to use language unstrategically, frames that do not resonate with the discursive opportunities when they seek to insist on (feminist) principles and/or to create alternative discourses. For example, sexual harassment activists have continued to frame sexual harassment as violence against women in the United States and within the EU, insisting on this gendered frame in the face of developments that make violence against women invisible. As we will see, these frames tie sexual harassment to different ways of conceptualizing injustices with different implications for equality for women.

At the heart of the struggles over policies and laws is who gets to define the meanings. Ferree and Mueller argue that "need definition is a political struggle over whose version of reality will be translated into public policy and social practices" (2004: 7). Frames not only give a name to problems but provide an interpretation of what the problem is about, who is responsible for it, and the possible solutions. Is sexual harassment about protecting women from men's sexual advances or creating equal gender cultures? Should we handle it as a women's rights issue or one of workplace health and safety? How feminist frames were translated into laws is a measure of short-term success, but it is crucial because these laws institutionalize ways of thinking about sexual harassment. Moreover, these laws provide enforcement and implementation mechanisms. For example, (gender) equality officers or factory health and safety inspectors could be in charge of enforcement. As we will see, these institutional agencies *do* make a difference.

Comparing movements across different countries also raises thorny questions about naming the actors. Notions of "feminism" are highly debated among academics and activists (Kaplan 1992). Some key actors who promoted the evolution of sexual harassment policies were self-identified radical feminist activists; others have included women and some men in institutions, state bureaucracies, unions, parties, courts, or outside legal consultants and experts. Many of these individuals might not identify themselves as feminists, especially in Germany, where "feminism" is used exclusively by the radical, cultural feminist branches of the West German autonomous women's movement. This book refers to actors as feminists or pro-feminists if they share a feminist interpretation of sexual harassment rooted in gender inequality and an abuse of power, as well as if they promote the creation of more equal gender culture in the workplace.

Industrial relations

Because sexual harassment occurs in the workplace, the paths for policy and legal changes are structured by systems of workplace governance. Industrial relations and the institutional structures of welfare states are important factors in understanding contextual differences in the United States and the EU. Studies of the "varieties of capitalism" show that countries differ in their systems of labor management, including regulations, laws, and policies on hiring, firing, and training (Hall and Soskice 2001), and the roles of state agencies, courts, employers, and unions. The United States has a laissez-faire, liberal, market-oriented system, while Germany has a socially conservative or neocorporatist system, and the EU is a combination (Gottfried and O'Reilly 2002).

Depending on the nature of workplace regulations or the variety of capitalism, unions are more or less crucial actors in the policy field of sexual harassment, and hence potentially important allies for change (Gelb and Palley 1982; Gelb 1989). Unions in the United States had little influence at the federal level on the EEOC or court rulings and were not able to hinder or support reforms. The evidence from EU member states so far is mixed – unions can both hinder and support. Researchers have highlighted the positive influence of trade union mobilization in the EU, Netherlands, and United Kingdom (Collins 1996; Gregory 2000; Husbands 1992; Roggeband and Verloo 1999). In some countries, however, unions have advocated strongly against sexual harassment laws. Baer (1995) claims that women in Germany faced opposition from strong unions. Elman (1996) points out how the strength of trade unions might actually have hindered the institutionalization of policies in Sweden. Systems of industrial relations circumscribe the role of labor unions, employers' associations, and state agencies in establishing sexual harassment as a policy issue as well as in implementing and enforcing antisexual harassment policies.

State agencies and sexual harassment

The politicization of sexual harassment has coincided with the creation and expansion of "women's policy machineries," such as state offices for women, and state equality agencies, such as the EEOC and Human Rights Commissions. From an institutional perspective, these offices became actors with their own interests, for example, the US EEOC sought aggressively to expand its institutional capacity through legal strategy (Pedriana and Stryker 1997, 2004). Offices of "state feminism" demonstrate the complex relationship of women's movements to the state. Women's movements have moved into state governments by creating and/or staffing these policy machineries. Scholarship has sought to explain what effects women's movements and institutionalized gender politics have on feminist policy outcomes (Katzenstein and Mueller 1987; Watson 1990; Sawer 1990; Eisenstein 1995; Banaszak, Beckwith, and Rucht 2003). These comparative studies have examined the mutually constitutive dynamics between women's movements and the state.

The Research Network on Gender Politics and the State has focused on the role of these *femocrats* (the name given to Australian women bureaucrats) as "intervening variables" in designing gendered public policy, because these femocrats bring women's movement activists into the state and potentially can bring feminist discourse into policies (Sawer 1995; Stetson and Mazur 1995; Stetson 2001; Mazur 2001). Amy Mazur, cofounder of RNGS feminist comparative policy studies, states that there is "no magic bullet for successful feminist policies . . . [because] feminist policy success is a product of the complex combination of factors that vary on a case-by-case basis," which also depends on the particular policy field (2003: 518). Mazur (2002) found that state equality agencies in Ireland, Sweden, France, and Great Britain were key players in the formulation of equal employment policy.

The timing of legal reforms also corresponds to states' responsiveness to violence against women. Australia, Canada, and the United States had the most comprehensive policies toward violence against women by 1994 (Weldon 2002). Weldon found that violence-against-women policies resulted from the interaction of women's movements and state institutions. In particular, government responsiveness "seems to be determined to a large degree by the presence of a strong, autonomous women's movement that draws on and reinforces state institutions designed to promote the status of women. When these 'women's policy agencies' have considerable material and institutional resources, and when they maintain consultative relations with activists, they greatly improve government responsiveness to violence against women" (2002: 5). Weldon, however, does not consider workplace sexual harassment policies as part of violence-against-women policy.

We find the earliest court responses in countries in which women's movements focused on anti-discrimination in the workplace, but which also had radical feminist movements that addressed violence against women. This picture of liberal welfare states taking the lead in policies against sexual harassment contradicts much of the gender and welfare state literature, in which these states are considered "residual" welfare states (see also O'Connor, Orloff, and Shaver 1999). The relationship between women's movements and state institutions is crucial because sexual harassment is an issue *both* of violence against women, and of the workplace. We need to study explicitly the interaction of violence-against-women agencies with other state agencies and workplace regulation systems because state agencies can provide activists with institutional vehicles to address issues.

There is one further parallel between sexual harassment policies, violence against women, and anti-discrimination laws which goes against the grain of comparative (feminist) policy studies. Research on gender equality policies finds that left-wing governments have been more supportive of egalitarian policies toward women. Yet, sexual harassment policy adoption in the EU cannot be explained by the left–right spectrum of ruling parties. Conservative or center governments in Sweden, Spain, and Germany easily fit "protecting women's dignity" into their agenda. Leftist parties were hesitant to embrace broader notions of sexual harassment; in France, Sweden, and Spain, social democratic governments excluded coworkers (Valiente 2000). Similarly, Mazur finds that equal employment policies that focus on anti-discrimination and positive action were adopted in Sweden, the United Kingdom, and Ireland under conservative or liberal rule, while feminists had least success in France under left-wing rule (2002: 99).[19] Nor were leftist governments more responsive than conservative ones on policies on violence against women (Weldon 2002).

Thus, the diffusion of sexual harassment policies from North America to the EU and its member states brought both opportunities and challenges to national-level advocates in EU member states. Legal structures and traditions are important because they explain the timing and the "legal path" for defining sexual harassment as sex discrimination in liberal welfare states. Finally, because these paths also reflect differences in systems of workplace regulation and institutionalized forms of gender politics, we need to examine how feminists built alliances with unions and state agencies, and how both can be vehicles as well as targets for change. What has been the impact of these different paths on the concessions feminist advocates had to make? Is the path through courts both faster and more able to reflect feminist ideas of sexual harassment? Does the path based on consensus through parliaments and collective bargaining agreements dilute feminist ideas about sexual harassment

---

[19] Cross-national differences in equality laws in the form of anti-discrimination measures generally speaking have different patterns than mother- or family-friendly policies in gendered welfare regimes (Gardiner 1997). See also Ronnie Steinberg (1980) for useful comparative criteria for gender equality policies.

and provide less effective forms of enforcement and implementation? These questions require systematic analysis of the implementation of sexual harassment laws.

The implementation of sexual harassment laws

Many industrialized Western countries and the EU passed sexual harassment laws in the late 1980s and 1990s (see Table 1.1), but there is broad variation in how these laws have been applied. Empirical assessment of these "policy outcomes" is challenging because the impact of sexual harassment laws is difficult to assess in quantifiable terms. What difference will laws make in the workplace? In their most narrow reach they provide legal redress for individuals who have been harassed and hold perpetrators or employers responsible in court. But more generally their effectiveness as a tool for social change depends to a great extent on their ability to change human behavior and employer practice. They can create awareness and hence change attitudes and interpretations. But this depends on enforcement and implementation.

Because of these thorny empirical questions, little research has been conducted on implementation of sexual harassment laws across different countries. Most comparative research focuses primarily on legal approaches and finds great variation in how laws define sexual harassment, provide access to courts, and hold perpetrators and employers responsible (Baer 1995; Bernstein 1994; Cahill 2001; Elman 1996; Hodges 1996; Husbands 1992; Saguy 2003). Laws can be on the books but lack effective enforcement and implementation mechanisms. We need to look beyond legal texts to see how a complex issue such as sexual harassment gets translated into workplace policies. Barely a handful of comparative studies of sexual harassment focus on employer responses (Rubenstein 1987; Cahill 2001; Saguy 2003). These studies show that laws are generally vague in defining sexual harassment and what employers need to do, and therefore leave much room for interpretation of what compliance is.[20] Implementation is itself a political process in which the identities and interests of actors are negotiated and contested.

There are several paths for implementation and enforcement of sexual harassment laws. The United States has embarked on the legal–regulatory route, where individuals hold employers responsible, and file complaints with the state agency and/or the courts. With relatively weak

---

[20] See also US implementation of family leave and anti-discrimination laws (Kelly and Dobbin 1999, 1998; Edelman, Erlanger, and Lande 1993).

legal redress, the German strategy of statutory corporatism relies primarily on collective bargaining between unions and employers as the main implementation and enforcement strategy. In Spain, France, and the Netherlands factory inspectors can also impose fines on companies if they do not comply with the sexual harassment laws.

In a comparison of the implementation of sexual harassment law, it is important to consider three main dimensions: (1) internal workplace policies and procedures; (2) prevention efforts such as training and awareness programs; and (3) agencies and services outside the workplace that implement, monitor, and enforce laws. These dimensions capture the difference legal reforms have made in the workplace.

The most visible difference between the United States and Germany is the sanctions employers face if they do not comply with the laws. Though the US state's capacity has been considered "weak," the EEOC, the state agency with the task of monitoring and enforcing, has actively pursued civil rights litigation, slowly extending its own institutional capacity (Pedriana and Stryker 2004; Dobbin and Kelly 2004; Dobbin and Sutton 1998). No German agency has such responsibility. The legal threat may be exaggerated by media reports and human resource professionals (Edelman 1990, 1992), but US laws are strict and employers risk legal costs from complaints, including punitive damages for failure to take adequate action.[21] In Germany, compensatory damages are insignificant, the concept of punitive damages does not exist, and, not surprisingly, many employers ignore the law. Yet, growing numbers, in particular public-sector employers, are beginning to consider sexual harassment a legitimate concern and address it through workplace policies, most often in the context of anti-mobbing policies.

The processes through which internal workplace policies and procedures are created can vary. Various actors are involved in constructing organizations' approach to sexual harassment. Unions can play a prominent role depending on the system of industrial relations. The US procedures are mostly designed by management, human resource managers, and external consultants. Only in the public sector, where unionization is more prevalent, have collective actors such as shop stewards been involved in creating policies. In EU member states, procedures are often negotiated between employers and workers' representatives. Collective agreements have some important advantages over employer-designed policies. They contribute to a process for change from "below"

---

[21] Since the 1991 Civil Rights Act, US courts can assign monetary compensation, including compensatory and punitive damages.

rather than enforcement from "above." Unions, as targets of change, can also be vehicles for change: they can play an important part in raising awareness by mobilizing women and men to promote gender-neutral workplace cultures. Feminists have found some unions an important and crucial ally for change, both in the unions themselves and in the workplace in general. Especially in the United States, private actors, such as insurance companies that cover employers' legal costs, have also become enforcers of the laws because they pressure employers to adopt policies and procedures.

Perhaps the most understudied phenomenon is how informal or formal women's networks – organizations formed across hierarchies – have brought the issue to the attention of employers (see, for example, Katzenstein 1998). These informal groups easily escape the eyes of researchers. Because they work behind closed doors, their forms of protest are rarely publicized. Yet, these groups have strategies to hold employers responsible. Even before Germany passed sexual harassment laws, some employers adopted policies because of the pressure these networks exerted. Similarly, cities adopted policies because various actors brought the issue to the attention of municipal officers.

Transatlantic learning

What lessons can the United States and the EU and its member states draw from one another? What are the advantages and disadvantages of the US approach, which relies on individual legal redress but allows employers to eradicate all "sexualized" behavior in the workplace, even consensual relationships, as Schultz (2003) argues? What are the advantages and disadvantages of the EU approach, which relies more on consensual forms of political change through parliaments and collective agreements? The EU states have embarked on an ambitious project to address the violation of integrity and dignity of *all workers*. What can the United States specifically learn from the EU effort to "mainstream" sexual harassment as a way to address justice and fairness for all workers? These broader questions will be investigated by asking how these paths can mobilize employers and unions, individual women and men in the workplace, to renew the gender contract and create a workplace culture that is inclusive for everyone.

Data

This study employs data from extensive fieldwork, including ninety-one interviews, and archival research in the United States, the EU, and

Germany (see Appendix B). To examine the *origins* of sexual harassment laws, the analysis took in archival materials, including legal texts, official documents, newspapers, and research where it exists. The *process of policy adoption* was examined through interviews with policy-makers, legal experts, feminist activists, trade unionists, and others. For *enactment and enforcement* in Germany and the United States, I compared court rulings in individual cases. To evaluate workplace changes, I compared employer policies and procedures and the consultation literature for employers. I interviewed those who handle sexual harassment complaints: human resource personnel, trade unionists, and (gender) equality advocates. Finally, I analyzed observations from training seminars, along with texts such as training manuals and information brochures, to assess how employers communicate the issue to employees. Because sexual harassment is still such a politically sensitive issue, most interviewees spoke to me only under conditions of confidentiality, and I chose not to use any names, unless the interviewees agreed to it (see Appendix A).

Chapter overview

Chapter Two examines the origins of the concept of sexual harassment and the key role played by a diverse feminist movement in constructing the issue as a legitimate public policy field in the United States. Drawing on the Civil Rights Act of 1964, US feminists framed sexual harassment as sex discrimination, a legal problem and issue for employers. This revolution led to a radical change in public perceptions, and media attention during the 1990s peaked with several political scandals. Legal developments were the most visible success, but individual lawsuits did not create the change alone; feminist actors used legal and lobbying strategies at the state and federal levels. This early process was characterized by struggles over meanings as well as ambivalence in finding legal and administrative solutions.

Chapter Three examines why the EU was an innovator, ahead of most member states. It examines how policy action moved between the EU and its member states and traces the influence of nonbinding EU measures. The TAN on gender equality, created with EU encouragement and assistance, was vital in the expansion of the EU legal framework on equal treatment to include sexual harassment in the Directive of 2002. Europeans viewed sexual harassment as a "cultural import" from the United States; the TAN was instrumental in making it a "European issue."

The in-depth study in Chapter Four shows how external factors, including supra- and international influences, shaped the German approach. It offers insights into the relationship between state actors and women's movements in a corporatist system. The German workplace system can be characterized by minimal state involvement and reliance on collective bargaining between employers and unions. Labor courts did not play an active role in shaping laws, despite their potential. Nor did grassroots women's organizations or unions put sexual harassment on their priority lists. The German Federal Employee Protection Law of 1994 resulted from the efforts of institutional actors – state offices for gender equality. These state feminists drew on transnational expertise to argue that Germany needed to implement EU measures. The resulting consensus-based law for the protection of dignity is relatively weak, with few enforcement mechanisms.

Chapter Five examines the difference these legal changes make in the workplace. US employers send male employees to "charm school" to teach nonsexualized "good" behavior. EEOC agencies and courts take an active role in shaping enforcement and create a perception of legal threat. An industry of legal consultants helps employers design internal procedures and training programs. German agencies have few monitoring and enforcement tools. Labor court decisions, while embarrassing for employers, do not carry punitive damages or significant compensatory awards. Unions and works councils participate in the design of policies and procedures based on consensual processes; the resulting broad, non-gender-specific, anti-mobbing policies subsume sexual harassment as a violation of workers' dignity.

The final chapter highlights the importance of a gender approach for the comparative study of social policies. Comparing the translation of feminist frames into laws reveals the links among frames and the institutional arrangements that can provide political opportunities for movements. The chapter discusses the implications of this study for broader questions of how social movements affect policy change in general, and feminist policy in particular, thereby addressing the reciprocal relationships between social movements and institutions. Comparative research allows us to reevaluate what we take for granted, how we think of sexual harassment, and which laws and strategies best combat sexual harassment in the workplace. The chapter draws lessons from the transatlantic comparison of employers, feminist movements, and unions in shaping the future of sexual harassment politics, paying special attention to different approaches to combating sexual harassment in the interest of promoting gender-fair workplace cultures.

2   Equality through litigation: sexual harassment in the United States

"The development of law against sexual harassment, and its transformation from private joke to public weapon, is one of the more successful
legal and political changes women have accomplished."(Catharine
MacKinnon 2002: 12)

The United States was the first country in the world to recognize sexual
harassment as sex discrimination, and today probably has the most sophisticated legal and institutional apparatus to handle such complaints in
the workplace and the legal system. It is important to note that although
there is a public perception that sexual harassment law has gone too far, in
fact it is by no means as broad as most people think it is – not only the
European but also the US public is frequently misled by misconstrued
and exaggerated interpretations of the reach of the law. Feminist advocates and legal scholars, however, are concerned that sexual harassment
laws have not gone far enough, as they still invite sexist interpretations and
possibly unfair applications of the law. Feminists continue to debate the
pitfalls, weaknesses, and problems of sexual harassment laws and their
applications (MacKinnon and Siegel (eds.) 2004).

Despite the criticism against the law from many sides, the revolution
of sexual harassment law in the United States can be considered a
feminist success story (Brownmiller 1999). The US law reflects and is
deeply influenced by feminist legal arguments; most importantly, US
courts have accepted a definition of sexual harassment from the victim's
perspective – as unwanted sexual behavior – or, as Gwendolyn Mink put
it, "the law begins with a woman's word" (2000: 4). Furthermore, under
the law sexual harassment is clearly linked to sex equality. It is a problem
that happens to women because they are women, because it constitutes
sex discrimination. In fact, victims of harassment have to prove in court
that they were discriminated against based on their sex.

The argument is that the feminist content of the laws against sexual
harassment is due to the particular legal–regulatory path the United States

took to address sexual harassment, which allowed the laws to be shaped by experiences of victims and feminist legal experts. The history of sexual harassment as a public issue – and as the object of legal and policy debate – is a complex one that began with injustice felt by individual women who lost their jobs because they did not want to have sex with their bosses in order to stay employed. Surprisingly, federal lawmakers have never explicitly prohibited the behavior or declared employers responsible for preventing it. Instead, the revolution in sexual harassment law has taken place mainly in the judiciary. The development of sexual harassment law has happened in court rooms. Victims filed lawsuits against their employers, arguing that their rights had been violated because of the sexual harassment they encountered at work and, moreover, that their employers had not taken their complaints seriously or acted on them appropriately. Judges, not elected lawmakers, have determined the kinds of behaviors that constitute sexual harassment and what employers' responsibilities are.

These legal changes have occurred in court rooms, but the individual lawsuits that triggered them did not occur in a vacuum. A broad, diverse movement against sexual harassment grew out of the second-wave women's movement, and these feminist actors used various strategies and tactics to frame sexual harassment as a legitimate policy issue. To understand how this came about, we must understand the context in which individuals came to challenge their employers in court and in which feminist activists worked. That context includes the civil rights movement and the legal reforms that resulted from it, embedded in a national legal history emphasizing civil law and individual rights.

In a common law legal system, these attorneys could build on strong existing anti-discrimination law, the Civil Rights Act of 1964, to convince the courts to recognize sexual harassment as sex discrimination. Individuals, but also feminist legal experts and a broad women's movement focused on workplace sex equity, used these laws. The emerging movement against violence against women was crucial to supplying new ways of conceptualizing intimacy and turning private issues into political ones. These factors, coupled with extraordinary publicity from several high-profile sexual harassment scandals, coalesced in the legal structures and the structures of public consciousness around sexual harassment in the United States, where the topic remains contentious.

This particular legal–liberal path is a common strategy of social movements in the United States. Courts have been the target and the site of struggles over social issues from abortion rights to cigarette company liability for damage from tobacco consumption.[1] Expanding existing law

---

[1] See O'Connor 1980; Gelb 1989; Handler 1978; McCann 1994; Morris 1984.

through the courts is a powerful strategy in common law legal systems, where attorneys can base their arguments on previous rulings and judges must take precedents into account when interpreting law. The development of case law through litigation provides the opportunity to use litigation as a strategy. Social movements can support a specific case if they expect it to be precedent-setting. The legal path is open for all groups involved. The civil rights movement used litigation to challenge segregation and the exclusion of Blacks from the vote beginning in the 1950s.

Perhaps because the model of the US liberal state is based on minimal state intervention, and convincing lawmakers to adopt new laws is a cumbersome strategy requiring much lobbying work and powerful allies in Washington, for the anti-harassment movement in the United States these particular institutional arrangements meant that legal strategies proved to be more successful than lobbying for sexual harassment laws, especially during the 1980s era under President Ronald Reagan.

The objective of this chapter is not to follow the chronological developments of case law around sexual harassment; this has been done already by some of the pioneering sexual harassment feminist legal scholars such as Catharine MacKinnon (see MacKinnon and Siegel 2004). The chapter focuses rather on the legal–regulatory path of addressing it, which both constrained and enabled feminist contributions to changes in public sensitivity, laws, and the workplace. It tells the story from the perspective of the actors involved in building revolutionary sexual harassment law – individuals, political groups, and organizations that initiated, contributed to, and shaped the legal and policy approach.

What becomes apparent is that a broad movement against sexual harassment began on several fronts in the mid-1970s. Some of this work appeared in the public eye, but much occurred behind closed doors in legal institutions and workplaces. First, individuals took their employers to court. Second, feminists founded organizations concerned with sexual harassment. There was some federal response to their concerns, but legal developments were mainly shaped in the courts. Finally, the media contributed significantly to increasing awareness of sexual harassment, though they also did much to misrepresent sexual harassment law.

Early discrimination court cases

Increasing numbers of women entered the workplace in the 1970s. Because employers were being forced to dismantle discriminatory practices, women entered previously male-dominated fields such as mining, factory jobs, and the police, although they remained a small minority in these occupations. As they broke gender barriers, they often experienced hostility. Male colleagues asked them out repeatedly, put up porno- graphic posters, told sexual stories, and so forth (Prieto 1983). There was no public awareness of what we now call sexual harassment, al- though the experiences of the plaintiffs in the early cases demonstrate the gravity of the problem.

In 1975, Lois Jenson, a single mother on welfare, decided to start a new life by taking a job at Eveleth Mines in Minnesota. It paid much better than any job she had held before. On her second day at work, another miner said, "You fucking women don't belong here. If you knew what was good for you, you'd go home where you belong" (Bingham and Gansler 2002: 14). A few months later, her male instructor urinated on a tire. Then he "zipped up his fly . . . Far from being embarrassed, the miner seized the moment to tell her about the time he pulled two tampons out of his wife, and to regale Jenson with stories of deer having sex." Seventeen women coworkers who had similar or worse experiences joined Jenson in filing the first class-action suit on sexual harassment alleging a hostile work environment. Their case, *Jenson v. Eveleth Taco- nite Co.*,[2] was decided on September 1, 1999 – almost twenty-five years later and after one of the victims had died.

In many occupations, supervisors' power has meant that they could demote, transfer, or fire women who refused their demands for sexual favors. Adrienne Tomkins,[3] a secretary for Public Service Electric and Gas Company (PSE&G), alleged that her supervisor made sexual ad- vances with threats of reprisal if she did not comply. She told the court that her boss asked her out for lunch and gave her an "ultimatum to engage in an affair with him or lose my job." He had said, "I want to lay you," and "I can't walk around the office with a hard-on all the time." When she refused, he held her forcibly and kissed her. After she com- plained, she was first transferred to a less desirable position and later fired (Baker 2001: 55).

Women who experienced unwanted sexual advances had few options, partly because sexual harassment in employment was not illegal. Further- more, they had few words with which to name their experience. As we will see, it was not until 1975 that feminist activists coined the term "sexual harassment." Women's complaints about sexual jokes and comments were frequently not taken seriously by employers, state agencies, or courts. Many employers did not have a process for handling complaints. Women who took the matter to a superior were often met with disbelief.

---

[2] 824 F. Supp. 847, (D. Minn. 1993) (settled January 4, 1999).
[3] *Tomkins v. Public Service Electric & Gas Co.*, 562F. 2d. 55 (3rd Circuit 1976).

Even managers who believed them did not take the complaints seriously, especially if no physical touching was involved. Women were told they were overreacting and were blamed for being too sensitive or for bringing it on themselves through dress and behavior. The men's behavior was often excused by a "boys will be boys" attitude. Supervisors who did take action often transferred women out of the unit, leaving the perpetrators in their positions. Most often, nothing happened, though if word got out, women experienced retaliation for being whistle-blowers.

Women who left their jobs could not file for unemployment, because state agencies did not recognize sexual harassment as cause for quitting. Carmita Wood, an administrative assistant at Cornell University who left her job in 1974 because harassment had made her physically ill, was denied unemployment payment (see discussion below). In the same year a district court ruled in a case of religious discrimination[4] that employers violate Title VII of the Civil Rights Act of 1964 when they create conditions under which "an employee involuntarily resigns in order to escape intolerable and illegal employment requirements." To claim "constructive discharge," the employee had to show that the intolerable or illegal conditions were based on race, color, religion, sex, or national origin. Sexual harassment was not considered discrimination on the basis of sex. Only in 1981 did a court rule[5] that sexual harassment in the form of hostile environment could result in constructive discharge and eligibility for unemployment benefits (Mink 2000: 4 n. 9).

Women who experienced sexual assault or severe physical overtures and could provide proof in court could use tort law to argue for infliction of emotional distress. But they faced (and still face) the problem that sexual harassment usually occurs without witnesses, behind closed doors, so in court one word stands against the other. Neither employers nor state agencies nor the legal system were responsive to complaints by individual women. Most women therefore did not speak up, tried to avoid harassing situations, and in general took for granted that they had to put up with sexual harassment on the job.

The legal situation changed dramatically when courts began to recognize sexual harassment as sex discrimination. In the early 1970s, several women filed complaints with equal employment offices and decided to file suits against their employers because they had lost their jobs for refusing the sexual advances of their supervisors. How did women come

---

[4] *Young v. Southwestern Savings and Loan Association*, 509F. 2d. 140, 144 (6th Circuit 1975).

[5] *Caldwell v. Hodgeman*, 25 Fair Employment Practice Case (BNA) 1647, 1649–50 (D. Mass. 1981).

to the belief that supervisors and colleagues should treat them with respect in the workplace? Why did they believe that courts would give them justice and reinstate them in their jobs?

The 1970s was a time of turbulent gender politics. The civil rights movement had heightened people's awareness of racial injustice. For African American women, sexual and racial harassment were intertwined, so it is not surprising that the plaintiffs in three of the six leading 1970s sexual harassment cases were African American women. Some of them worked in public offices dedicated to racial equality yet experienced sexual inequality in their work lives. Many were not in middle-class jobs; they included a payroll clerk, office worker, assistant collection manager, and information specialist. Margaret Miller, who filed for both sex and race discrimination, testified that her white male supervisor "promised her a better job if she would be sexually 'cooperative' and caused her dismissal when she refused." He showed up at her home with a bottle of wine, saying "I've never felt this way about a black chick before" and that he would get her "off the machines" if she cooperated with him sexually (cited in Baker 2001: 55).[6]

The battle over whether sexual harassment constitutes sex discrimination was fought with these court cases. Arguing that the civil rights had been violated because they had been discriminated against based on sex, the attorneys filed suits under Title VII. Most plaintiffs lost their cases at lower levels. For example, Judge Stern in *Tomkins* argued that "Title VII was enacted in order to remove those artificial barriers to full employment which are based upon unjust and long-encrusted prejudice. Its aim is to make careers open to talents irrespective of race or sex. It is not intended to provide a federal tort remedy for what amounts to physical attack motivated by sexual desire on the part of a supervisor and which happened to occur in a corporate corridor rather than a back alley." Thus, while Judge Stern took the harassment seriously as a physical attack, he did not see it as a workplace issue, because he considered it a private, personal matter that only happened to occur in the workplace.

Other judges agreed with defense arguments that the incidents were a private matter and employers should not be responsible. For example, the judge in *Corne v. Bausch & Lomb, Inc.*[7] reasoned: "By his alleged sexual advance, Mr. Price was satisfying a personal urge." The judge argued that the woman's dismissal had little to do with gender inequality,

---

[6] *Miller v. Bank of America*, 418F. Supp. 233 (N.D. Col. 1976), 600F.2d 211 (9th Circuit 1979).

[7] 390f. Supp. 161 (D. Ariz. 1975), 562F. 2d. 55 (9th Circuit 1977).

reasoning "she was not terminated because she was a woman, but because she had refused sexual advances."

Plaintiffs, their lawyers and advocates, and feminist theorists argued that sexual harassment was sex discrimination because "women are sexually harassed because they are women" (MacKinnon 1979: 191). They also linked harassment to gender inequality in the workplace, an unfair working condition. The Equal Employment Opportunity Commission supported this argument in *Corne* with an amicus curiae brief arguing that the supervisor's sexual advances had been directed toward the plaintiffs because they were female. Accordingly, Title VII should apply because it prohibits "irrational impediment to job opportunities." Sexual harassment was an "irrational, or unwarranted, working condition" that affected the employment of women, since "the choice between frequent unsolicited sexual advances and being unemployed has a significant and clearly unwarranted effect on employment opportunities . . . If Title VII does not provide such elementary protection against sexually motivated conduct, its promise to women is virtually without meaning" (cited in Baker 2001: 63).

The first court to accept that sexual harassment was sex discrimination actionable under Title VII was the trial court in the District of Columbia in *Williams v. Saxbe*[8] in 1976. Diane Williams, an African American woman who worked as a public information specialist with the Justice Department Community Relations Service, alleged that her black male supervisor harassed her. When she resisted his advances, including his promise to enhance her employment status if she had an affair with him, he began a "conscious campaign" to retaliate. She did not get a promised promotion and was reassigned to a position of less responsibility. Her attorney argued that the "continuing pattern and practice of harassment and humiliation because of her sex had denied her equal opportunities for advancement and promotion" (cited in Baker 2001: 52).

In this groundbreaking case, the white male judge, Charles Richey, reasoned that sexual harassment was discriminatory to women because men and women were being treated differently: women had to put up with harassment, while men did not, so "the conduct of the plaintiff's supervisor created an artificial barrier to employment which was placed before one gender and not the other." He compared sexual harassment to discriminatory employer policies that exclude married women or women with preschool children.

---

[8] 413 F. Supp. 654 (D.D.C. 1976).

Judge Richey's precedent-making decision had an enormous impact on sexual harassment law. With *Williams* in hand, attorneys challenged lower court decisions, and appellate courts for several plaintiffs overturned those decisions. The women were reinstated into their jobs and received some financial compensation for lost income, attorney fees, and so on; these awards were all less than $50,000. With these federal cases as precedents, lower courts began to recognize *quid pro quo* sexual harassment in which supervisors offer advantages in exchange for sexual favors or threaten disadvantages for failing to comply.

Most important for the creation of public awareness, these cases triggered the interest of the mainstream media. Print and broadcast media gave much coverage to the issues, though mostly ridiculing, trivializing, and mocking the *Williams* decision (Baker 2001: 70). Some argued that "the so-called Sexual Revolution is over." Sexual harassment now also attracted legal scholars and commentators, which gave an impetus for the development of jurisprudence.

Because the 1964 Civil Rights Act focuses on employers, only a few courts have held individual perpetrators legally responsible under Title VII (Stein 1999: 68; MacKinnon 2004). As in labor law, courts limit the reach of the act to the contract between employers and employees by making employers legally liable, though victims have the option to use state tort law to sue individuals for intentional infliction of emotional distress or invasion of privacy.

The courts left up to employers how to sanction perpetrators, but were more sympathetic to victims if employers had not taken their complaints seriously. For example, the court in *Munford v. James T. Barnes and Co.*[9] concluded that the employer has an affirmative duty to investigate sexual harassment complaints and take appropriate action against offenders. Some courts ordered employers to adopt company policies and conduct training programs. In *Tomkins*, the court argued that the employer, by not responding to her complaint, was complicit and therefore liable. The employer was now required to notify all employees that sexual harassment is against the law, to inform supervisors that they would be disciplined, and to contribute to awareness by showing a film informing employees about their rights.

Thus the legal revolution against sexual harassment in the United States began with individual women who were brave enough to risk their necks (Brownmiller and Alexander 1992). These cases were not initiated or sought out by women's organizations, and some plaintiffs were disappointed that the organizations did not support them in lower-level courts

[9] 441 F. Supp. 459 (E.D. Mich. 1977).

(Marshall 2001: 133). This lack of assistance might have been due in part to the fact that collective forms of action against harassment began only in the mid-1970s. Several feminist public law organizations did take an interest in some cases when they reached federal appellate courts. In the following years, these organizations continued to support individual cases. They helped women find counsel, helped attorneys prepare, and submitted amicus briefs in support of the plaintiffs if they thought a case would set an important precedent.

The origins of sexual harassment litigation are a puzzle for social movement theorists because, as Anna-Maria Marshall (2001) points out, non-activists played a crucial role. These individual lawsuits did not happen, however, without the context of the civil rights and women's movements, which had created what Marshall calls an oppositional consciousness. Based on interviews with plaintiffs and attorneys, Marshall found a "spectrum in forms of oppositional consciousness that ranged from committed activist, in the case of some of the lawyers, to the influenced nonactivist, in the case of some of the plaintiffs" (2001: 140). Some plaintiffs were feminist-identified, but most did not see themselves as spearheading a social movement. Several had turned to civil rights organizations for help in locating attorneys – feminists, civil rights lawyers, and other lawyers who could build on the legal successes of the civil rights and women's movements. Feminist discourse and emerging legal theories helped attorneys make their cases. In turn, the movement against sexual harassment benefited from these court cases in legitimizing it as a serious issue to which employers and politicians should pay attention. These cases gave feminists who began to organize against sexual harassment an important "legal weapon" to work with and build on.

The social movement context for sexual harassment politics in the 1970s

The attorneys in these early US cases had an important advantage over their colleagues in most European Union countries, where anti-discrimination laws were passed only during the 1970s. The Civil Rights Act of 1964 and the establishment of the EEOC to implement and enforce this and other anti-discrimination laws provided an important base for the fight for equal employment protection. This is not to say that legislators intentionally built laws that would help feminists fight sexual harassment. But activists did benefit from the foundations laid by the Civil Rights Act of 1964 and the 1963 Equal Pay Act, both of which preceded the second-wave women's movement. Lobby groups had advocated for equal pay legislation for many decades, but no organized movement had done so for the 1963 Act (Gelb and Palley 1982: 175). The Civil Rights Act of 1964 was intended primarily to address racial segregation and inequality. "Sex" was added at the last minute as an amendment by Representative Howard Smith of Virginia, a Southern Democrat hoping to delegitimize the legislation. As with the first introduction of the Equal Rights Amendment (ERA) later, women's groups were divided over the inclusion of sex, for fear that protective legislation for women would be dismantled, and the EEOC was at first hesitant to pursue sex discrimination cases (Kenney 1992: 51).

The civil rights movement also provided attorneys and activists with the "master frame" of individual rights (Tarrow 1994; Snow and Benford 1992; O'Connor, Orloff, and Shaver 1999). Previous cases addressing race discrimination were used along with feminist discourse and emerging feminist legal theories to bolster arguments in sexual harassment cases. MacKinnon became the single most influential and visible feminist legal scholar on sexual harassment. Her path-breaking 1979 book, *Sexual Harassment of Working Women*, provided the academic concept of sexual harassment; she had circulated previous drafts already to attorneys and some courts. It made the case that civil rights law was the best way to formulate sexual harassment because the civil rights framework is equality-based and protects women not as individuals but as members of a group. Litigation based on the Civil Rights Act of 1964 uses "group-based" logic rather than treating sexual harassment as a moral problem or an individual harm as criminal or tort law would. Civil rights law would get to the root of the problem: gender inequality. MacKinnon also drew from feminist theories on rape and violence and from scholarship that combined sociological and historical explanations of sexual coercion in the workplace. Her distinction of sexual harassment as *quid pro quo* and hostile environment was adapted by the EEOC and later affirmed by the Supreme Court case *Meritor Savings Bank v. Vinson* in 1986.

Linking sexual harassment to sex discrimination was crucial for several reasons. First, activists did not have to convince lawmakers to pass a new law. Second, the US notion of individual rights to equal and "fair" treatment resonated with individuals, made sense to attorneys, and fit into an increasingly mainstream notion of injustice as violating the individual right to equal treatment in the workplace. Third, with sexual harassment understood as discrimination based on sex, anti-discrimination laws provided powerful tools for promoting *employers'* actions, because they helped formulate an employee's right vis-à-vis his or her employer. Fourth, existing implementation and enforcement structures, most prominently the EEOC, could be used to make sure sexual harassment law would be taken seriously.

The Civil Rights Act of 1964 provided an important political opportunity. The EEOC was created to enforce and implement the Civil Rights Act, and employers created EEO or affirmative action (AA) offices in their workplaces (Dobbin and Sutton 1998; Edelman 1990; Pedriana and Stryker 2004). The plaintiffs in the early cases used workplace and state EEO offices to file complaints, a process far less costly than filing tort or criminal suits. Once the federal courts accepted sexual harassment as sex discrimination, the EEOC provided a range of tools for implementation and enforcement. These early court cases were thus important, beyond their success for the individual plaintiffs.

During the 1970s, a broad second-wave women's movement was active in Washington. With a Democratic president, Jimmy Carter, women's groups were at the height of their influence as lobbying groups. Much of the effort of the national US women's movement at this time was focused on the Equal Rights Amendment and the achievement and defense of abortion rights (Gelb 1989; Costain 1992). Another arm, a network of national women's organizations, pursued gender equality in the workplace. US feminists were most successful in pursuing "liberal" gender politics oriented toward "sameness" (O'Connor, Orloff, and Shaver 1999). For example, the Equal Credit Opportunity Act of 1974 allowed women equal access to credit transactions, prohibiting discrimination based on sex or marital status. These groups also worked to strengthen anti-discrimination legislation in employment and education. In 1972, the women's lobby was able to find allies to convince Congress to pass Title IX, prohibiting discrimination in education programs that receive federal funds. Women's groups had argued that protective laws such as working time restrictions and protection of pregnant women from hazardous working conditions were discriminatory; despite opposition from women in unions, some of these laws were dismantled (Kenney 1992). When the Supreme Court did not rule in favor of including pregnant women in employers' disability provisions, a coalition of 300 groups forged the Campaign to End Discrimination Against Pregnant Workers and fought successfully for the 1978 Pregnancy Discrimination Act (PDA), which amended Title VII (Gelb and Palley 1982). Thus, during the 1970s, an informal network of organized women's groups was quite successful at finding allies and lobbying "friendly" policy-makers for the passage of laws that extended the Civil Rights Act.

By contrast, feminists mobilizing on sexual harassment were not able to promote new legislation at the federal level. Some activists and experts did lobby for new laws in several congressional hearings. But given the controversial nature of the issue (even among feminists), it is not surprising that feminists could not build a consensus on how to define sexual harassment and how to hold employers or perpetrators responsible. Advocates might have argued for a specific law against sexual harassment as the protection of women's particular vulnerability to sexual coercion by men. But in the dominant frame of gender politics, "gender sameness," an argument for such a law would have been hard to make. Furthermore, the positive climate for feminist agendas in Washington changed dramatically in the 1980s under Reagan. It is unlikely that any law to prohibit sexual harassment that might have costs for businesses could have passed during that period. In fact, the EEOC under Reagan investigated how to limit employers' liabilities. So activists worked with established women's organizations to expand the Civil Rights Act, not to introduce a new law.

Feminist activism and strategies

Just as US courts were the first to rule that sexual harassment was sex discrimination, second-wave feminists were also the first to mobilize explicitly around the issue. While the early court cases were taking place, a broad, loosely connected network of women's organizations became concerned with sexual harassment (Farley 1978; Brownmiller and Alexander 1992; Segrave 1994). The movement grew from two main arms of the women's movement: a locally organized grassroots movement against violence and nationally organized networks advocating for working women. Typical of strategies at this time, some feminists built independent women's organizations focusing on sexual harassment, and these made important contributions to the development of sexual harassment protections.

Working Women United (WWU) was founded by forty women in Ithaca, New York, in 1975. When Lin Farley, an activist, was teaching an experimental course on women and work at Cornell University, students began talking about losing summer jobs because of sexual coercion. When Farley learned that Carmita Wood, a Cornell employee, was seeking help, she, Susan Meyer, and Karen Sauvigne used their experience in organizing and mobilizing women to address sexual harassment. The very notion of sexual harassment was born in Ithaca. According to Susan Brownmiller, Sauvigne remembered: "Eight of us were sitting in an office of Human Affairs brainstorming about what we were going to write on posters for our speak-out. We were referring to it as 'sexual intimidation,' 'sexual coercion,' 'sexual exploitation on the job.' None of those names seemed quite right. We wanted something that embraced a whole range of subtle and unsubtle persistent behaviors. Somebody came up with 'harassment.' Sexual harassment! Instantly we agreed. That's what it was" (Brownmiller 1999: 281).

A separate Working Women United Institute founded by Meyer and Sauvigne, also in 1975, became a clearinghouse for inquiries, drawing on local and national networks of crisis counselors and lawyers. While they hoped to influence public policy, their primary purpose was to create awareness and mobilize women to resist collectively using the public protest form called speak-outs. Working Women United had roots in the women's working movement and close contact with academic researchers. They attempted to mobilize and include women workers in Ithaca in their organization, and later moved to New York City to build a broader base for their operations (Baker 2001). Working Women United Institute women had connections to a network of national women's organizations that pursued gender equality in the workplace. For example, they knew Karen DeCrow, president of the National Organization for Women (NOW), and used their NOW contacts to create awareness of the sexual harassment issue in feminist organizations (Baker 2001: 95).

The second single-issue organization, the Alliance Against Sexual Coercion (AASC), the first grassroots organization against sexual harassment, was founded in Boston in June 1977. From their work as rape crisis counselors, its founders were aware of the problems women faced when they experienced sexual harassment in the workplace. "Knowing these women's centers and rape crisis centers were already overworked, the founding AASC members decided to set up separate services specifically for sexual harassment" (Alliance Against Sexual Coercion 1981: 79). The organization was oriented toward providing services for victims and creating awareness in organizations and workplaces.

Other workplace-oriented organizations included Women Office Workers (WOW), founded in 1973 by 300 New York workers, which like the Working Women United Institute originated in consciousness-raising efforts (Segrave 1994). Most of the early organizations had disintegrated by the 1980s, but 9 to 5, the National Association of Working Women, has remained a visible organization concerned with sexual harassment. A clerk-typist, Karen Nussbaum, founded this organization for women office workers with Ellen Bravo in 1973 in Boston. Its goal was to attract the attention of both management and the trade union movement. Nussbaum was later appointed by President Bill Clinton as director of the Women's Bureau in the Department of Labor.

Thus, a few single-issue independent women's organizations concerned with sexual harassment emerged. They had ties to other second-wave organizations, and borrowed a variety of strategies from the civil rights and women's movements to combat sexual harassment. But using courts to combat sexual harassment was not their main strategy, nor was lobby work in Washington a priority.

Feminist discourse

The foremost important contribution of the organizations I have discussed was to identify sexual harassment as a social problem and create legitimacy for it as a political problem. Like the emerging antiviolence movement, these activists were aware of the importance of finding a language to discuss sexual harassment. It is important to remember what workplace culture looked like for women in the 1970s. Increasingly aware of gender and expecting to be treated fairly and equally, women began to rebel when asked to perform tasks such as making coffee, which were not included in job descriptions but expected because they were women (Karen Nussbaum, interview, 2002). Gendered expectations also included serving, performing emotional work such as keeping others happy, and looking pretty and smiling. Women began to question why they were expected to wear a mini-skirt and listen to sexual jokes and innuendos. The topic of "sex in the office" was certainly not new, and popular culture had a whole genre of jokes about sexual relations between secretaries and bosses, doctors and nurses, and so on. Feminists wanted to draw attention to the fact that much of this was unwanted and not consensual. They set out to demonstrate not only how widespread the issue was but that sexual harassment was not merely a problem of individual women but a structural issue of gender discrimination. Lin Farley, who documented the emergence of the notion in *Sexual Shakedown: The Sexual Harassment of Women on the Job* (1978), summarized the experience at Cornell: "The male behavior eventually required a name, and sexual harassment seemed to come about as close to symbolizing the problem as the language would permit" (1978: xi).

These feminists used organizational and protest forms similar to those around abortion and violence. Speak-outs were held to empower individual women through talking about their personal experience and realizing its political dimension. Two hundred women gathered at the first speak-out in Ithaca, speaking openly about their shame, embarrassment, and feelings of guilt, and also expressing their anger. Thus, instead of (self-) blaming women, these activists created a language to make perpetrators of sexual harassment responsible, and to find a way to make employers accountable.

Feminists not only gave sexual harassment a name but transformed it from a taboo moral issue into a woman's rights issue. Using the argumentative strategy developed for rape, they insisted that sexual harassment was not a matter of "sexual desire" or "flirtation gone wrong" but an "expression of power," more specifically an abuse of (hierarchical or masculinist) power over women (Farley 1978; MacKinnon 1979; Backhouse and Cohen 1981: 36ff). In particular, feminists in AASC drew parallels to sexual assault and rape, shifted attention to issues previously considered "private," and explored cultural, social, institutional, and organizational factors. To hold employers accountable, they framed sexual harassment as a problem of the workplace: Farley defined it as "unsolicited, non-reciprocal male behavior that asserts a woman's sex role over her function as worker" (Farley 1978: xi). Sociologists provided an organizational analysis, tying sexual harassment to hierarchical workplace structures and linking gender inequalities to race and class (Gutek 1985; Acker 1990; Cockburn 1991).

These organizations were also involved in creating expertise, "factual" knowledge about sexual harassment. They coordinated several surveys whose responses (though they did not satisfy academic standards of representativeness and had other methodological problems) gave feminist advocates legitimacy and supported the argument that sexual harassment was widespread and serious (Gillespie and Leffler 1987). Historical studies also helped link women's subordinate status and vulnerability as domestic workers and factory workers to persistent abuse of male authority and power. The discourse and expertise feminists created proved to be very useful in the courts. Supportive state officials, lawmakers, and employers picked up feminist discourses to justify their concern. Finally, as we will see in later chapters, sexual harassment activists and researchers abroad benefited from this early theorizing and expertise in the United States.

Activists in the 1970s also used the media strategically to stimulate and influence public debates and increase awareness among the broader public. AASC and Working Women United members wrote extensively for magazines and newspapers (Weeks et al. 1986). They sent out news releases, supplied journalists with information, and responded to their questions. Unlike in most European states, popular media also took on a feminist viewpoint of the issue. Karen Nussbaum convinced Jane Fonda, a friend from the antiwar movement, of the importance of the problem (Brownmiller and Alexander 1992). In 1980 Fonda starred in and produced the box office hit movie *9 to 5* (Bravo and Cassedy 1992).

Farley and other activists in Ithaca organized in support of Carmita Wood's lawsuit. After Wood lost her case, however, WWU limited its engagement with litigation to helping individual women find lawyers and supporting attorneys with expertise and knowledge. AASC was critical of bureaucratic, legal solutions and a strong promoter of grassroots, extralegal solutions. Its publications suggested that women should organize collectively and write letters to harassers, detailing the offense and the potential of legal/extralegal actions if the behavior continued (Alliance Against Sexual Coercion 1981). It recommended protests and demonstrations outside harassers' homes and workplaces and posters in the community identifying the harasser and the offenses.

Thus, sexual harassment activists used direct-action strategies, borrowing from the antiviolence and working women movements. They mobilized women, used the media strategically to create public awareness, and, most important, created alternative discourses, knowledge, and expertise through research. Providing opportunities for empowerment and "self-help" for women confronted with sexual harassment, rather than calling on institutions to protect women, was a central concern.

Neither WWU nor AASC focused on legislative change or litigation as a strategy. Nor were they lobbying to persuade policy-makers, Congress, and acting president Gerald Ford to pass a new law. Instead, they built on early court victories and used informal networks, particularly in the legal community and with the media, to further their cause. Nevertheless, a broad policy network of organizations, feminist activists, and women lawyers and journalists had become influential in monitoring the implementation and enforcement of sex discrimination laws and regulations. This feminist legal community formed around litigation strategies and used the particular political opportunity structure of the Civil Rights Act of 1964 in Washington D.C. to advance their goals through the legal path. Sexual harassment ended up on their agenda, too.

Feminist–state interaction

While the federal government did not pass new sexual harassment laws, Congress, state agencies, and state governments did help legitimate the issue. Feminist organizations had a voice in the first federal initiatives. Representative James M. Hanley, Democrat from New York, called for the first congressional hearings on sexual harassment. Hanley, chair of the House Committee on Post Office and Civil Service and of the Subcommittee on Investigations, held two hearings in 1979 and 1980. The committees heard four days of reports, testimonies, and expert witnesses, including EEOC chair Eleanor Holmes Norton, and representatives of other state agencies, unions, and organizations, for example, the American Federation of Government Employees and Federally Employed Women.

Unlike any official hearing in the EU or Germany, US public hearings on sexual harassment included first-hand reports and experiences of victims in their own voices. Diane Williams, one of the early plaintiffs, spoke, as did representatives of feminist organizations, including staff members from the Women's Legal Defense Fund and the National Organization for Women, and Mary Ann Largen, director of New Responses, a national lobby group for the feminist antiviolence movement. By 1980, feminist organizations were accepted as a legitimate pressure group.

As an important consequence of these hearings, the federal government began to take measures in the public sector and beyond. The US Merit Systems Protection Board was commissioned to investigate sexual harassment in the federal workplace; its report became the first representative study (U.S.M.S.P.B. 1981, 1988, 1995). The Office of Personnel and Management was instructed to issue policy directives and initiate training. Finally, the EEOC guidelines, though drafted before the first hearing, encompassed both federal government and private-sector employers.

Under Norton's directorship, the EEOC between 1977 and 1981 took an active role in sexual harassment as a legal and policy issue. Norton, appointed by President Carter, was an African American, a strong supporter of civil rights, an advocate for working women, and a major influence on sexual harassment policy. Norton was a *femocrat*, though not in charge of a state office for women but in an office for discrimination issues. For Norton, sexual harassment was similar to racial harassment. She called on the federal government to set an example of how to combat it and called on all employers to take action: "As in its actions to curtail racial and other forms of discrimination, the federal government should set the tone of other employers in trying to rid the workplace of this manifestation of the culture's bias against women. The Commission believes that sexual harassment must be brought to the surface as a workplace issue and dealt with affirmatively and aggressively by the employer" (Norton 1981: 93).

Norton used the feminist argument that sexual harassment was an economic problem women faced. She drew the analogy to racial discrimination by suggesting that integration of women and men would solve the problem: "The overall problem of sexual harassment will only be abated when women cease meeting artificial barriers to their career advancement; when they are present at all levels of employment, and represented in all job categories. A man contemplating sexual harassment reacts differently when he knows that there are women in his chain of command, and a man who would ignore sexual harassment by his colleague reacts differently when he understands that it could also happen to his wife or daughter" (90–98).

During Norton's leadership the EEOC supported several suits with amicus curiae briefs arguing that Title VII should be applied in sexual harassment cases (for example *Corne*, *Tomkins*, and *Bundy*). Most important for sexual harassment policy, however, were the 1980 guidelines. Norton explained that the commission also intended to issue policy guidance for private employers: "Because EEOC was also concerned about the plight of women in non-federal jobs, the commission decided that the clearest, most meaningful, and most consistent way to convey to all employers the unlawfulness of sexual harassment was through the issuance of an interpretative guideline applicable in other public and private employment" (42). The EEOC guidelines, she argued, merely confirmed EEOC practice of treating sexual harassment as a violation of the Civil Rights Act of 1964. But the EEOC went beyond the legal precedents of early federal appellate cases and defined harassment as *quid pro quo* and hostile environment, following MacKinnon's differentiation. Though not binding for the courts, the guidelines were later affirmed by a 1986 Supreme Court ruling. Employers took notice of them and began to implement measures in the workplace.

The EEOC used several means to influence sexual harassment policy, in particular issuing guidelines for employers and asking courts to clarify the Civil Rights Act of 1964. The EEOC can be an advocate for victims. When the commission gets a complaint, it is authorized to seek a voluntary settlement. If no settlement can be achieved and the commission feels the complaint has sufficient merit, it can bring the complaint before the courts on behalf of the complainant. The justification for interference in workplace regulations here is based on the ideal of fairness. In the neoliberal market ideology, the state has the duty to ensure the free play of market forces. If fairness and equality of opportunities are not guaranteed, market mechanisms cannot work. Though the EEOC itself does not have enforcement powers but must rely on the courts for the final say, it is nonetheless an agency with potentially substantive regulatory power.

The early phase of policy initiation came during a politically favorable climate, and feminist organizations had unofficial input through the submission of policy suggestions, proposals, and legal definitions. The crucial EEOC guidelines were passed in 1980, under President Carter and in the last year of Norton's directorship. Women's organizations had established strong ties to Norton, who continued to be a vocal advocate even after she left her post. For example, she spoke on behalf of forty-eight women's organizations in favor of continuing efforts to combat harassment in a hearing before the Senate Committee on Labor and Human Resources in 1981.

NOW and other women's organizations have not always had an amicable relationship with the EEOC, nor has the EEOC consistently been a strong ally of advocates for gender equality and sexual harassment measures. Historically, the agency did not want to take on cases of sex discrimination. Along with generally monitoring and promoting women's rights in Washington, the very reason feminists founded NOW was to push the implementation of sex discrimination law which had been ignored by the EEOC. However, to the surprise of European observers, the EEOC at times allowed NOW to assist in monitoring settlements and consulted NOW before signing consent decrees with employers (Meehan 1985: 127).

The fact that much of MacKinnon's conceptualization of sexual harassment made its way into federal policy reflects the high appreciation for feminist legal expertise in the agency during that period. Yet, feminist organizations did not "write" the entire EEOC guidelines. A major compromise with conservative forces was the inclusion of sexual favoritism. Sexual favoritism occurs when an employee experiences disadvantages and a coworker receives preferred treatment because the coworker is having a sexual relationship with their supervisor. Critics argued that the EEOC had bought into sexist stereotypes of women who used sexual favors to "sleep their way up" (Baker 2001: 326). Only in the US context, in which sexual harassment is depicted as an issue of "fairness," did this concept of sexual favoritism take hold. Employers have subsequently used it as an excuse to prohibit even consensual relationships between coworkers in the workplace.

Changes in political constellations and in EEOC leadership reflect the advantages and disadvantages of a "politicized" administration (Gelb 1989). Because presidents appoint the EEOC head and allocate the agency's resources, its role has changed over time, depending on the president. Without support from presidents Reagan and G.H.W. Bush in the 1980s, the EEOC suffered budgetary constraints that limited its function. For example, the existing backlog of cases increased over time (Abramson 1979; Skaine 1996). In subsequent years, feminist interest groups lost what voice they had had in it.

Even more remarkable changes occurred in EEOC politics on sexual harassment. In 1981 Reagan appointed Clarence Thomas to replace

Norton. Not surprisingly, given what would later be learned about what went on in the EEOC itself, under Thomas sexual harassment policy was by no means the focus of EEOC attention. In line with pro-business philosophy, Thomas even considered reducing employers' burden for supervisors who harassed subordinates (Hill 1997: 76–7). Anita Hill was assigned the task of assessing EEOC policy, which made her aware of her own struggle: "I was flooded with embarrassment at my own experience. Still, it never entered the discussion as I reviewed my conclusions with Clarence Thomas." She recommended keeping the existing policy on employer liability, which Thomas hesitantly accepted (76–7).

It is curious that employers did not lobby the EEOC more strongly to cut back emphasis on employer liability and the need for policies and preventive measures. Norton painted a picture of employers supportive of measures against sexual harassment: "The great majority of the comments from the business community on the [guidelines] were also favorable."[10] One can speculate that the Republican party and employers underestimated the seriousness of the issue for women and did not foresee the consequences of the policy in numbers of complaints and lawsuits. After the 1986 Supreme Court ruling that sexual harassment constituted sexual discrimination, there was no turning back.

An alternative explanation for employers' lack of reaction might be that they reframed the issue in ways that benefited them. Even in the early 1980s, business magazines fell in line with some feminists' argument that "sexual harassment is bad for business," and discussed the loss of image/reputation, productivity, and legal costs (Lootens 1986: 13). However, Schultz (2003) argues that US employers were happy to embrace laws against sexual harassment because they allowed them to "sanitize the workplace" by eliminating sexuality in the workplace. Some other unintended consequences of policy enforcement are legitimacy for increased surveillance and control of employees. In addition, zero-tolerance policies give employers more power to dismiss unwanted employees. Yet, no matter what employers' interests were, it is striking that there was no organized resistance to the changes in policy.

In contrast to the EU, where national women's offices were important in creating sexual harassment laws, the Women's Bureau in the US

[10] Committee on Labor and Human Resources, January 28 and April 21, 1981.

Department of Labor did not initiate major policy changes. This was in part a consequence of framing sexual harassment as sex discrimination. The Bureau is more a service agency than a policy initiator or advocate, and plays no official role in implementing the Civil Rights Act of 1964. Stetson also points out that feminist organizations did not use the Women's Bureau as an ally to promote a feminist policy agenda (Stetson 1995: 269–70). Only a few of its directors, such as Elizabeth Koontz and Karen Nussbaum, had such agendas. Furthermore, at the time the Bureau agenda was dominated by issues such as pregnancy discrimination (1970–78) and job training (1975–92) (Stetson 1995).

Policies against sexual harassment evolved in a period marked by a conservative, hostile political environment toward gender equality politics at the national level. Before the 1980s the Women's Bureau had contributed to formulation of gender equality policies in the workplace and was central in organizing a policy network on sex equality (Stetson 1995: 283), but during the Reagan and G.H.W. Bush administrations its influence declined. It has continued to collect information on women's work issues and provide information for individuals and groups to take action on sexual harassment. For example, in 1994 it published a brochure entitled "Sexual Harassment, Know Your Rights."

How responsive were the federal and state governments to feminists' demands to take sexual harassment more seriously? Their responsiveness has been strikingly uneven. On the one hand, several agencies were forerunners in acknowledging sexual harassment as sex discrimination by creating research, reports, policies, and training manuals. On the other hand, scandals in politics, the military, and the police, as well as lawsuits by individual women in state offices, demonstrate how close to home the issue has been for government institutions themselves. Finally, even today, employees who have to leave their jobs because of sexual harassment do not necessarily receive timely unemployment benefits, because state laws vary in their recognition of sexual harassment as a "good cause" for leaving a job. The federal government never issued a regulation to consider sexual harassment a "good cause," so feminists have had to fight the same fight fifty-one times at the state level.

Like other social movements, the movement against sexual harassment has had an uneasy relationship with the state. Lobby activities were stifled through the politically less receptive climate in Washington D.C. during the 1980s. Yet, the development of sexual harassment law took a life of its own. There were setbacks but even in the negative political climate feminists in the courts could persistently push for the improvement of the law.

Legal revolution

Given that there have not been federal laws explicitly prohibiting sexual harassment, the courts have remained the major site for the development of law and policy. The concept has been modified and refined through a series of cases. Courts decided, for example, that university students should be protected against sexual harassment by laws holding the university liable. In the groundbreaking case of *Alexander v. Yale University*,[11] attorneys argued that sexual harassment should be actionable under Title IX, which prohibits sex discrimination in education.

After the 1980 EEOC guidelines, courts began to recognize that sexual harassment that created an intimidating and offensive working environment similar to that created by racial intimidation was itself sex discrimination and thus actionable under Title VII. Sandra Bundy, a corrections department employee, testified that supervisors and co-workers had physically and verbally harassed her. When she complained, her supervisor promised an investigation, but stated: "Any man in his right mind would want to rape you." The judge in *Bundy v. Jackson*[12] reasoned that this working environment of intimidation, ridicule, and insult based on sex was discriminatory, even though Bundy remained in the job and did not suffer job-related consequences for refusing co-workers' invitations to lunch and vacations. In *Henson v. City of Dundee*[13] the court ruled that an environment that is merely offensive is not sexual harassment: the harassment has to be "sufficiently pervasive so as to alter the conditions of employment and create an abusive working environment." This criterion became part of a five-part catalogue subsequently used by courts to test the hostile environment claim.

The first case in which the US Supreme Court ruled on sexual harassment was a hostile environment case. The plaintiff, Mechelle Vinson, a twenty-eight-year-old African American bank teller, had lost her job for excessive use of sick leave. Vinson alleged that her black supervisor, Sidney Taylor, had repeatedly asked her to have sexual intercourse and that she had complied out of fear of losing her job. She also said that he had fondled her in front of other employees and had

---

[11] 621 Federal Reporter 2d 178 (1980) US Court of Appeals for the Second Circuit.
[12] 641F.2d 934 (D.C. Circuit 1981).
[13] 682F.2d 897 (11th Circuit 1982).

raped her. Taylor denied ever having sex with Vinson but testified that she had made sexual advances to him, which he had declined. The Supreme Court ruled in *Meritor Savings Bank v. Vinson*[14] that both quid *pro quo* and hostile environment forms of sexual harassment constituted sexual discrimination and were actionable under Title VII. The court affirmed both the federal appellate courts of the late 1970s and the EEOC guidelines, and provided a powerful basis for sexual harassment law by extending the Civil Rights Act of 1964. In this decision the EEOC, under Thomas, was on the side of the bank,[15] arguing that sexual harassment should be treated differently from other forms of discrimination because it was too subjective.

Several areas of sexual harassment law have remained a source of contention in both case law and public conversation. Debates have centered on whether policies interfere with freedom of speech when they discourage the use of offensive language and jokes, especially in academic settings. How to define "unwantedness" and consent has been a constant issue. Since 1986 the Supreme Court has chosen to hear several cases involving issues on which lower courts held diverging rulings. I discuss here three important questions the court has addressed: how plaintiffs can convince courts that behavior is severe enough to be considered harassment, same-sex harassment, and employer liability for harassment by supervisors and coworkers.

First, the EEOC definition of sexual harassment as hostile environment defines it as "unwanted behavior of a sexual nature which inappropriately interferes with the work environment." In legal practice, the question was how plaintiffs could prove that the harassment had been "sufficiently severe and pervasive." The court ruled in *Harris v. Forklift System, Inc.*[16] that a victim did not have to prove that psychological harm had already occurred: "Title VII comes into play before the harassing conduct leads to a nervous breakdown." Teresa Harris worked as a manager in a company that rented construction equipment. The president of the company harassed her in sexual and nonsexual ways. For example, questioning her expertise, he said, "You're a woman, what do you know?" and "We need a man as the rental manager." He referred to her as a "dumb ass woman." He suggested they should go to a hotel to negotiate a raise and occasionally asked her to get coins from his front

---

[14] 106 S. Ct. 2399 (1986).

[15] Other agencies and groups which filed briefs on behalf of the bank were the Chamber of Commerce, the Trustees of Boston University, and the Equal Employment Advisory Council.

[16] 510 US 17 (1993).

pants pocket. The court decision that victims did not have to prove psychological harm was important for a number of reasons, including that employers would not necessarily be granted access to plaintiffs' psychological or medical files. Victims had to show, however, that sexual harassment led to discrimination.

Second, because of a narrow conception of "sex discrimination" and the equation of heterosexual desire and gender, US courts have had a difficult time handling harassment experienced by men and, in particular, harassment between men. While lawmakers in European countries explicitly wanted to protect men against cross-sex sexual harassment and to include harassment between women or between men, US courts battled over same-sex harassment until 1998. The Supreme Court settled the diverging opinions of lower courts in *Oncale v. Sundowner Offshore Services*[17]. Joseph Oncale worked on an oil platform in the Gulf of Mexico and was harassed by a group of male coworkers, suffering physical attacks and assaults in which the men threatened to rape him. The court recognized that harassment experienced by a man from other men might constitute sex discrimination.

The third issue courts have struggled with is employer responsibility. The 1980 EEOC guidelines held employers liable for supervisor harassment and for coworker harassment if they knew or should have known of it. Courts also used a model in which they held employers more strictly liable for *quid pro quo* harassment than for hostile environment. But the Supreme Court ruled in 1998 that the distinction is not useful in determining employer liability. In addition, the court has increasingly set the expectation that employers have effective policies, in-house grievance procedures, and prevention efforts. Courts have been more sympathetic to victims and awarded higher damages and penalties if employers did not have such apparatus in place or respond appropriately to complaints (Juliano and Schwab 2001).

One source of unresolved controversy in the late 1990s was the conditions under which employers can limit their liability. Do victims have to use in-house complaint procedures and mediation offers? Or can they quit and take their employer to court without filing an official report beforehand? The Supreme Court weighed in on the side of employers, who can now use efforts to combat sexual harassment as an affirmative defense to limit their liability in court. The court ruled in two decisions in 1998, *Faragher v. City of Boca Raton* and *Burlington Industries Inc. v. Ellerth*.[18] Kimberly Ellerth, a salesperson, charged that she endured a

---

[17] 523 US 75 (1998).
[18] 111F.3d 1530 (1998); 123F.3d 490 (1998).

steady stream of sexual harassment from her supervisor's boss, including pats on the buttocks and sexual remarks such as comments about her breasts. On a business trip he told her to "loosen up," with the warning, "You know, Kim, I could make your life very hard or very easy at Burlington" (156). The court supported the notion that the intent of the Civil Rights Act of 1964 was to have conflicts solved in the workplace and since then victims are well advised to use existing internal grievance procedures.

Hence, these Supreme Court cases solved controversies among lower courts, including issues of employer liability, same-sex sexual harassment and what effects sexual harassment has to have in order to be actionable in court. This legal–regulatory path meant that legal reform occurred through the courts and through the administrative state offices. The legal route to expand and refine law through juridical interpretation of case law, by building on precedent-setting cases, has been much quicker in responding to victims of sexual harassment than the statutory routes to pass laws against sexual harassment in most European member states. In these path-breaking rulings, sexual harassment victims were in court to hold employers liable – not the perpetrators of sexual harassment.

Legal outcomes: tracing feminist discourse

The expansion and refinement of sexual harassment law took place in court rooms based on women's experiences. Sexual harassment is a highly powerful, intensely emotional issue that involves complex, ambivalent, even contradictory feelings of fear, shame, embarrassment, disgust, anger, and a whole range of other emotions that result from sexual advances when they are perceived as offensive, intimidating, and demeaning. Not only victims but everyone involved in these trials has to face and sometimes share these emotions. In the United States, sexual harassment law evolved through judges who faced individual women as victims, heard their stories, and ruled against or in favor of these victims. This legal route created the opportunity for victims' voices to be "heard" more than through the statutory route to effect change.

Civil rights litigation was used mainly by victims who took their employers to court because the employers failed to protect them and/ or discriminated against them after they complained about the harassment. This set-up potentially allowed for judges to be more sympathetic toward the victims, because sexual harassment victims were pitted against their employers and not against the male perpetrators. Judges and juries decided on sanctions against the employers who had failed their responsibility vis-à-vis the victim of sexual harassment, but they did not decide how to punish (male) perpetrators, hence they did not have to choose between sympathy for the victim or the perpetrator of sexual harassment.

This legal–regulatory route also meant that victims of sexual harassment could make use of feminist expertise. Though most judges consider themselves to be on the politically conservative side, or are considered thus, they do not seek re-election, and are therefore less dependent on public opinion than politicians are. Hence, feminists did not need to create consensus among predominantly lawmakers who seek re-election, instead they needed to find convincing, legal arguments for public officials, judges, and later juries. This legal route provided the unique opportunity for feminist legal arguments to make their way into the continuous modification of sexual harassment law.

Most striking was the attempt to capture women's subjective experience. The EEOC guidelines defined harassment from the subjective viewpoint of the victim, as "unwanted attention of a sexual nature." Supported by psychological and sociological research, courts have increasingly recognized that perceptions, interpretations, and reactions to sexual harassment vary by gender. MacKinnon (2002) calls sexual harassment law "women's common law," as courts took women's experiences into account and based their decisions on women's perspectives. Instead of a "reasonable person" standard, feminist legal scholars have argued the need to apply a "reasonable woman" standard and to judge women's specific reactions in sexually harassing situations (Abrahms 1998). In 1991, a federal court ruled in *Ellison v. Brady*[19] that because gender differences exist in perceptions of what constitutes sexual harassment, courts need to apply a reasonable woman's standard to assess whether behaviors are pervasive enough to constitute harassment.

Though this concept has not been extensively applied in the court room (Juliano and Schwab 2001), the notion is revolutionary in that it challenges the belief that "objective," universal standards of behavior can be applied to judge what constitutes sexual harassment. Yet, in its current version, the theoretical concept has also been criticized by a number of scholars for falsely stating homogeneity in women's experience. Crenshaw (1988), for example, argues that applying the reasonable woman's standard might lead to privileging white, heterosexual, middle-class women's perspectives over those of minority women.

---

[19] 924F. 2d 872 (9th Cir. 1991).

Interestingly, even though sexual harassment as a policy area emerged in the United States in the context of equal treatment and sex discrimination, and therefore might be seen as an approach to gender "sameness," the application of laws and policies has raised debates on gender differences in perception, interpretation, and reaction to sexual harassment. Feminists have been able to advocate for legal concepts that recognize and take into account these gender differences. Hence, in practice, sexual harassment challenges the frame of gender "sameness." For example, the concept of the reasonable woman's standard is based on the argument that gender differences need to be taken into account to achieve equal treatment – as a way to achieve gender equality. In addition, feminist theories of sexual harassment used traditional notions of gender differences in sexuality. For example, they did not challenge the perception that men are more sexually aggressive and women more sexually vulnerable (Baker 2001). They instead used it to make a case that women needed to be protected.

Courts have also reproduced traditional views, myths, and stereotypical depictions of gender relations and sexual harassment. Certain forms of "victim blame" have crept into decisions. Courts have evoked popular beliefs that women might be "asking for sexual harassment" by the way they behave or dress. Cultural understandings of what victims should look like and how they should behave have affected what "unwelcome" means. Perpetrators try to show that the women consented, that they believed the women welcomed their behavior. In the 1986 *Meritor Savings Bank v. Vinson* case, Supreme Court Chief Justice Rehnquist insisted that a plaintiff's "sexually provocative speech and dress" could be relevant in determining how welcome the sexual advances of the harasser were (68–69).

This was a setback, and went against the intention of lawmakers who had established rape shield laws for sexual assault cases in criminal courts during the 1970s. Feminists had argued that it was the behavior of perpetrators, not victims, that should be on trial, as they had successfully lobbied at the state level to introduce laws protecting the privacy of victims in the courts. In 1978, Congress passed Rule 412 of the Federal Rules of Evidence, establishing that evidence offered to prove that a victim engaged in other sexual behavior, or to prove a victim's sexual predisposition, is generally inadmissible in any civil or criminal proceeding involving alleged sexual misconduct. By contrast, in sexual harassment law, courts continue to allow perpetrators to make a case of how women showed their "consent" or demonstrated how they welcomed the behavior (Fitzgerald 2004). Hence underlying notions and androcentric views of gender and sexuality continue to focus the attention on victims rather than on perpetrators.

Feminist legal scholars have long been occupied with the problems involved in using laws to address violence against women. The difficulty is to capture psychological and physical harm while acknowledging the agency of individual women. All of these issues raise thorny questions of consent. Hence, feminists have challenged the basic assumptions of "rational" actor models that use gendered notions and expectations for the behaviors of victims and perpetrators (Smart 1995).

On the positive side, anti-harassment advocates had a number of possible ways to seek influence through the courts. The primary currency and resources needed in court are legal arguments, legal discourse, and expertise. The opportunity for feminists to seek influence in the courts gave them strong incentives to create "alternative discourses," but also to professionalize this knowledge, in terms of building expertise based on research, in order to support cases in court.

A loose network of consultants, scholars, and other advocates established breadth and depth of research in psychology, sociology, and human resources in the 1980s and this strengthened throughout the 1990s. Attorneys have drawn on this knowledge by calling these experts as witnesses to testify about the phenomenon of sexual harassment, its psychological aspects, what victims could be expected to do, and so on. Some of the women involved in early research and activism, including Freada Klein, one of the founders of AASC, became consultants and served as expert witnesses in several court cases. The list of expert witnesses included people such as Louise Fitzgerald, James Gruber, and Susan Webb. Their knowledge and expertise helped promote important cases. A few individuals were also able to make a living as consultants by becoming experts not only for courts but also for employers.

While the majority of women who file sexual harassment lawsuits today have no direct support from or ties to feminist organizations, women's organizations have built an important infrastructure for individual lawsuits. Since the 1980s, a network of feminist organizations oriented toward achieving change via legal change have picked up the issue of sexual harassment, including the Women's Legal Defense Fund, National Women's Law Center, NOW, NOW Legal Defense Fund, and Fund for the Feminist Majority.

Perhaps the most direct voice feminist organizations have used in the courts are amicus curiae briefs. In all Supreme Court decisions, feminist organizations coordinated amicus curiae briefs in support of the plaintiff.

A broad network of women's movement organizations and allies supported Vinson's case; the seven amicus curiae briefs on her behalf included those from the Working Women United Institute, unions (AFL-CIO and CLUW), Women's Legal Defense Fund, women's bar and lawyers' associations, and members of Congress. Patricia Barry and Catharine MacKinnon made her case in court. Thus, a broad range of organizations, some not founded specifically to combat sexual harassment, supplied important infrastructure for feminists to continue their efforts to improve the law. They have been at the core of the dynamics to change the US legal system.

The opportunities to have an impact on court decisions are very different from political paths of change, where legal texts have to be agreed upon by a legislature. Most significantly, there is no need to reach "consensus" among diverse groups of actors such as unions, employers, and politicians. Public opinion plays less of a role in the decisions of judges because, unlike lawmakers, once appointed, they do not need to be re-elected. Some critics of the political nature of judicial decisions argue that making decisions in court is fundamentally undemocratic, because they are made not by elected politicians but by judges who are not directly accountable to society.

Despite the opportunity to file class-action suits, women have used the courts collectively to hold employers accountable in only a very few cases. Juliano and Schwab (2001) found that only three of approximately 500 sexual harassment cases were filed as class-action suits. The fact that most sexual harassment suits are brought by individuals may indicate that women themselves perceive it as an individual problem, and that feminists have not been successful in organizing women to use the law collectively. The first, as noted above, was *Jenson v. Eveleth Taconite Co.*, decided in 1999. The EEOC, particularly under President Clinton, supported highly visible class-action suits, including a 1998 settlement with Mitsubishi over $34 million in damages on behalf of 300 women; a 1999 settlement with Ford for $8 million to be paid to 19 female employees because of sexual harassment, racial harassment, gender harassment, and retaliation when they complained; and a 1999 suit on behalf of mostly Mexican illegal immigrant women at the border against a large agricultural company, Tanimura & Antle. In these settlements the companies agreed to pay damages to the plaintiffs and conduct mandatory training. Ford agreed to take additional steps by increasing the number of women in supervisory positions.

The early court successes that defined sexual harassment as sex discrimination were filed before feminist organizations began to mobilize around sexual harassment and before the public paid any attention to the issue. This path to legal change was very fruitful for feminist and civil rights lawyers and experts because it allowed them to contribute to the creation of law. It shaped the movement by creating demands for feminist discourse on sexual harassment. Much important, creative advocacy work occurs behind closed doors in the form of discursive battles and debates among experts in psychological, legal, and EEO/AA professional consultant journals, so research has also been shaped by legal disputes. For example, early psychological research tried to determine whether there are in fact persistent gender differences in the awareness, perception, and experience of sexual harassment.

The drawback of the dominance of the legal path means that further refinement and modification depend on individuals continuing to bring lawsuits. This is particularly problematic for sexual harassment cases, because the issue is that individuals have a difficult time speaking out and using the legal system. Cases do not lend themselves easily to collective action. They are particularly difficult to pursue because they are as expensive as other employment discrimination lawsuits, and the complaints are of a deeply emotional, personal nature in which embarrassment and psychological dimensions affect everyone involved. Solidarity among women cannot be taken for granted. Consequently, by contrast with pay equity litigation, organizations concerned with sexual harassment, though supportive of lawsuits, did not primarily pursue a litigation strategy.

Media coverage of high-profile cases

Aware that legal changes alone would not bring about the cultural change, activists strategically used the media to spread knowledge and to raise public awareness. The media have paid most attention to lawsuits and to highly publicized cases involving politicians and public figures. Coverage of the 1970s court trials and the 1986 Supreme Court case led to increasing numbers of women seeking help from Working Women United Institute and other women's organizations, and the scandals in the 1990s did much to generate public awareness. Even before Hill's testimony, several scandals occurred in the military and in the Senate. In 1995, Senator Bob Packwood, Republican from Oregon, resigned when the Ethics Committee voted for his expulsion after they found that he had sexually harassed at least seventeen women, mostly Senate employees and campaign workers (twenty-nine women had made accusations against him). These scandals demonstrated not only the increasing willingness of the media to write about the "private" behavior of men but also women's growing sense of injustice and unwillingness to put up with it.

The military has figured significantly in media representations of sexual harassment. An incident during the 1991 Tailhook Convention, the annual meeting for Naval officers, fueled broad public discussions about sexual harassment. Navy and Pentagon investigations found that male naval aviators had assaulted and sexually harassed eighty-three women in the Las Vegas Hilton Hotel. The Navy sanctioned only a handful of the men for failure to stop it with small fines or reprimands, sent them into early retirement or denied them promotions. Ironically, it was not the Navy but the hotel that was finally held responsible. A federal jury trial ruled in favor of former Navy Lt. Paula T. Coughlin who had sued the hotel chain for negligence for failing to set up adequate security – she was awarded compensatory damages of $1.7 million for emotional distress.

In 2000, Army Lt. Gen. Claudia J. Kennedy, the highest ranking woman in the US military, portrayed as the role model for women's equality in the armed forces, came forward with allegations of inappropriate sexual advances (*New York Times*, April 6, 2000: A1). She made public a previously informal complaint against another army general because he was about to be promoted into a position with authority to resolve sexual harassment complaints.

The most prominent case of sexual harassment to draw media attention was certainly Paula Corbin Jones's suit against President Clinton, in which she alleged that he sexually harassed her when he was governor of Arkansas in 1994. In 2003, Arnold Schwarzenegger, in his successful campaign for governor of California, was accused by sixteen women of physical and verbal harassment on film sets dating back to the 1970s. The media are attracted by these scandals involving the hot issues of sex and power, when women publicly accuse politically powerful men of sexual misdeeds. While most of these incidents did not lead to successful lawsuits for the plaintiffs, their public statements would not be possible without a legal and social context that framed sexual harassment as potentially unlawful.

Among the scandals, none has been so identified with sexual harassment as Hill's allegations against Thomas. This incident brought out Americans' emotions and attitudes about sexism and racism and spurred a national debate. During the 1991 Senate Judiciary Committee's confirmation hearings on Thomas, President G.H.W. Bush's nominee for the US Supreme Court, Hill came forward with accusations that Thomas had sexually harassed her when she worked under him at the EEOC. She testified that she had been the object of his improper sexual behavior, including discussions of sexual acts and pornographic films, after she rebuffed his invitations to date him.

The hearings were broadcast live, and millions of Americans watched as this all-male, all-white panel of fifteen senators questioned Hill's testimony. When Thomas denied the allegations, the typical "he said–she said" situation arose. Thomas defended himself by bringing racial rather than gender politics to the fore. Despite the fact that Thomas had previously scolded African Americans for using race as a "crutch," he called the hearings "a high-tech lynching for uppity blacks." Hill argued that she believed he used that language "because he knew how effective it would be."[20] The Senate ultimately confirmed Thomas's appointment in a 52–48 vote.

These hearings demonstrated how the all-white, all-male Senate Judiciary Committee "just didn't get it." The composition of this panel also highlighted the unequal representation of women and people of color in the political sphere. Hill explained that she spoke out because she knew that Thomas, as a Supreme Court judge, would have the power to influence sexual harassment law. Her public statement changed her life: "I am no longer an anonymous, private individual – my name having become synonymous with sexual harassment" (Hill 1997: 2). Similar to rape victims, she became the focus of investigations; her veracity, mental stability, and morals, rather than the behavior of the perpetrator, were questioned. She experienced retaliation in her job and subsequently left the University of Oklahoma for Brandeis University in Boston. She has been invited to speak on campuses, to political groups, and at other meetings.

Following her example, more women than ever before stood up and complained about sexual harassment. Cases filed with the EEOC jumped from 6,127 in 1991 to 10,532 in 1992 and in the mid-1990s peaked with 15,889 in 1997. Only after the 1998 Supreme Court decisions and Jones's lawsuit against then President Clinton did these numbers decline. In 2004, 13,136 cases were filed – 15 percent of these were filed by male victims.

European media covered the hearings extensively, bringing sexual harassment into the news for the first time in many countries. The hearings also galvanized US women's rights supporters; many argue that the Year of the Woman was a consequence of women's politicization through the Senate hearings. The 1992 Year of the Woman was coined by feminists and the media for several reasons. More women became

---

[20] *http://news-service.stanford.edu/news/2002/april3/anitahill-43.html* (downloaded May 20, 2004).

involved in politics: women voters turned out in record numbers, and more women than ever before were elected to Congress in 1992. Twenty-four new women were elected to the House and five to the Senate, which signified the largest increase in history. The same year women voters also contributed to President Clinton's electoral success.

Although American women have maintained their political representation in Congress, it is strikingly below that of most EU member states. According to the Inter-Parliamentary Union, the United States holds a dismal fifty-seventh world ranking for its low numbers of women in Congress. Only 15 percent of the seats in the House and 14 percent of those in the Senate are held by women.[21] Hence, not only did Hill stand for the lack of women's power in the workplace, where they have to endure sexual harassment, but her testimony signified the lack of women's power in the centers of political decision-making.

Though lacking formal political power, US women activists could now build on informal networks created by advocates during the 1980s. On learning that the Judiciary Committee had planned a closed hearing, NOW demanded an open hearing on Hill's allegations.[22] In the aftermath, women's groups throughout the country lobbied employers to adopt effective policies or revise existing ones. After the hearings, NOW members demonstrated against Thomas, wearing T-shirts emblazoned with "I believe Anita Hill."

For the first time, a broad coalition of women's groups lobbied successfully for a law strengthening the position of sexual harassment victims. This window of opportunity came with efforts to amend the Civil Rights Act of 1964. The main purpose of the Civil Rights Act of 1991[23] was to affirm the federal civil rights protections the courts had weakened during the 1980s. Most important, Congress reversed the Supreme Court decision in *Wards Cove Packing Co. v. Atonio.*[24] The Act, passed by a Republican Congress and signed by G.H.W. Bush, reestablished the legitimacy of statistical evidence and placed the burden of proof back on the employer. Media attention on the Hill-Thomas hearings and the subsequent national debate heightened awareness of the issues. Women's groups used this impetus and possibly the embarrassment of some members of Congress over their colleagues' behavior to lobby for the passage of the Act. As a consequence, federal lawmakers for the first time aided victims of sexual harassment through legislation.

---

[21] *http://www.ipu.org/wmn-e/classif.htm* (downloaded January 5, 2005).
[22] *http://www.now.org/issues/harass/anitahil.html* (downloaded May 20, 2004).
[23] 42 USC. § 2000e-5(k) (1996).
[24] 490 US 642 (1989).

Ironically, the law did not prohibit sexual harassment itself. Its purpose is "to provide appropriate remedies for intentional discrimination and unlawful harassment in the workplace,"[25] but it does not define what harassment is. Thus, lawmakers basically validated the Supreme Court and EEOC definitions without going beyond them.

The 1991 amendments improved the rights of victims in two ways. Plaintiffs now have the right to a jury trial and can recover punitive damages. Compensatory damages such as back pay, attorneys' fees, and other costs were already allowed under the 1964 Civil Rights Act. Now damages include "future pecuniary losses, emotional pain, suffering, inconvenience, mental anguish, loss of enjoyment of life, and other nonpecuniary losses" (102 (b) (3)). These damages can be awarded only if there is evidence that the employer acted with malice or reckless indifference. Critics have argued, however, that in race discrimination cases no upper limits for punitive damages have been set. Yet, Congress decided to set a maximum limit for the fines depending on the size of the employer: for employers with 15–100 employees, $50,000; for 101–200 employees, $100,000; for 201–500 employees, $200,000; for more than 500 employees, $300,000.

In practice, attorneys have often attached state tort claims to federal or state employment discrimination claims through which plaintiffs could receive non-wage-based compensatory and punitive damages and, in some situations, jury trials. Because attorneys can now use these guidelines to demand damages, the Civil Rights Act of 1991 effectively strengthened sexual harassment law under Title VII.

Advocates might have expected that feminist projects in general would receive more support under Clinton, who was elected in 1992 and re-elected in 1996 by disproportionate numbers of women. But the Clinton administration's relationship to issues of violence against women, including sexual harassment, was paradoxical. The antiviolence movement received support for the 1994 Federal Violence Against Women Act (VAWA). VAWA helped sexual harassment plaintiffs in court, since it extended the logic of rape shield laws to civil sex offense cases (Mink 2000: 104). In addition, the EEOC was more active and supported several class-action suits. But the late 1990s were a difficult and challenging time for women's organizations' stance on sexual harassment. Supporting Hill against the Republican party was no problem, but Jones's suit against Clinton presented difficult dilemmas.

---

[25] Civil Rights Act of 1991, Sec. 3 (1).

Jones v. Clinton

Unlike Hill, who did not file a sexual harassment suit, Jones pursued a legal case against Clinton. Most victims of sexual harassment use the Civil Rights Act of 1964 to hold their employers responsible, but Jones took to court the individual man by whom she felt harassed.

A former Arkansas state employee, she alleged that Clinton, while governor of Arkansas, exposed himself and propositioned her in a hotel room. *Jones v. Clinton*[26] was dismissed by federal district court judge Susan Webber Wright. In the course of the suit, however, Jones's lawyers had subpoenaed Monica Lewinsky, a former White House intern, with the intention of establishing Clinton's pattern of sexual relationships in the workplace. Clinton initially denied a sexual relationship with Lewinsky, and even lied under oath, although he later admitted the affair. In the 1998 out-of-court settlement, Clinton agreed to pay $850,000 for damages, including "physical and personal injury, civil rights violations, emotional distress, and legal fees and expenses."[27] Of this money Jones received $200,000 – the rest was divided among her lawyers and the Rutherford Institute, a conservative think-tank, that supported her.[28]

Public debates were less concerned with women's rights in the workplace than Clinton's perjury and the moral questions of the extramarital affair and Lewinsky's detailed account of it. The debate was about whether Jones's account was true or part of a "vast right-wing conspiracy." And if Jones was right, did Clinton's behavior amount to sexual harassment under the law?

Several women's organizations in Washington at first maintained their alliance to the Democratic party. Their spokeswomen and other feminists contributed to the discussions with interpretations of sexual harassment law. Some took Clinton's side, arguing that even if Jones was telling the truth, it did not constitute harassment under the law. Mink summarized their reasoning that sexual harassment has to occur in multiple instances and be egregious. Feminists defended Clinton because "he didn't force Jones to give him oral sex, didn't ask her for it more than once, and didn't fire her when she refused him" (Mink 2000: 123). Mink has argued that feminists failed not only Jones but sexual harassment victims in general (119–25). The very few feminists who criticized the court ruling publicly included MacKinnon and Martha Davis, legal director of the NOW Legal Defense and Education Fund

---

[26] 990F. Supp. 657 (E.D. Ark. 1998).
[27] *http://www.ardemgaz.com/prev/clinton/acsettletext14.html* (downloaded June 16, 2004).
[28] *http://www.tribuneindia.com/1999/99mar07/world.htm#3* (downloaded June 24, 2005).

(Mink 2000: 121). MacKinnon (2004) pointed out the irony that law and public perception can be far apart. The public considered Thomas's behavior toward Hill sexual harassment, and did not believe that Clinton harassed Jones. Yet, during the time Thomas as EEOC director told jokes to Hill, a judge might or might not have found them severe enough to constitute sexual harassment.

Judge Wright finally found that the alleged incident with Jones, if it occurred, "was certainly boorish and offensive" but not "one of those exceptional cases in which a single incident of sexual harassment, such as an assault, was deemed sufficient to state a claim of hostile work environment sexual harassment."[29] MacKinnon criticized this ruling because Wright did not apply the Civil Rights Act of 1964: "Instead of measuring the severity of Paula Jones's allegations by sex equality standards – asking whether the challenged activity was gendered unequal or whether it was central to the historical subordination of women as a sex or whether men in that workplace had to work under similar conditions or whether sex equality at work could be achieved if such acts were tolerated–Judge Wright seems to have asked whether the acts were bad" (2004: 690).

Clinton had signed VAWA, so it was ironic that his attorneys tried to discredit Jones's testimony by pulling her sexual private life into the public eye. At this point feminist organizations did speak up, and NOW president Patricia Ireland came to Jones's aid. NOW also supported and welcomed the three Supreme Court decisions on sexual harassment the same year, and, in the context of a Women Friendly Workplace and Campus Campaign, announced a ten-point action plan targeting government and business leaders with the goal of ending sexual harassment. The new campaign was consistent with NOW's earlier "Global Campaign Aims to End 'Seku Hara,'" which mobilized around the 1998 EEOC – Mitsubishi lawsuit.[30]

Thus, Washington's women's organizations had a difficult time during the Clinton-Jones-Lewinsky scandal. NOW had supported the Mitsubishi workers and filed amicus briefs in the 1998 Supreme Court decisions, but Ireland announced NOW would not write a brief on behalf of Jones because the case was not suitable to set precedent: "We do not intend to encourage higher courts to consider and possibly create legal precedent that would injure everyday women in the workplace, based on the allegations and evidence of a politically charged case. The fact that this case is so highly politically charged and that such a broad national consensus exists surrounding the allegations, make it an imperfect case,

[29] 520 US 681 (1997).
[30] *http://www.now.org/nnt/11-96/mitsu.html* (downloaded June 16, 2004).

at best, to use as a test case to advance important legal principles. In plain English, hard cases make bad law."[31]

While race was a challenge for the public in the Hill–Thomas hearings, class became the implicit issue for judging whether Jones's working-class "white trash" background or her support by the Rutherford Institute, a foundation close to the Republican party, stood in the way of feminist organizational solidarity with her.

If the American public, including feminists, have been misinformed about what sexual harassment law is, then European observers' ideas about US law have been even more confused. For Europeans the issue seemed to be that Clinton was in trouble for his affair with Lewinsky. They learned more about the details of Lewinsky's and Clinton's sexual affair from her testimony that was posted in full text on hundreds of websites than they had ever heard about the details of the Jones sexual harassment case. Not surprisingly, the European media expressed sympathy for Clinton, and politicians called for the protection of the private life of public figures, because they interpreted the situation as an illegitimate political strategy initiated by Clinton's opponents.

In European countries, even when extramarital affairs or deviations from traditional marriages have become known, state officials have generally not suffered politically. For instance, German chancellor Helmut Kohl (1982–99) had a long-term affair with his secretary, and French Socialist president François Mitterrand (1981–95) acknowledged a daughter whose mother he had not married. In Germany, both Foreign Minister Joschka Fischer (Green) and Chancellor Gerhard Schroeder (Social Democrat) have been married more than three times, a personal history that might be a problem for high-powered US politicians.

The European perception was that Clinton was in court for his affair with Lewinsky, not the Jones lawsuit. Lewinsky, however, always insisted that her relationship with Clinton had been consensual. Her statement did not occur in court, but in August 1998 she was called before an investigative grand jury by Kenneth Starr to answer questions about her relationship with Clinton during his presidency. Because Clinton had lied under oath about the relationship, he subsequently was impeached by Congress, although the Senate did not convict him.

These political scandals tell a cautionary tale for feminist organizations' ability to shape public debate on sexual harassment. Sexual harassment itself is neither a right nor a left issue, but it carries so much embarrassment, shame, and moral significance that it can be exploited from either

---

[31] *http://www.now.org/press/04-98/04-22-98.html* (downloaded June 15, 2004).

side. In such an environment, discussions about the gender dimension tend to disappear. Instead, the conversation is on the sexual aspects and debates about "morality," for example whether Schwarzenegger's or Clinton's behavior was sufficiently "bad." The focus on the details of what happened brought ridicule, joking, and insensitivity back into the media, along with the myth that women cannot be trusted because they will bring false allegations or report behavior because of ulterior motives. The recent scandals have depicted women as vengeful creatures who prey on innocent politically powerful men for political or financial goals.

The legal–regulatory route for change attracts much attention to individual legal cases and high-profile lawsuits can potentially be meaningful beyond the individual case if they can set a precedent. However, it is important to acknowledge that sexual harassment law can evolve only if victims take perpetrators and employers to court. If we de-legitimize victims of sexual harassment and restrict individuals' legal redress, the driving motor for sexual harassment legal change is gone (see Mink 2000).

Conclusion

The path for the creation of sexual harassment law in the United States went primarily through the courts. Individual harassed women and some men challenged their employers in court and these individual cases have continuously been the motor for legal changes. Courts have been responsive to women's plight, and there is more sophisticated case law in the United States than in any other country. Perhaps this is because these laws were not agreed upon by politicians through consensual paths of decision-making; judges' decisions based on listening to women's experiences and feminist (legal) expertise were the foundation for the next cases. But there is little public consensus on what sexual harassment is and what behavior should and should not be illegal.

The forerunner role of the United States is due to the successful efforts of litigants, lawyers, and advocates who convinced the courts and state agencies to take the issue seriously. These attorneys and advocates were helped immensely by being able to build on a tradition of individual rights and, even more important, expand an existing law – the Civil Rights Act of 1964. Racial harassment or intimidation, which the courts had already accepted as a violation of Title VII, served to conceptualize sexual harassment as sex discrimination.

The Civil Rights Act created a supportive context for individuals to challenge their employers. These lawsuits revolved around employers, not perpetrators, and judges left it up to employers to find appropriate sanctions for the perpetrators of sexual harassment. In this institutional framework, women filed complaints at workplace EEO offices or the EEOC. Hence, the development of case law on sexual harassment built on, and is unthinkable without, the civil rights movement and the laws it created – these provided the opportunity for women to expand on preexisting anti-discrimination law.

The discrimination frame was particularly successful because it resonated with cultural understandings of gender sameness – a predominately individual–liberal orientation of equality that assumes that gender equality can be achieved by treating women the same as men. At the same time, however, feminists drew on traditional understandings of gender difference by pointing to women's need to be protected against masculine aggressive sexuality. This approach appealed to judges, policy-makers, and elites. But feminists also made the case to consider sexual harassment as sex discrimination, a core frame of the women's movement at that time. In fact, workplace issues moved into the core of mainstream gender politics in the United States during the 1970s. The broader second-wave women's movement generated gender awareness, and thus also opened space to discuss sexual harassment in institutions such as the police, military, politics, and the workplace. Activists benefited from the willingness of courts and state agencies to examine gender issues at work. For example, advocates for policy change had the opportunity to address gender workplace issues in congressional hearings.

The opportunities to effect legal changes through the courts also shaped the movement on sexual harassment. Because the common law legal system provided the opportunity for judges to expand on and create legal norms without the involvement of lawmakers, activists did not need to lobby for legal change. They did not have to mobilize and create a broad-based movement in Washington to convince policy-makers, Congress, and the president to pass a new law. Instead, they used existing informal networks, in particular the feminist legal community. A major contribution of the early activists was the development of alternative discourses to promote changes of awareness among the public and gain allies in the women's legal organizations. A loosely connected policy network of organizations sometimes supported individual lawsuits, among them feminist activists, lawyers, journalists, and other actors who had been influential in monitoring the implementation and enforcement of regulations. Thus, important parts of the women's movement which contributed to the development of sexual harassment law and policy stayed outside the media; their strategies were not public protest activities or demonstrations but working with existing institutions.

"Having the law in their hand" enabled these feminists to promote legal change at the state level, in workplaces, and in organizations. Lawmakers in some states, for example California, have gone beyond the narrowly defined workplace to prohibit the abuse of power in service–client relationships, for instance, doctors and patients or landlords and renters. In many states, lawmakers passed laws to hold employers with more than five employees responsible for creating workplace environments free of sexual harassment. Several states adopted regulations requiring employers to have policies and grievance procedures and training programs. Given the continuing controversial nature of the issue itself, it is hard to imagine how feminist advocates could have convinced federal lawmakers to pass a law specifically outlawing sexual harassment.

The media contributed to bringing the issue to broader awareness by following court cases and publicizing allegations against high-profile figures. Sexual harassment is an issue of neither liberals nor conservatives, yet, as the political scandals show, the political constellations in Washington did matter. Political parties have an indirect influence through the appointment of judges, and the EEOC chair used the agency's potential to be an ally to sexual harassment activists more under Democratic presidents Carter and, to some extent, Clinton than in Reagan and G.H.W. Bush times. Yet G.H.W. Bush, under the pressure created by the Hill-Thomas hearings, had to support the first federal law that aided victims, the Civil Rights Act of 1991. Here, public opinion and some feminist organization lobbying paid off. Because of the US system of labor relations, unions do not play a major role at the national level, though there is some evidence that they were allies to feminists at the state level.

Without feminist reconceptualization of sexual harassment, not as a moral issue but as one of women's rights prohibited under Title VII, it is unlikely that the legal revolution would have occurred in the United States. In the 1970s and 1980s, feminists worked to create awareness among officials, employers, and individual women that sexual harassment should no longer be allowed in the workplace. We can see feminist legal scholars' influence on the development of several aspects of law, such as the concept of unwantedness and, perhaps most visible, the reasonable woman's standard. US feminists not only created alternative discourses for Americans, they also inspired their European counterparts to take on the issue. US courts have been much more responsive to victims of sexual harassment than those in most EU member states, as we will see in the next chapter.

3 Diffusion through supranational actors: sexual harassment in the European Union[1]

European Union Commissioner Anna Diamantopoulou, celebrating the passage of the directive on sexual harassment,[2] announced at a press conference: "The general level of awareness of sexual harassment in Member States is very poor. Now sexual harassment, absent from most national laws today, will finally have a name" (Commission Press Release April 18, 2002). The 2002 Equal Treatment Directive passed despite the objections of several European member states and the European employers' associations. They had actively criticized the European Union's efforts to combat sexual harassment and long resisted it. They declared sexual harassment a culturally specific issue for which EU-wide regulations could not be developed, and sought to protect businesses against overregulation and additional costs. For example, a spokesman for the United Kingdom right/center Tory party explained: "Sexual harassment has got absolutely nothing to do with the EU" (Philip Bushill-Matthews, Member of the British Parliament, 2002). The Tories not only argued that the EU was intruding on domestic affairs but demanded the dismantling of the European Commission's Equality Directorate, arguing that this office had become "an engine of costly left-wing legislation that was plaguing business with rules and red tape" (Evans-Pritchard 2002).

The Commissioner had tried to convince businesses of the value of anti-harassment laws: "In my mind, the chief purpose of this directive is preventive . . . At the end of the day, a clear and predictable working environment free of sexual harassment is also in the interest of business itself"(Commission Press Release June 7, 2000). The Commissioner also took a clearly feminist stance and referred to her goal of making

---

[1] Parts of this chapter have been published previously in *Social Politics* (Zippel 2004).
[2] Directive 2002/73/EC of the European Parliament and the European Council of September 23, 2002 amending Council Directive 76/207/EEC on the implementation of the principle of equal treatment for men and women as regards access to employment, vocational training and promotion, and working conditions.

sexual harassment and violence against women visible. In her announcement of the new directive she drew on feminist notions of laws as empowerment and defined sexual harassment as a problem that affects women, and young women in particular, as a collective group: "The fact that we are announcing that there will be a European policy on sexual harassment will give women the internal courage to stand up and have their say" (Commission Press Release June 7, 2000).

Surprisingly, the EU has been an innovator in this policy field, ahead of most member states since the mid-1980s. As Ada Garcia, a feminist researcher and advocate for sexual harassment laws from Belgium, explained at a conference in 2005 when she referred to EU support of violence issues in the workplace: "We are lucky that the European Union exists." Despite the fact that the first European Community policies of the early 1990s were not directly binding for member states, and that sexual harassment was perceived as an "American import," most member states did adopt some laws against sexual harassment during the 1990s. The EU contributed to diffusing sexual harassment policies and was a catalyst in legal reforms in the member states, but their diverse legal approaches demonstrate how specific national institutional arrangements of gender and workplace contribute to shaping the politics of sexual harassment in the member states. Generally speaking, EU measures have been more "feminist" than these national laws, whose weakness has also been in the lack of implementation and in their erratic, uneven enforcement through courts and tribunals because of gender bias and sexist attitudes.

The latest measure, the 2002 Equal Treatment Directive, required the twenty-five member states to revise or adopt sexual harassment laws by October 2005. This directive reflects feminist demands to define sexual harassment from the victim's perspective, as "unwanted behavior." With this directive, sexual harassment is a workplace issue and clearly linked to sex equality, because it is defined as sex discrimination. Moreover, the EU has invented a particularly "European" notion of sexual harassment as the violation of dignity. The legal context is a broader directive on gender equality in the workplace, and policy-makers added an important feminist demand, the recognition not only of sexual behavior but also of nonsexual forms of harassment based on gender as sex discrimination. The directive also lifted any limitations on damages for victims of discrimination in general, but member states have been left to decide how to require employers to take preventive steps and how to implement and enforce these laws.

The forerunner role of the EU has surprised many observers, not least those feminists who have been highly critical of globalization and have viewed the European integration process with its neo-liberal, free market ideological orientation as catering primarily to business interests. In EU member states there is in fact little understanding of how acts and directives are passed in the supranational organization; a common perception has been that Brussels bureaucrats and business elites make deals behind closed doors. How, then, can we explain how the EU has been a promoter of gender equality – at least regarding sexual harassment in the workplace?

The chronology of EU policies on sexual harassment beginning in the 1980s and their subsequent implementation by member states during the 1990s[3] suggests that sexual harassment law resulted from a twenty-year process on policy development between the EU and its member states that resembled a ping-pong effect. At the EU level there has been a slow process of incremental policy change, especially compared with the US legal revolution. Member states in the 1980s were reluctant to agree to a binding EU law, so the European Commission resorted to several soft-law measures in the early 1990s. Only in 2002, almost twenty years after sexual harassment was first mentioned in Community documents, did the EU modernize the 1976 Directive on Equal Treatment to include a binding definition of sexual harassment as sex discrimination. The 2002 Equal Treatment Directive required member states to revise or adopt laws to encourage employers to prevent sexual harassment by 2005.

The paths these policy changes took in the EU and most member states were strikingly different from that of the United States. US courts were the main site of change. Grassroots women's organizations had named "sexual harassment" and brought it to public attention in the mid-1970s. In the EU, there was a process of bureaucratic measures and negotiations among national governments, with complex interaction between member states and the EU. Even though many successes in the area of EU gender equality laws came through litigation (Alter and Vargas 2000; Cichowski 2002; Shaw 2000), in the case of sexual harassment individuals did not bring sexual harassment to the European Court of Justice. Only a small number of EU reform-oriented women's organizations had mobilized on the issue by the early 1980s. Instead, women in EU institutions, and in particular the emergent state offices for women – femocrats who built networks with women within unions –

---

[3] The states that founded the European Community in the 1950s were France, Belgium, West Germany, Italy, Luxembourg, and the Netherlands. Denmark, Ireland, and the United Kingdom joined in 1973, Greece in 1981, and Spain and Portugal in 1986. Sweden, Austria, and Finland joined the EU in 1995. In the largest enlargement, in 2004, Cyprus, the Czech Republic, Hungary, Estonia, Latvia, Lithuania, Malta, Poland, Slovenia, and the Slovak Republic joined. This chapter focuses on the developments in member states until 2004.

drew on (feminist) legal experts to become the driving force for these legal reforms in the EU and its member states.

The multi-level policy-making process in the EU has provided some surprising avenues for feminists to play a role in the politics of sexual harassment. For example, the EU Commission and the Parliament have been particularly open to feminist demands because they have tried to build legitimacy by responding to neglected domestic groups (Hoskyns 1996). The path to effect change in the supranational organization of the EU requires working on various policy levels, and at the EU level requires convincing multiple national leaders in discursive struggles about the legitimacy of EU intervention, etc. While national policy-makers have to take public opinion more into account, the EU has no public sphere and only an emerging civil society. Instead, feminist advocates, feminists, and pro-feminist experts were influential because they provided the trans-national expertise, ideas, and discourses on sexual harassment.[4] This expertise was needed by the EU Commission and Parliament to expand the narrow focus of the 1976 Equal Treatment Directive on equal pay to sexual harassment, an issue framed as sexual violence. These trans-national ideas and discourses provided legitimacy for this new field of gender equality policy within the EU and in its member states.

Hence, within the EU, feminist mobilizing around sexual harassment took a particular form that was shaped by the path for legal changes within the particular institutional arrangements of the EU and its member states. An emerging transnational advocacy network on gender equality took advantage of the emerging political opportunity structures at the supranational level; it also participated in shaping and creating opportunities for policy change in the EU and in the member states. Transnational advocacy networks are, according to Keck and Sikkink (1998), broad "principled" transnational networks that form around shared values in areas such as human rights, violence against women, and environmental destruction. These networks can include various actors: nongovernmental organizations (NGOs), researchers, experts, policy-makers, and "friendly governments." They have the capacity to create transnational expertise through the exchange of information and knowledge across borders and among activists, experts, and policy-makers. Hence, feminists mobilizing around sexual harassment could use the TAN on gender equality to enhance elite learning and diffuse transnational expertise successfully.

---

[4] See also Vivien Schmidt (2002) for a discussion on how important discourses are in explaining Europeanization in policy areas.

This EU TAN drew extensively on the US feminist debates on sexual harassment. But the influence of the "American way" of handling sexual harassment has provided Europeans both a model to follow and a model to avoid. Once US feminists had defined and named the concept of sexual harassment in the mid-1970s, feminists in Europe did not need to reinvent it. But during the 1990s, the EU discourse on sexual harassment became more important for feminists to draw on because the US model was seen as an "import" and misconstrued in the media with persistent critiques of sexual correctness and the overuse of law in the United States.

This chapter proceeds chronologically, beginning by tracing the origins of sexual harassment politics in the European Community and its member states in the 1980s. It then discusses the development of soft-law measures during the late 1980s and early 1990s, when the EC was the innovator in this policy field, passing nonbinding measures before most of its member states acted. It addresses how these EC measures contributed to the diffusion of sexual harassment law at the national level during the 1990s and its implementation in member states. Finally, it describes how, in 2002, policy-makers in the EU updated the 1976 Equal Treatment Directive to include sexual harassment.

The origin of EU measures

The evolution of sexual harassment as a legitimate field for policy-making in the member states and in the EU can be traced to feminist actors who protested the everyday experience of women in workplaces. Feminist mobilization around the issue benefited in the beginning from exchanges with activists and academics in the United States. Politics against sexual harassment emerged in the early 1980s, when feminists and women in unions mobilized around the issue in the member states, drew media attention, and demanded legal and policy changes. As in the United States, the issue at first lacked political legitimacy in EU member states, and advocates who raised the issue frequently faced laughter and ridicule. Advocates for change needed to create awareness and convince political actors in their countries that sexual harassment was a legitimate problem that required the attention of employers, unions, and states.

No national law at the time defined sexual harassment as a violation of working women's rights. European Community law required member states to adopt measures on equal pay and equal treatment, and by 1980 all member states had some form of gender equality law in the workplace. Yet most member states did little to enforce and implement these laws, and individuals had little legal recourse to hold employers responsible for sex discrimination in general and sexual harassment in particular.

Few women brought cases we would now consider as involving sexual harassment to courts under labor law or civil law. Civil and criminal courts heard some cases regarding unwanted physical sexual advances, especially if they amounted to rape and sexual assault by supervisors (Holzbecher et al. 1990; Rubenstein 1987). Labor courts heard cases under unfair dismissal laws, but they often did not acknowledge the severe consequences on victims, even of physical harassment. The major problem individuals faced was that courts, employers, and unions lacked sensitivity on the issue. Treating sexual harassment as a private matter between individuals, they frequently did not take women's complaints seriously (Holzbecher et al. 1990).

Only in the United Kingdom and Ireland did courts apply sex discrimination law to cases of sexual harassment during the 1980s (Rubenstein 1987). One of the earliest cases that specifically recognized sexual harassment as a violation of equal treatment of women occurred in Northern Ireland, when a woman facing severe harassment in a male-dominated occupation took her employer to court. In an interview with the BBC, the Equal Opportunity Commission for Northern Ireland stated that the "sexual harassment amounted to unlawful sex discrimination" (Collins 1996: 26). Based on this public attention and the EOC statement, a young woman who was training as a motor mechanic in a Belfast garage brought the first case of sexual harassment to a tribunal. Evelyn Collins summarizes the case:

She had been subjected to lewd comments and unwanted physical contact from two male colleagues, which resulted in injury. The industrial tribunal found that the men's behavior was entirely unacceptable and that the harassment was dictated by prejudice because she was female. The tribunal concluded that sexual harassment constituted unlawful discrimination.[5]

This way of interpreting sexual harassment as a gender workplace issue rooted in discrimination was an import from the United States. Indeed, the concept of sexual harassment first traveled from the United States to Europe through both informal and formal transnational women's networks. Women labor unionists, activists involved in anti-violence movements, (pro-) feminist labor experts, and academic women diffused the concept in international conferences throughout the 1980s (Collins 1996). For example, Elske ter Veld, then at the Dutch women's secretariat of the peak union organization and later state

---

[5] *M v. Crescent Garage Ltd*, IT Case 23/83/SD; cited in Collins (1996: 26).

secretary for Social Affairs and Emancipation, wrote an article about a study trip to the United States, where sexual harassment at work was much discussed (Kuiper 2002). Feminists were particularly apt to use transnational forums to draw on and create expertise by introducing alternative perspectives and discourses (for example, to consider sexual harassment not as a private issue but as sex discrimination), and by exchanging information about the problem of sexual harassment and solutions to it.

On both sides of the Atlantic, feminists framed sexual harassment as constituting violence against women, abuse of supervisors' hierarchical power, and sexual exploitation of women. Feminists in Europe and the United States were reading the same books on violence against women and workplace sexual harassment (Brownmiller 1975; MacKinnon 1979). In France, women's organizations had connections to Québec, the French-speaking part of Canada. French feminists took the notion of "harcèlement sexuel" from the Quebecois, rather than translating "sexual harassment" themselves.[6]

Feminists in Europe were aware of the 1980 guidelines on sexual harassment developed by the US Equal Employment Opportunity Commission and the 1986 US Supreme Court decision on *Meritor Savings Bank v. Vinson*,[7] in which the court ruled that sexual harassment is actionable under the Civil Rights Act of 1964, recognizing that it constitutes sex discrimination. These actors in the emerging TAN on gender equality borrowed the notion of sexual harassment from the United States and translated the term into European languages.

Activists in some EC member states also borrowed strategies from the US movement, such as consciousness raising, documenting sexual harassment through surveys, and mobilizing protests around specific incidents. In the early 1980s, media attention on sexual harassment in a few member states began to raise public awareness of the issue. Forms of activism that subsequently emerged included Dutch feminists' 1981 replication of the survey on sexual harassment in the US women's magazine *Redbook* in the Dutch magazine *Viva* (Roggeband and Verloo 1999). The researcher Mieke Verloo found that 90 percent of respondents indicated having an experience with sexual harassment (Kuiper 2002). Public interest and awareness in Belgium was also the result of publicized research on sexual harassment. In the aftermath of a 1982 scandal in the West German Green party, Sybille Plogstedt, a feminist

---

[6] Thanks to Abigail Saguy who pointed out this Québec connection to me (communication March 2004).
[7] 106S. Ct. 2399 (1986).

journalist and sociologist, convinced the German Trade Union Confederation to publish the results of a survey on women's experiences with sexual harassment and state institution and union responses (Plogstedt and Bode 1984). In France, beginning in 1985, a coalition of feminists from the women's policy agency, trade union confederation, feminist jurists, and the Ligue du Droit des Femmes (LDF) mobilized and advocated for policy change (Mazur 1994).

Women in labor unions not only in West Germany but also in the United Kingdom and the Netherlands placed the issue on the agenda of national trade unions (see Collins 1996; Roggeband and Verloo 1999).[8] A resolution of the German trade union association (DGB) in 1986 found: "It is necessary to lead an open process of discussion, and to make sexual harassment part of union interest representation."[9] Similarly, in 1983 the British Trades Union Congress published a guide to recognizing and preventing sexual harassment at work that was widely circulated across Europe. It called on trade unions to take action: "It is a legitimate concern for trade unions that the workplace can become a threatening environment for women, and trade unions have a duty to make members aware of, and sensitive to, the nature and scope of the problems involved, and to take action to prevent sexual harassment from occurring" (cited in Rubenstein 1987: 158).

Yet the issue of sexual harassment lacked legitimacy in both the national and EC arenas. Neither women's movements nor trade unions put it high on their list of priorities, and no national government in the EC passed laws addressing it. Only three single-issue women's organizations in EC member states emerged that had the goals of assisting victims of sexual harassment and advocating for policy changes. The Association Européenne Contre les Violences Faites aux Femmes au Travail (AVFT), founded in 1985 by Yvette Fuillet, became the most visible autonomous single-issue organization devoted to sexual harassment in France but with an explicit orientation toward affecting change in the EC. Women against Sexual Harassment (WaSH) in the United Kingdom has provided services to victims and has played a role in monitoring EEO offices. In the Dutch case, both the government and trade unions proved more responsive. The organization Stichting Handen Thuis (Keep Your Hands to Yourself, or short: Hands Off) was founded in the Netherlands with state and trade union support as the

---

[8] For example, a guide from the UK Trades Union Congress, published in August 1983, was widely circulated throughout Europe. In West Germany, the public-sector union ÖTV Berlin had a traveling exhibit on "Sexism in the Workplace" in 1985.

[9] Resolution of the 13th DGB-Federal Congress 1986.

country's national office dealing with sexual harassment (Roggeband and Verloo 1999). Indeed, Roggeband and Verloo point out that the Netherlands was a pioneer in this policy field. For example, the Dutch group received state funding to establish a national complaint center, with a twenty-four-hour hotline for victims of sexual harassment and an information and training center for trade unions and employers. When the state funding ran out in 1990, Alie Kuiper, who had been one of three paid staff members, founded a private consultation agency (Kuiper 2002). These women's groups also began to address the issue at the EC level because their own countries offered strong resistance to legal reforms and limited political opportunities.

Opportunities at the EU level

Given the controversial nature of the issue of sexual harassment, it is surprising that the EU has been an innovator and assumed a leadership role in this policy area. Why were feminists more successful at the EU than at the national level? The European Community created a new arena for activism for feminists concerned with issues for women in the workplace and provided new political opportunities for supranational influence. Emergent supranational organizations tend to be less fully institutionalized than nation-states; therefore, they often provide a more open and flexible field of opportunities for influencing policy. This new level of political opportunity also reshapes domestic conflicts (Imig and Tarrow 2001). Roggeband and Verloo (1999) argue convincingly that the EU not only adds an additional layer of opportunities for social movements but transforms national political structures themselves. Unlike any other supranational organization, the EU wields considerable authority in economic issues and also has power in areas of workplace gender equality in its member states. Policy-making in this system of "multilevel governance" occurs at the regional, national, and supranational levels. Incremental steps in policy action at each level can continuously interact with and influence each other.

At the EU level, the main actors in the development of this policy field have been the European Commission, the Council of Ministers, the European Parliament, and, most recently, the social partners (EU-wide employers and trade union associations). The European Commission is the quasi-governmental body of the EU, but the member state governments together with the European Parliament have decision-making power over EU laws. Until the 1993 Treaty of the EU, and during the time feminists first mobilized around sexual harassment, approval by the

Parliament was not necessary, and the Council of Ministers alone – that is, the representatives of the member states – had the final word. Today, the Council needs the approval of the Parliament; both decide together in the co-decision-making procedure. Regulations, such as sexual harassment law, are determined in the Council by qualified majority voting.

The 1970s mobilization of feminists and a number of legal cases before the European Court of Justice forced the Commission to increase its attention to this potential area of intervention (Cichowski 2002; Mazey 1998; Hoskyns 1996). The Commission also pursued gender equality because it had been looking for issues that would consolidate its power and influence and help establish its profile as an active policy-maker. Aware of the exclusion of women's interests in the member states, the Commission, under Jacques Delores, promoted and built an agenda of gender equality in the European Community. This strategy was aimed at elevating the Commission's political profile and expanding its area of intervention.

Both creating policy innovation and convincing member states to take action require an important resource: transnational expertise. Transnational expertise bridges cultural, political, and legal differences among countries and helps create "European" issues. In organizations like the EU, administrative bodies drive policy areas such as gender equality. This bureaucratic model contrasts with democratic or parliamentary forms of policy-making, in which political parties and governments dominate the process. Administrative policy-making relies more on transnational expertise than on public opinion. Policy-makers need information about the possible impact on member states of measures at the supranational level. In addition, support of now twenty-five member states is needed for approval of policy initiatives. Thus, professional, scientific language becomes the currency in transnational communication between administrators, policy-makers, and politicians.

The role of the transnational advocacy network during the 1980s

The particular ability of transnational advocacy networks to create the transnational expertise so crucial for EU action has forged important relationships among EU-level policy-makers, experts, and activists. TANs create policy expertise through the exchange of information and knowledge among activists, experts, and policy-makers, with insiders and outsiders sharing an interest. The EU actively supported the development of TANs in general and the TAN on gender equality in particular. As Sonia Mazey points out, this development gave EU institutions access to "several transnational women's networks and Brussels-centered interest group coalitions, who have become sophisticated policy actors" (1998: 135, see also Cichowski 2002; Hoskyns 1996; Sperling and Bretherton 1996; Stratigaki 2000). The emerging TAN on gender equality, which included European Parliament and Commission members sympathetic to the issue, also proved instrumental in placing the specific issue of sexual harassment on the EU policy-making agenda.

Women's organizations that focused on sexual harassment and became part of this TAN and served as EU-level pressure groups included the Paris-based AVFT, the British WaSH, and the Dutch activists in Hands Off (Roggeband and Verloo 1999; Mazur 1994; Collins 1996). In a classic boomerang effect (see Keck and Sikkink 1998), both the French and Dutch groups, facing resistance at the national level, lobbied to place sexual harassment on the agenda of supranational organizations. As we will see, the politics of sexual harassment in the European Community jumped back and forth from member states to supranational level, hence we need to extend the boomerang effect to a ping-pong effect.

AVFT from the beginning employed a strategy that not only pressured the French government to reform its penal code and labor laws but also sought legal reform in the EC (Louis 1994). The group succeeded in soliciting initial financial support from the European Commission and government funding in subsequent years. In 1989, AVFT organized the first international meeting specifically on sexual harassment; it included international activists and experts as well as French politicians (Mazur 1994; Saguy 2003).

Despite the fact that Hands Off had received funding from the Dutch government, Dutch activists could not convince the government to legislate against sexual harassment. The government maintained that the EC should legislate, although it did support efforts to place the issue on the EC agenda (Roggeband and Verloo 1999). When the Council of Ministers was under Dutch presidency, it commissioned the first EU-wide study on sexual harassment, promoting the creation of transnational expertise.

The result, Michael Rubenstein's report on "The Dignity of Women at Work" (1987), became an influential tool at both the EC and national levels. Rubenstein, a legal expert on industrial relations, reported that consciousness about the issue varied greatly from state to state and that only a few member states, including the United Kingdom, Ireland, and Belgium, had adequate laws providing legal redress for victims. Yet empirical studies showed that such workplace harassment did indeed affect many women and some men throughout the Community. Rubenstein made several suggestions for directives and a code of practice. His study was widely cited because it offered expertise: a professional, transnational European examination of sexual harassment. In subsequent years the study provided legitimacy for national and EU advocacy groups because it offered models for a "European way" to address sexual harassment. It also provided the impetus for national governmental action to acquire more expertise. The German Ministry of Women, for example, commissioned the first nationwide study on sexual harassment, published in 1990 (see Chapter 4).

Rubenstein, a pro-feminist himself, who had left the United States in the 1950s, was a key expert who "imported" legal concepts of sexual harassment in the United Kingdom and for the Commission, consciously developing an improved "European" model. As he explained:

"I think . . . we were carving out a distinct, and I would argue more sophisticated, 'European' approach to sexual harassment, in contrast to the American approach of prohibiting certain behaviours at work such as touching between colleagues or telling off-colour jokes. We were also making it clear that a woman does not have to accept the mores of a male-dominated workplace or lose her right to complain about behaviour merely because other women have not objected to being treated in the same way" (Personal Profile, *http://www.michael-rubenstein.co.uk/*).

The development of professional expertise to talk about sexual harassment publicly was crucial because it created a language also to discuss the problem itself. For example, while the Rubenstein report was positively perceived, Rubenstein remembers: "It was said that the Social Affairs Commissioner at the time, Madame Papandreou [from Greece], did not wish to answer questions at press conferences as to the types of behaviour that would or would not constitute sexual harassment" (Personal Profile, 2005, *http://www.michaelrubenstein.co.uk/*).

In this early phase, the TAN on gender equality relied on an informal network of feminists and other gender-minded actors within and outside EC institutions. These actors were particularly apt to use transnational forums to draw on and create the transnational expertise policy-makers needed.[10] This TAN's most important contributions were placing sexual harassment on the EC agenda, providing research findings to justify their claims, and developing policy models. They also introduced alternative discourses and developed new ways to frame sexual harassment as an issue requiring EC intervention. For example, women in the European Parliament, as well as many women's organizations, initiated dis-

---

[10] The European Women's Lobby was founded in 1989 with EC funding. The organization began to coordinate the lobbying efforts of national women's organizations in the 1990s.

cussions on sexual harassment and demanded EC-level action. As early as 1983, the socialist member of the European Parliament, Yvette Fuillet (France), and her communist colleague, Maria-Lisa Cinciari-Rodano (Italy), presented a draft to the European Parliament demanding action against the sexual exploitation and blackmail of women in the workplace (*TAZ*, February 2, 1983; *Frankfurter Rundschau*, February 8, 1983).

The TAN framed sexual harassment both as a workplace issue and as an issue of violence against women. A 1984 Council of Ministers recommendation acknowledged the problem of sexual harassment for the first time and called on member states to take action to promote "respect for the dignity of women at the workplace." In the mid-1980s, the European Parliament passed a similar resolution on violence against women, recommending action on the part of the Commission (OJC 175, July 14, 1986). This resolution suggested methods for preventing sexual harassment and demanded both protection against it and assistance for its victims. The resolution asked governments, equal opportunity committees, and trade unions to conduct awareness campaigns. Finally, the European Parliament called upon the council to harmonize member states' legislation on this issue.

The struggle at the EC level centered on whether the issue was an important social problem that warranted EC action. Member state governments resisted the expansion of gender equality law at the EC level. Opponents argued that sexual harassment falls outside the purview of EC institutions because of its cultural embeddedness and should be handled at the national level. For example, within the Commission a list of behaviors that would constitute sexual harassment could not be agreed on. Northern Europeans did not necessarily object to pornographic images; southern Europeans did not object to kissing, touching, and hugging (Collins 1996). Kisses on the cheek, for example, are a common greeting practice for women and men in many southern European countries.

Advocates needed to draw on existing Community laws to establish justification for intervention. The Commission's mandate for action on gender issues was limited, and domestic violence, rape, and other forms of violence against women still lay beyond reach, but sexual harassment was a workplace issue, within the mandate. Community intervention was defined by the Equal Treatment Directive of 1976, which prohibits all forms of sex discrimination in the areas of access to employment, including promotion, vocational training, and working conditions. Thus, proponents of EC action linked sexual harassment to the existing legitimate field of intervention on equal treatment of women and men in the workplace. Advocates argued that sexual harassment constituted a problem of unequal working conditions for women, and the 1976 Directive became the legal foundation for EC action on sexual harassment.

Advocates also broadened the concern of sexual harassment as a gender-specific issue by framing it in the context of workplace health and safety, another area of EU social policy. This frame emphasizes the effects of sexual harassment on individuals, such as socio-psychological stresses in the workplace in general, but does little to promote awareness of it as a problem of gender inequality. Feminists advocated for measures that would link sexual harassment clearly to unequal power relations between men and women and emphasized the gender-specific nature of the problem.

The TAN succeeded in placing the issue on the Community agenda and began to increase awareness of sexual harassment as a concern to women in the workplace. The TAN created new alternative discourses, the Commission began to gather information from the member states, and transnational expertise emerged that subsequently aided the formulation of the EU soft-law instruments against sexual harassment.

EU soft-law measures

Within the Commission, Evelyn Collins proved instrumental in the creation of the EU soft-law measures of the early 1990s. Collins, a civil servant from Northern Ireland, was on assignment in the Equal Opportunity Unit of the European Commission. She drew from her legal expertise in the United Kingdom, where case law on sexual harassment had advanced farthest. In addition, she worked closely with Rubenstein, author of the influential EC-wide study on sexual harassment, to draft the policy documents.

Advocates promoted without success a legally binding law on sexual harassment for member states. A binding directive would require that member states create or modify their national laws to comply with EC law. Breach of such hard laws entails sanctions, and the European Court of Justice and the Commission can hold member states accountable for taking action under them. Advocates faced obstacles within the Commission to establishing the issue's legitimacy and even greater resistance from member state governments to agree on a legally binding framework. Collins was, however, able to promote consensus among member states for soft-law measures. In December 1990, the Council of Ministers passed a resolution entitled "Dignity of Women and Men in the Workplace"[11] (see Table 3.1).

---

[11] Council resolution on the protection of the dignity of women and men at work (OJ No C 157, June 27, 1990).

Table 3.1. *European Union measures against sexual harassment*

Phase 1 Origin of EU measures:
1976 Directive on Equal Treatment
1984 Council of Ministers: Recommendation on the promotion of positive action for
    women
1986 European Parliament Resolution on violence against women
Phase 2 Soft-law measures and the implementation in member states
1990 Council of Ministers' Resolution
1991 Commission Recommendation
1991 Commission Code of Practice
1996 Social Dialogue (failed)
Phase 3 The Directive of 2002 and beyond
2002 Revision of the 1976 Directive on Equal Treatment

In the absence of member state consensus on hard law, the Commission typically uses soft-law measures to establish new policy fields. In the area of gender equality politics in the 1980s and 1990s, the Commission used various soft-law measures, including recommendations and resolutions.[12] These have the drawback of being nonbinding, with no sanctions if member states do not observe them. With what is now called the open method of coordination, the Commission encourages voluntary policy transfer between member states and workplace organizations. This strategy promotes diffusion and exchange of policy models and best-practice models among policy-makers and experts.[13] In 1991, the European Commission issued a recommendation and corresponding Code of Practice on sexual harassment in the workplace, and requested that member states take action in the public sector to set a positive example for the private sector.[14] Both the recommendation and the Code of Practice focused on the importance of national legislative reform to ensure individual legal redress, called on states, employers, and unions to engage in prevention efforts, and encouraged employers and unions to adopt collective agreements to ensure that

---

[12] The Commission issued four such recommendations in the 1980s and six in the 1990s (Rees 1998: 55).
[13] See Rianne Mahon (2002) for a discussion of best-practice model on child care in the EU.
[14] Commission recommendation of November 27, 1991 on the protection of the dignity of women and men at work (92/131/EEC) (OJ No L049 February, 24 1992).

policies and specific procedures would allow victims to file complaints at the company level.

The success of the TAN in creating these soft-law measures depended on various actors: Evelyn Collins's dedicated promotion of the issue in the European Commission was aided by demands of outside advocacy groups and support from within the Commission. Because resistance proved so strong, it was fortuitous that the Commissioner for Social and Employment Affairs, Vasso Papandreou, a socialist woman from Greece, supported the proposal. According to Collins (1996), it is also unlikely that the Commission would have taken on the issue of sexual harassment without the lobbying efforts of advocacy groups such as AVFT, WaSH, and Hands Off. Coincidentally, the International Lesbian and Gay Association (ILGA) and the UK-based lesbian, gay, and bisexual lobby organization, Stonewall, were lobbying the Commission to take action on discrimination against lesbians and gays.

The demands of advocacy groups are most visible in the Code of Practice, which went beyond the council resolution in defining sexual harassment in explicitly feminist language and specifically defining harassment as a matter of women's equality and status in the workplace:

As sexual harassment is often a function of women's status in the employment hierarchy, policies to deal with sexual harassment are likely to be most effective where they are linked to a broader policy to promote equal opportunities and to improve the position of women.

The Commission's recommendation resembles the US EEOC guidelines on defining sexual harassment in its definition of *quid pro quo* and hostile environment harassment by supervisors or coworkers. It differs from the EEOC guidelines in three important respects. First, sexual harassment is defined as a "violation of dignity," linked to sex discrimination only with the vague statement that "such conduct may, in certain circumstances, be contrary to the principle of equal treatment and thus covered under Directive 76/207/EEC." This reflects the contentious nature of sexual harassment as sex discrimination across the member states.

Second, the Code recognizes sexual harassment of men and the specific vulnerability of persons because of disability, sexual orientation, and race. By contrast, US courts only belatedly recognized same-sex harassment and the possibility that men could also be victims. Only in 1998 did the US Supreme Court decision in *Oncale v. Sundowner*

Offshore Services, Inc. clarify that same-sex sexual harassment can be prosecuted under the 1964 Civil Rights Act.

Third, following the US model, the strategy of enforcement is predominant by ensuring individuals' access to the courts, by emphasizing legal claims in case of violation, and by ensuring protection against retaliation, for example dismissal for instigating a legal claim. But, unlike the EEOC guidelines, the Code also provides explicit guidance to collective bargaining partners (trade unions and employers) for developing agreements about preventive measures and complaint procedures against workplace sexual harassment.

Thus, the soft-law model of combating sexual harassment in the workplace contained the following elements: member states should adopt laws against sexual harassment to strengthen individuals' legal redress, and state agencies should implement and enforce these laws. In addition, the EU has emphasized the role of collective bargaining partners in devising instruments against sexual harassment in the workplace. These measures translated sexual harassment into a European context – in particular, by formulating sexual harassment as violation of dignity and by including collective bargaining partners in the process of implementing workplace policies.

The soft-law measures, however, also have limitations. Feminists in particular have been rather critical of their lack of enforcement. A widespread concern was that governments, employers, and trade unions would ignore nonbinding measures. For example, the Committee on Women's Rights of the European Parliament and the Committee on Economy and Social Affairs criticized the Code of Conduct for being a recommendation rather than a regulation or a directive.[15]

During the 1990s, the Commission continued the open method of coordination, supporting the creation of TANs of activists, legal experts, and policy-makers, which helped to slowly establish sexual harassment as a valid policy field. The transnational expertise TANs create is crucial in policy fields dominated by taboos, myths, and stereotypes, as is the case for sexual harassment. Beyond bringing together experts, the EU generated and stimulated research within and across member states. Cross-national, comparative research initiatives, conferences, and symposia constructed a layer of transnational expertise. The EU funded networks of experts, called observatories, and several international

---

[15] Report of January 27, 1994 of the Committee on Women's Rights on a new post of "Confidential Counsellor" at the workplace (European Parliament Session Documents, A3-0043/94), page 10.

meetings were convened, often cofinanced by the Commission. These were no longer limited to furthering the exchange among experts, but were also capable of diffusing information to participating nonprofit organizations, activists, attorneys, and other practitioners. In the mid-1990s the Commission financed a comparative study updating Rubenstein's original report on the prevalence of sexual harassment and initiated national-level research activities, particularly in countries that had previously not conducted extensive research (e.g., Greece and Portugal) (European Commission 1999).

With the Council resolution, the Commission had a mandate to work on sexual harassment, but the issue was not a high priority. For example, after Collins left the Equal Opportunity Unit, no replacement was assigned responsibility for addressing sexual harassment. Given the heated debates in EU member states, reaching agreement at the EU level was unlikely, and the Commission did not propose a directive. Instead, in 1996, it resorted to the new social dialogue and initiated a process of consultation with its social partners, the EU-wide employer associations and trade unions. The European Trade Union Confederation had strong interest in establishing this dialogue at the EU level and favored a collective European agreement on preventing the violation of dignity. But the negotiations failed because the Union of Industrial and Employers' Confederation of Europe (UNICE) maintained that the issue should be addressed at the national level and dismissed the argument that sexual harassment constitutes sex discrimination. Although the European Women's Lobby did not play a formal role in this process, it supported the trade union and issued a strong statement criticizing the breakdown of negotiations.

The soft-law measures of the early 1990s resulted from feminist efforts to draw attention to sexual harassment as a concern of working women. In this phase, the TAN drew extensively on transnational expertise, from EU member states and also from the United States. The US policy model proved exemplary in formulating measures against sexual harassment. Although EU policy was shaped by processes of administrative policy-making, it also needed consensus among member states. In the course of creating these policy tools, feminist demands were diluted: the member states could not reach consensus that sexual harassment constituted a gender-specific problem, that of sex discrimination. Instead, sexual harassment was broadened to include violations of dignity of both women and men. Nor did the member states agree to binding measures. As we will see, these soft-law measures did have an important impact because they subsequently helped activists promote action also in the member states.

Implementation of soft law in the member states

It is striking that between 1989 and 2000, twelve of fifteen member states adopted some kind of legislation against sexual harassment (see Table 3.2). The timing reflects the two main external factors – the influence of the controversial US discussions and the catalytic role played by the EU measures in legitimizing the new policy area. Before the EU-level action the issue of sexual harassment had lacked political legitimacy in most member states. Proponents for measures frequently had elicited laughter when introducing the issue. But the EU soft-law measures and transnational expertise now provided legitimacy and authority to national-level actors.

In this phase, the impact of US developments on public debates and legal reforms was mixed. Europeans were watching and reading reports about the 1991 US Senate hearings in which Anita Hill accused Supreme Court nominee Clarence Thomas of sexual harassment. Consequently, European media attention increased, but sexual harassment was depicted as an American problem Europeans did not have. The hearings generated widespread debate across Europe about the perceived American phobia about sexuality. Mainstream European media obsessed over "American excesses," portraying Americans as Puritans constantly on their guard against sexual expression and Europeans as sexually liberated (Bernstein 1994; Mazur 1994, 1996; Baer 1996; Valiente 1998; Saguy 2003). The impact was so negative in several member states that one might speculate as to whether the states would have agreed to the 1990 Council Resolution had the US Senate hearings preceded it.

Table 3.2. *First member state laws or court rulings*

1984	**Council of Ministers' Resolution on Positive Action**
1986	UK (tribunal decision)
1989	Spain, Denmark (court decision)
1990	**Council of Ministers' Resolution**
1991	**Commission Recommendation & Code of Practice**
1991	Sweden
1992	France, Austria
1994	Germany, Netherlands, Italy
1995	Belgium, Finland
1996	**EU Social Dialogue fails**
1998	Ireland
2000	Luxembourg
2002	**EU Equal Treatment Directive (1976 revised)**

Yet the public awareness the US debates generated served to direct attention also to the EC measures. Although many critics of soft-law measures on sexual harassment in the early 1990s expressed skepticism that the measures would have any effect, they did, in fact, influence national-level policy-making in a number of ways, some quite unexpected. Compliance with EC measures became an explicit and successful argument for promoting laws at the national level. Although it was not outright obligation, the need to comply with EC soft laws provided an additional argument for taking national-level action, and helped advocates in member states to overcome resistance and win approval for legislation.[16] Advocates also used this argument in applicant countries such as Austria, Sweden, and the Czech Republic, which sought to bring their laws in line with EC/EU legislation before joining (Elman 1996; Cahill 2001).

Even in countries with women's organizations like AVFT and Hands Off, national legislation passed only after EC soft-law measures existed: the need for compliance with the EC rather than direct concern about sexual harassment itself helped overcome national-level resistance. Institutional actors in equality offices played an important role. Mazur (2002) argues that not just the "feminist campaign" of AVFT and LDF (the French women's organization La Ligue des droits de la femme) but a host of factors contributed to the passage of the French law against sexual harassment in 1992. These factors included "a Cabinet reshuffle that brought in a pro-EC Prime Minister and a Deputy Minister of Women's Rights who wanted to present her own bill, the formulation of EC policy recommendations on . . . sexual harassment, and the successful adoption of Yvette Roudy's private member's bill" (2002: 167). The EC provided "an additional reason for state decision makers to place controversial issues on their . . . agendas" (Mazur 1996: 48–9).

Even in the countries considered leaders in gender equality law, the EU measures were necessary for gaining recognition of sexual harassment as an issue warranting action. Elman points out that "comparative examination of Swedish and EU sexual harassment policy suggests that, whatever its varied shortcomings, the EU served as a positive catalyst in the development of Swedish reform (and not vice versa)" (2000: 15). Thus, we can see here the next phase of the workings of the TANs: now national-level actors could draw on and make use of supranational policy measures to legitimize their demands at the national level.

---

[16] In 1996, the ECJ ruled that member states could not entirely ignore these soft-law measures.

The EU soft-law measures served to "Europeanize" the issue.[17] For example, those who opposed the establishment of laws argued that sexual harassment demonstrated how feminism and individual rights in the United States had gone too far, and provided another instance of "American prudish culture."[18] The authors of a working paper in the Women's Rights Series of the European Parliament also warned explicitly against adopting the US model: "National provisions must establish a balance between the need to protect individuals against sexual harassment and the risk of excessive legal proceedings" (Subhan and Boujan 1994: 28).

Advocates for national-level laws drew on the soft-law measures to justify a "moderate" European way of defining sexual harassment and designing policies. They also used the transnational expertise the EU had helped to create. For example, advocates in Spain avoided mentioning US laws or studies to make their case, referring instead to the 1987 Rubenstein report and the recommendation and code on sexual harassment (Valiente 1998). Ironically, this EU definition was almost identical to that of the United States. Advocates also used legislation in other EU member states to legitimate their demands for reforms. In Greece, for example, the French model of criminalizing sexual harassment became the policy template that legal experts and advocates promoted.

Most member states adopted the "European" concept that sexual harassment is a violation of dignity.[19] While the United Kingdom and Ireland followed the United States' lead in defining sexual harassment as sex discrimination, they too adopted the European interpretation of the issue as a violation of dignity. The British government did not believe that further legal measures were necessary; instead, it promised and conducted an awareness campaign, reasoning that "this problem cannot be solved by the law alone. The question is one not of the law but of general workplace relationships; this has to be tackled on a *voluntary basis*, everybody must co-operate and be engaged in solving the problem."[20] The Irish EEO issued a National Code of Practice entitled "Measures to Protect the Dignity of Women and Men at Work." Most member states also followed the EU's concept that sexual harassment

---

[17] For the role of ideas and discourses in EU policy change see also Vivien Schmidt and Claudio Radaelli (2004).

[18] This was particularly the case in Spain (Valiente 1998) and France (Mazur 1994, 1996; Saguy 2002).

[19] See also laws adopted in Austria, Belgium, Germany, Spain, France, and Portugal.

[20] European Standing Committee B, House of Commons: Dignity of women and men at work, Parliamentary Debate of December 18, 1991 (HMSO, London 1991), cited in ILO (1992: 270), emphasis by the author.

could take both verbal and physical forms. However, the initial laws member states adopted varied greatly as to whether they followed the definitions set by the EU soft-law measures (a topic addressed in more detail below).

There is also a cultural dimension of the European integration process in which countries compare themselves with each other. During the late 1980s, Spanish feminists, for example, used the argument that Spanish gender relations needed to be Europeanized (Valiente 1998). The EC research report triggered competition between EC member states in promoting gender equality issues. In Germany, the Ministry of Women had been embarrassed not to be able to provide research and information in 1987. France took pride in being the first country to pass a law following the EC recommendations. Finally, while Sweden prides itself on having the most progressive policies for women, the lack of adequate laws against sexual harassment constituted a sore point. Elman (2000: 23) critically observes:

Sweden formally recognized that it had no specific prohibition against sexual harassment the year that it entered the EU. While governmental references to European contexts had been made in the past, they often concluded that Sweden was ahead of the game. Indeed, Swedish identity is, in part, predicated on being superior to the rest of Europe, particularly with regard to sexual equality. On the issue of sexualized harassment at work, such exceptionalism proved impossible to substantiate . . . Sweden's definition of harassment was significantly less extensive than Europe's. Moreover, the very composition and context of the act provided only the most remote possibility for redress.

The contradiction of Swedish progressive policies for working women on the one hand, and a lack of awareness of sexual harassment on the other hand, is striking. Swedes seem to believe – in much the same way as Germans and French – that sexual harassment is an American problem. A common perception among them has been that, compared with the United States, "Swedes are more 'natural' about sex and that relations between genders are more natural," as Hauserman found (2002: 96). In February 1998, the US EEOC brokered a $9.9 million settlement on behalf of sexual harassment victims with Astra, a Swedish pharmaceutical company. In May 1996, *Business Week* broke the story about Lars Bildman, the CEO of the United States-based Astra, and other executives who had "fostered an environment in which relatively young saleswomen were badgered to engage in sex or to endure the sexual innuendoes, gropes, and grabs of senior management" (cited in Hauserman 2002: 89). The business culture included parties on yachts with prostitutes for visiting businessmen. Though Astra had agreed already to at least eleven settlements because of sexual harassment,

Swedish media trivialized the issue and portrayed it as a US problem (Hauserman 2002: 95). Hauserman argues: "Definitions that trivialize sexual harassment trivialize the whole concept of sexual harassment, inaccurately portray most cases, and cast the complaining victims, usually women, in the role of overly sensitive females" (2002: 95). Hence, the rivalry with other European member states to be at the forefront of gender equality in Sweden has competed with the perception of sexual harassment as an import from the United States. As we will see, the development of a "European" concept of sexual harassment as the violation of dignity helped in the future to overcome this cultural resistance not only in Sweden but also in other EU member states.

Implementation through national gender equality offices

In EU member states, feminist legal experts, feminists, and gender-minded actors in state offices and unions, rather than autonomous women's organizations, became the proponents for legal redress for sexual harassment. Gender equality offices in France, Germany, Belgium, and Spain were key actors. The implementation process through these national offices demonstrates how feminists capitalized on existing political opportunities and how the TAN on gender equality created new opportunity structures. Member states established institutionalized bodies for gender equality to monitor and implement EU legislation on sex equality law. Their powers varied greatly, but they proved instrumental in implementing EU soft-law measures against sexual harassment.

Of course, their relative power in governments mattered greatly. For example, Mazur (1994) points out that, without the support of the French Deputy Minister of Women's Rights in the late 1980s, feminist organizations would have lobbied in vain. Valiente (1998) finds that the Spanish group Instituto de la Mujer (Women's Institute), together with women within unions, convinced the country's socialist majority to address the issue of sexual harassment. In subsequent reforms, the Women's Institute was a crucial actor in proposing and drafting laws. In Germany, the minister of women, Rita Süßmuth, a member of the Christian Democratic party, was a strong supporter of women's rights. She was a key actor in preparing legislative measures on sexual harassment by commissioning the 1990 study as well as initiating several measures against sexual harassment within her own ministry.

These offices reviewed the EU soft-law measures and took it upon themselves to expand their own policy influence. Because sexual harassment is of concern to both women in unions and anti-violence activists, gender-minded policy-makers could now organize hearings and conferences on an issue of interest to both groups. EU measures provided these state actors with templates for drafting policies on sexual harassment and lent legitimacy to their efforts. Gender equality offices in turn devoted resources to raising awareness, distributing the EU Code of Practice to employers and unions (Germany and Spain, for example) (European Commission 1996), publishing their own guides and codes of practice (Ireland), and commissioning research studies on sexual harassment (Germany, Austria).

Because equality offices also fielded victims' complaints, their expertise in the field of sexual harassment grew. Individuals and unions can report sexual harassment to national EEO offices or other gender equality offices and agencies in a number of countries, including Austria, the United Kingdom, Northern Ireland, Spain, and Sweden. Some offices provide advice and legal support to victims, conduct investigations, or represent victims in court. One advantage of having specific offices handle sexual harassment complaints is apparent in the experience of a gender equality advocate who explains the difference between confrontational court proceedings and mediation-oriented committee hearings:

In Austria you can apply to the so-called Commission for Equal Treatment or to the labour court. The commission offers a different proceeding strategy. It is not as formal and confrontational as at court. In terms of sexual harassment the sensitivity of the members of this commission has increased since there are a lot of applications in this area. A kind of insensitivity still predominates at court. (Baur 2002)

The Austrian Commission for Equal Treatment[21] has become known for handling harassment cases which constitute the single most common form of sex discrimination complaints since 1992.

Only a few countries, such as the Netherlands and Spain, allow state inspectors to impose sanctions on employers who do not have adequate policies. For example, Alie Kuiper (2002) explains:

Inspectors of the National Department of Social Affairs can force individual organizations to have a policy in place and to develop a complaining-procedure. Last week a director HRM of an international company in Holland called me for an urgent consultation. First he complained about the governmental inspectors that forced him to take complaints of some female workers seriously and then he asked me to help him. He risks paying a fine when he can't show the inspectors within the time fixed that he took adequate measures.

---

[21] The commission consists of three government representatives, four employer representatives, and four employee representatives.

In practice, having these state officials in charge of enforcement of sexual harassment has serious drawbacks, as a French inspector explained (2005): "We do not have any training on discrimination or sexual harassment issues. When I go to a company I do not have the right to talk confidentially to women." Hence, if inspectors do not receive educational and awareness programs or have powers to conduct investigations into sexual harassment incidents, this enforcement mechanism remains flawed.

Implementation through national courts

National courts, including tribunal and labor courts, also took note of and applied the EU measures.[22] Rulings of UK tribunal courts referred to these measures, even though one court used them to rule against a claim of harassment (Gregory 2000). In Germany, labor court judges referred to them frequently when affirming employers' duty to protect employees from harassment, thus justifying employers' decisions to dismiss harassers. In fact, men dismissed by employers because of complaints against them have brought about 77 percent of all sexual harassment cases in German labor courts (see Chapter 5). In Greece, where no national legislation existed, a judge used EU policies to rule in favor of a victim of sexual harassment in 1998 (Gregory 2000). Finally, the Spanish Constitutional Court referred to the definition of sexual harassment from the Code of Practice and Recommendation in a 1999 ruling.[23]

However, courts can also choose to ignore soft laws. In 2002, the highest appeals court in Italy overruled a lower court decision sentencing a public health manager to eighteen months in jail and a $4,000 fine. The accuser, a woman employee, alleged that the manager had sexually harassed her, including touching her behind, and subsequently threatened to block her career if she denounced him. The court found no evidence that he intended "an act of libido," reasoning that the pat appeared to be an "isolated" incident and "impulsive." The court thus based its ruling on a guess as to the perpetrator's intentions rather than the act of harassment itself. After the ruling, the woman was quoted in the newspapers as saying, "After all I've been through and I've suffered, maybe I would advise another woman not to go to court" (Associated Press, January 25, 2001). In 1999, the same court reasoned that a

---

[22] In *Grimaldi de Fonds v. Maladie Professionelles* the ECJ ruled that member states cannot simply ignore EU soft-law measures and that there is a duty to take them into consideration when looking at questions of European law (Case C-322/88, 1989 ECR 4407).

[23] Decision no. 224/1999, of December 13, 1999 (see ILO Labor Court Judges Meeting).

woman wearing tight jeans could not be raped, since she would have to help remove the jeans, which would be tantamount to consenting to sex. To protest the decision, some female lawmakers showed up in parliament wearing jeans and holding banners that read, "Jeans, an alibi for rape" (Associated Press, January 25, 2001; *Off our backs*, 2001, 31 (3): 3; *New York Times*, January 26, 2001: 8).

Even where anti-discrimination laws already existed, as in the United Kingdom, access to the courts has remained a major problem: complaints can take three years or more before an industrial tribunal hears the case.[24] The outcomes of these complaints also demonstrate the inefficiency of these laws in providing redress for victims of sexual harassment. Analysis of 54 UK tribunal cases between 1998 and 2001 reveals that only 63 percent of the cases (34) resulted in successful complaints (EOC 2003). In over 90 percent of these cases, the complainants had lost their job or resigned as a direct result of the harassment. Compensation ranged between £750 and £40,000, though the majority of awards were between £2,000 and £5,000, an amount that did not even cover their legal fees.[25]

Even when women are lucky to find courts that rule in their favor, the case of sales manager Michelle Walker demonstrates the dramatic consequences sexual harassment can have for victims. In 2004, the tribunal awarded her nearly £120,000 in compensation, because it found that Walker's boss had sexually harassed her and her employer, Phones 44, discriminated against her by ignoring her complaints. Yet, for her the experience was a nightmare. She explained: "He's been promoted and I haven't got a job and I think it's unfair" (Walker cited in Bevan 2004). Following the harassment Walker had suffered from a moderately severe depressive disorder and was unemployable.

Instead of focusing on the plight of women who have been harassed and the problems women face going through the courts, however, UK media (much the same as US media) focus on a few high-profile trials only.[26] For example, Elizabeth Weston, a lawyer working for Merrill

---

[24] *http://www.state.gov/g/drl/rls/hrrpt/2000/eur/856.htm*

[25] In addition, a survey of the Equal Opportunities Review found that the average award for injury of feelings in sexual harassment cases was £13,331 and the median £10,405 in the year 2000 (EOR no. 100 Nov/Dec 2001, cited in Equal Opportunity Commission 2005, "General Guidance." *http://www.eoc.org.uk/* downloaded June 25, 2005. The highest UK settlement on sexual harassment was the case of a secretary suing a union boss and was said to be £300,000 for damages and £300,000 for legal fees.

[26] An exception is Kerry Capell's (2004) article in *Business Week* in which she argued that these high-profile cases should be a wake-up call for European businesses.

Lynch with an income of £60,000, settled with the investment bank for £550,000 because of sexual harassment, dismissal, and victimization. She alleged that an executive had made "disgusting" comments about her breasts and sex life at the office Christmas party. One journalist expressed concern for gender equality over these recent high-profile cases. Wright (2004) worried in his article "Discrimination Cases May Do More Harm Than Good" that a "litigious mentality" might in future keep employers from hiring women. Surprisingly, however, he failed to mention that United Kingdom and EU law prohibits sex discrimination in hiring.

The legal cases in the United Kingdom remain an exception in EU member states; though victims of sexual harassment have brought cases to EU member state courts, the enforcement remains limited in comparison with the United States. Seeking justice through the legal system is the last resort for many victims. Despite the fact that victims might have more access to the courts, since legal fees are usually lower than in the United States and some unions have policies to support sexual harassment victims financially, compensatory damages in the EU are also comparatively low, although the future 2002 Equal Treatment Directive has lifted limits for compensation of discrimination cases now. While some penal codes have been amended to hold perpetrators of harassment accountable, the often high burden of proof in criminal courts (compared with labor courts) provides a major obstacle, especially because sexual harassment frequently occurs without witnesses.

The application of the French penal code which served as exemplary for other EU member states highlights the problems victims of sexual harassment can face in court. At a conference in Paris in 2005, Catherine Le Magueresse, the president of AVFT, maintained that this rather weak law against sexual harassment continues to fail to protect victims because judges have applied the law in unpredictable ways and unevenly also across appellate courts. For example, though the French penal code seems tough on perpetrators because punishment is a one-year prison sentence and a fine of up to €15,000, the law limited sexual harassment to the intentions of supervisors to obtain sexual favors from subordinates until 2002. Since then the law can also be applied to coworkers, but the victim still has to prove the perpetrator's intent. In court, judges' opinions of what should be considered sexual harassment enter into their rulings because the legal definition is so vague, despite the fact that criminal law is subject to strict interpretation. Though some men have been convicted of sexual harassment, since 1992 none has spent time in jail. A male police commissioner who raised a woman police officer's skirt, kissed her back, pinched her behind, and fondled her breast was acquitted by a court in Montpellier (October 21, 2004). The judge reasoned that the commissioner had applied no force and his behavior appeared to be normal in the context of the customs and culture of the police station (AVFT 2004).

After being acquitted, accused men frequently file defamation libel lawsuits. Hence, because of the weaknesses of sexual harassment laws in convicting perpetrators, sexually harassed women do not only risk their job if they complain but risk severe punishment through the courts when perpetrators turn around and take them to court. In France in 2003, one judge's ruling reflected his sympathies with the victim of sexual harassment. Because the woman could not prove her case against a male town mayor in the court, the judge convicted her but sentenced her to a symbolic penalty of €1, most likely because he was convinced that the mayor had physically assaulted her in front of a witness. Only the highest court brought justice to one victim in December 2004 when it overturned a three-month prison sentence on probation and a €15,000 fine against a victim of sexual harassment. The judge of the appellate court had used against her the fact that she had contested the first judgment and explained that she should know she was wrong in her allegations of sexual harassment and assault. In November 2004 an unsympathetic judge imposed a fine of €11,500 on a woman victim. This woman decided to pay the fine instead of appealing. After years of struggles in court, first against the perpetrator and then defending herself for having complained about rape, sexual assault, and sexual harassment, she concluded "justice is not for me" (Le Magueresse 2005; AVFT 2004).

The fact that more men use the courts to fight dismissals because of complaints of sexual harassment against them than do women to hold employers responsible for sexual harassment demonstrates that determining who will seek justice through the courts is a gender rather than a transatlantic difference. Stricter laws provide recourse for harassed individuals. They also have an important function in preventing harassment, because they can serve to justify employers' actions to create workplaces free of sexual harassment.

Implementation in the workplace

In contrast to the United States, many EU member states rely on the implementation of workplace regulations through collective agreements between unions and employers. Collective bargaining partners have the potential to be the institutionalized vehicle for raising awareness and designing workplace policies and complaint procedures, as some pioneers in the 1980s demonstrated. However, this European model, addressing sexual harassment through collective agreements, so far has proved to be an insufficient mechanism for implementation. An EU-wide study commissioned by the Irish government found very low levels of coverage: only 24 percent of the surveyed unions/employee organizations and 15 percent of the responding employer organizations were party to collective agreements that addressed sexual harassment specifically (Government of Ireland 2004: xiii). There seems to be great variation among member states: only 30 percent of Spanish collective agreements include sexual harassment, whereas 60 percent of Dutch agreements do (Roggeband and Verloo 1999).

Though several countries including Belgium and the Netherlands require employers to implement sexual harassment policies and procedures, we know little about how many employers in fact have adopted them. The most detailed information is available about the United Kingdom. Studies found that 72 percent of UK employers had a sexual harassment policy, usually part of a general harassment policy; half provided training to those involved in handling complaints; 40 percent provided training to employees. The public sector had more policies than the private sector. Fewer than half the businesses with fewer than fifty employees had a written equal opportunities policy (IRS study and Employment Trends Survey 1999; cited in EOC 2003).

The EU Commission's Code of Practice has become a resource for both employers and unions. The Europe-wide employers' association, UNICE, promoted the Code as exemplary strategies to prevent sexual harassment. Agnes Huber, former head of the Commission's Equality Unit, recalls that a transnational company ordered one million brochures distributed to its offices in Europe and North Africa (interview, June 2003).

Several trade unions have designed their own policies, or negotiated with employers ways to combat sexual harassment, which refer directly to the EU soft-law measures. In 1992, the European Trade Union Coalition Executive Committee adopted a resolution on the protection of the dignity of men and women at work and stated that these measures should be considered "part of the notion of 'equality,' so that women's opportunities are promoted in companies and sectors" (cited in ILO 1992: 279). The UK Trades Union Congress issued guidelines that reproduced the 1990 Council of Ministers Resolution (cited in ILO 1992: 269). The National Association of Italian Hosiery Manufacturers and the workers' federation in the clothing industry distributed the Council Resolution together with their own 1991 agreement (cited in ILO 1992: 214).

An important trend emerges when unions and employers negotiate these agreements: the notion of sexual harassment is broadened and conceptualized as affecting all workers. Citing the soft-law measures, Article 4 of the 1991 Italian agreement specifies that:

It is desirable that the employment relationship develops in an appropriate atmosphere and that behavior be conducive to the harmonious performance of work. To this end, all workers must be assured of *respect for their personal dignity in all areas*, including those relating to their sex. Particularly to be avoided is behavior based on sex differences, which may be offensive to the person towards whom it is directed, especially when such behavior detrimentally affects working conditions. In the event of sexual harassment in the workplace, the works council or the trade union, together with the management of the enterprise, shall endeavor to restore normal working conditions, ensuring as much privacy as possible for the persons concerned (emphasis by author).

Thus, the 1991 agreement broadened the interpretation of sexual harassment to include men as potential victims and to understand it as a general violation of personal dignity. While collective bargaining agreements on equal opportunities mention sexual harassment, the trend in company-level agreements has been to "mainstream" sexual harassment to protect the personal integrity and dignity of all workers, much in the same way as the agreement made by Italian Hosiery Manufacturers. Mainstreaming sexual harassment here means to include forms of harassment that are nonsexual and not based on gender alone.

Unions in the EU have various stakes in the issue of sexual harassment. Given the decrease in male membership, several unions have recognized the importance of enlisting women as members. The promotion of equal opportunities and measures against sexual harassment can be a strategy to recruit women. This has also aided women within trade unions and workers' representation bodies, who have made slow but steady progress in having their concerns recognized in male-dominated unions.

Member states' diverse responses to EU soft law

The wide variation in the laws ultimately adopted by member states demonstrates the limited reach of soft-law measures and the influence of nationally specific factors that worked to mediate both the EU and US impact. The parliamentary road of policy-making relies on compromises between policy actors. Governmental proposals have to win approval by political parties, and in some countries, since sexual harassment concerns workplace regulations, by employers and unions as well. This path for change relies on consensus, not only because it is shaped by policy-making structures but also because the EU measures are nonbinding and open to interpretation. Even EU gender equality laws, which are binding, have been translated into national contexts unevenly at best (Walby 2004; Liebert (ed.) 2003; Hoskyns 1996). When EU measures are transposed through national law, which means that member states adopt national laws to comply with EU laws, different historical and legal traditions, preexisting laws on gender equality and workplace regulations, gender ideologies, and gender regimes shape the legal and policy approaches (Ostner and Lewis 1995; Mazey 1998).

The Code of Practice suggested a variety of legal frameworks that could be applied in different countries. This catalogue of possibilities gave policy-makers a great degree of flexibility for defining sexual harassment and whether to promote legal reforms in labor law, penal, or civil codes. As a consequence, implementation by member states has been a slow process of incremental policy change. The statutory-political path of implementing nonbinding measures also explains the resistance of Greece and Portugal to adopting any new law.

In the most obvious departure from American practice, several EU countries rejected the notion that sexual harassment constitutes sex discrimination. Several countries further limited the scope of the law to abuse of authority (by a supervisor, for example) rather than abuse of "gender power" by men vis-à-vis women. Spain's 1989 Workers' Charter (prepared, as noted above, in anticipation of the EU measures) was the first to include an amendment on abuse by supervisors, to "ensure the respect for a person's intimacy and dignity, including protection against verbal and physical insults of a sexual nature" (Roggeband and Verloo 1999; Valiente 1998).

Like Spain, France and Sweden limited their laws in the early 1990s to abuses of power by supervisors, despite the fact that the EU soft laws included sexual harassment by both supervisors and coworkers. Curiously, the French labor law does not prohibit sexual harassment itself, only retaliation linked with sexual harassment. Similarly, the 1992 Swedish amendment on sexual harassment, attached to the act concerning gender equality, neither attempted to define sexual harassment nor prohibited it. Twisting the concept of *quid pro quo*, the amendment considers retaliation, not sexual advances themselves, as harassment: "An employer may not subject an employee to harassment because the latter has rejected the employer's sexual advances or lodged a complaint against the employer for sex discrimination" (cited in European Commission 1996: 29). France also fell short of covering harassment by coworkers; its 1992 Penal and Labor Code[27] defined sexual harassment

---

[27] Act of November 2, 1992, *Bulletin Legal Issues in Equality* No 2/ 2002, p. 21.

as "an abuse of legal power" by an employer, by his/her representative, or by any other person abusing his/her power.

Most of the other EU member states adopted laws against both coworker and supervisor harassment and have been oriented to holding employers responsible, rather than making harassment itself a punishable offense. In 1992, Belgium and Austria provided more encompassing legal definitions of sexual harassment. Austria amended its labor law on equal treatment to include the concept of a hostile or humiliating work environment. Belgium's Royal Decree on the protection of workers from sexual harassment in the law on labor conditions went farthest in requiring employers to take action to prevent harassment, though only a small percentage of the workforce was covered by this law. Referring to the EU soft-law measures, the Decree requires that employers adopt protective measures for workers and design a confidential counseling service for victims. In 1994, Germany and the Netherlands passed laws providing explicit definitions of sexual harassment. While Germany ensures individual rights to lodge complaints and requires employers to designate a specific office to hear them, its law applies no penalties or sanctions for noncompliance. By contrast, the Dutch law on labor conditions does not require specific mechanisms, and thus leaves more room for employers and employee representatives to work out means to handle harassment.

Feminist visions of sexual harassment laws were negotiated as part of the processes of reaching national consensus about what legal measures were deemed appropriate. For example, limiting harassment to acts by supervisors emerged from the perception that US laws were applied too broadly to everyday behavior. Thus, Spanish and French policy-makers intended to criminalize perpetrators of "serious" harassment and make it a punishable offense. Experiences of women with harassment, however, suggest that both supervisors and colleagues can be involved in severe verbal and physical forms of harassment (European Commission 1999). Male-dominated environments such as the police force and military are notorious for fostering hostile environments, where superiors *and* coworkers can create an environment that excludes women. It is important to point out that the concept of harassment was vigorously debated among feminists as well. The French AVFT and state feminists advocated a broader notion of harassment, but the majority of feminists in Spain did not (Mazur 1996, Valiente 1998).

National consensus about coworker harassment in these countries took longer. A second Swedish law, in 1998, finally defined sexual harassment and used language from the 1991 recommendation. The Spanish penal code of 1995 made sexual harassment by supervisors a punishable offense; the Spanish Social Offenses and Sanctions Act of

2000 considers sexual harassment "a very serious employer's offense when it takes place within his/her scope of control and organization, being irrelevant who the harasser is," and thus also covers coworker harassment.[28] France finally passed laws to cover sexual harassment by both coworkers and supervisors, but uses a very vague and limited definition: "Sexual harassment occurs when an employee is subjected to acts by another in order to obtain sexual favors of a sexual nature for himself or for a third party."[29] In short, only cases in which the perpetrator intends to have sex with the victim does the French law consider the situation as sexual harassment.

The European discourse on the violation of dignity

At the EU level, feminist groups demanded that sexual harassment be considered sex discrimination in order to have a gender-specific concept. Instead, in the soft-law measures the Council and the Commission defined sexual harassment as "violation of dignity." Drawing on the continent's tradition of workers' rights[30] and the international discourse of human rights, EU member states agreed with these measures on the principle of protecting their citizens' dignity and defined sexual harassment as the violation of dignity. Because American workplace rights to privacy remain very weak, some scholars have argued that the United States should adopt the European model. Bernstein (1994) argues for defining sexual harassment as violation of personal integrity and dignity, opening the offense to prosecution under tort rather than civil rights law. Feminist legal scholars, however, including MacKinnon, have vehemently opposed applying human rights and tort law to sexual harassment, arguing that it individualizes the problem.

Similarly, feminist legal experts in Europe, most prominently Susanne Baer (1996), have expressed skepticism about defining sexual harassment as the violation of dignity because it individualizes the problem of sexual harassment since it does not link the harassment to gender inequality. Dena DeSacco argues that this concept implies that "sexual

---

[28] "Even when the harasser is not the employer but a victim's colleague, the employer will be responsible if the conduct occurred in his/her undertaking and may be prosecuted by Inspectors of Employment and Social Security, having to face a very high fine of up to 15 million pesetas [article 40.1.c, Social Offenses and Sanctions Act 2000]" (see ILO Labor Court Judges).

[29] Act of May 9, 2001 concerning discrimination and Social Modernization Act of January 17, 2002.

[30] See Friedman and Whitman (2003) for a contemporary analysis and Whitman (2003) for a legal historical analysis on the use of the concept of "dignity" during fascist Italy and Germany.

harassment affects all workers equally rather than recognizing that it is overwhelmingly directed against women. The use of 'dignity' and of both sexes decontextualizes sexual harassment by turning it into an acceptable human rights issue rather than recognizing it as a gendered issue of workplace structure" (1996: 25). Yet the EU concept of sexual harassment as behavior that harms a person's integrity and dignity has been widely adopted throughout the EU in laws and in collective agreements.

The danger in the European approach is that it tends to subsume the issue under general violations of workers' dignity. There had been a clear shift even in the 1980s from the early EC/EU initiatives and documents that expressed concerns about the "dignity of women" (see, for example, Rubenstein 1987) to the soft-law measures that concerned protecting both women's and men's dignity. In the process of implementation, many member states have "mainstreamed" this concept even farther. For example, while Portugal did not pass a law against sexual harassment, its 2002 draft for a new health and safety law in the workplace states that "contemporary society, and particularly the 'European social model,' attributes growing importance to safeguarding workers' dignity and psychological integrity."[31] Yet, there is no mention of sexual harassment as an expression of gender inequality.

Since the mid-1990s, similar developments in public attention to bullying and mobbing have also been prevalent in Germany, France, the United Kingdom, the Netherlands, Sweden, and Spain (Friedman and Whitman 2003). Unions, labor courts, and policy-makers are considering prevention and ways to facilitate individual redress. It is worth pointing out that the French consensus to include coworker harassment came in the context of mainstreaming "sexual harassment" to "moral harassment." The French Social Modernization Act of 2002 introduced these provisions into the Labor Code and Penal Code and modified rules concerning sexual harassment. Moral harassment is defined as "No employee shall suffer repeated acts of moral harassment that induce a deterioration of working conditions which may affect his/her rights or dignity, damage his/her mental or physical health, or affect his/her career."[32]

Thus, the EU soft-law measures have contributed to diffusion of the concept of violation of dignity throughout EU member states and have Europeanized sexual harassment by providing advocates and

---

[31] European Industrial Relations Observatory online: *http://www.eiro.eurofound.ie/2001/01/ Feature/PT0101132F.html*
[32] Social Modernization Act of January 17, 2002, L.122–49, paragraph 1.

policy-makers with legitimacy, policy models, and transnational expert-ise. Even though the extent of member-state legislation on sexual harassment has not met the expectations of activists, the level of awareness of sexual harassment was certainly raised during the 1990s. But the implementation of sexual harassment measures in EU work-places, based on consensus models and collective bargaining agree-ments, has broadened sexual harassment to a non-gender-specific issue of abuse of power in workplaces. The limitations of the soft-law meas-ures are most obvious in the lack of implementation in Greece and Portugal, which failed to adopt any laws, and the inadequacy of many of the member state laws. The hesitation to "voluntarily" adopt adequate laws, however, provided impetus for binding legislation at the EU level.

New opportunities in the EU – the 2002 Equal Treatment Directive

Although Commissioner Pádraig Flynn stated in 1998 that a majority of member states opposed creating an instrument to deal with workplace sexual harassment,[33] only four years later the EU approved a binding legal measure against it. How quickly the tide can change demonstrates how windows of opportunity for TANs can open suddenly at the EU level.

The revised Equal Treatment Directive sets minimum standards for gender equality legislation in the member states, which must adopt or amend their laws by 2005. The revisions to the 1976 Directive reflect ECJ rulings on indirect/direct discrimination, compensation to be awarded in such cases, and discrimination against pregnant women (see Shaw 2000). The directive also requires member states to institu-tionalize equality bodies to implement and monitor EU gender equality law.

The most important revision in the directive is the binding, EU-wide definition of sexual harassment and its link to sex discrimination, following the US model. The directive maintains the European concept of harassment as the "violation of dignity," but clearly expresses the gendered nature of harassment: it prohibits both gender (nonsexual) and sexual harassment as sex discrimination. This formulation of har-assment is useful because it provides a gender-specific term clearly linking sexual harassment to gender inequality. It has also improved

---

[33] Notes of meeting of the European Parliament's Women's Committee (ETUC January 1998–March 1998, Bulletin no. 9, *www.etuc.org*).

mechanisms for implementation and enforcement of EU sex equality law in general. For example, the burden of proof for sexual harassment now lies with the employer to show that discrimination did not take place. Courts have more latitude in awarding damages because the directive prohibits award limits. While the directive does not explicitly require employers and unions to take action to prevent sexual harassment, EU member states are supposed to encourage preventive measures in workplaces.

The influence of changes within the Commission

These revisions to the Equal Treatment Directive came about through the work of institutional actors. Commissioner for Social and Employment Affairs Anna Diamantopoulou, who succeeded Flynn, played a major role in the 2002 Equal Treatment Directive. As early as 1999, she announced plans to promote a new directive on gender equality and to make sexual harassment one of her priorities. Given the stigmatization of victims, the Commissioner realized the importance of raising public awareness and made a bold public statement about having experienced sexual harassment herself when she was a nineteen-year-old employee in Greece. Because of this harassment and the lack of available legal remedies, she left the job (*Financial Times*, January 8, 2000). In the face of Greek government resistance to adopting soft-law measures, Diamantopoulou vigorously promoted stricter laws at the EU level. She also demonstrated her commitment to include feminists in her administration. For example, in 1999 she appointed Barbara Helfferich, former general secretary of the European Women's Lobby, to her cabinet.

The political environment for gender equality politics within the European Commission changed with the appointment of five women as Commissioners. There was broad support to update the 1976 Directive on Equal Treatment and adopt a binding law on sexual harassment. Female politicians and administrators saw inclusion of sexual harassment in the new directive as a "logical step" toward filling the gap in EU legislation (interview with Barbara Helfferich, June 2003).

Even violence against women had slowly made its way onto the agenda of EU institutions and was creating sensitivity within the Commission. Beginning in 1999, Commissioner for Justice and Home Affairs Anita Gradin, a socialist feminist from Sweden, promoted the issue of violence against women in the context of trafficking. The Commission had already proposed a program called Daphne that has provided funding since 1997 for research, awareness, and educational campaigns addressing violence against women. In response to the 1997 European

Parliament resolution to establish an EU-wide campaign for zero tolerance of violence against women, the Commission conducted a campaign in 1999–2000 to raise public awareness of the issue. Under Portuguese and German leadership in the council presidency, a number of conferences on the issue were held in 1999. This mobilization heightened awareness of these issues in the EU and helped advocates who were working for passage of laws to address sexual harassment.

Resistance to the directive

Convincing member states to agree to the new directive proved a major struggle for activists and EU institutional actors, who met resistance mainly from the United Kingdom, Sweden, Austria, and Ireland. Germany also expressed reservations. Member states supporting revisions included France, the Netherlands, and Luxembourg, as well as the Spanish presidency of the European Council at the time. The industrial and employers union UNICE lobbied strongly against the directive and the definition of sexual harassment as sex discrimination. Therese De Liedekerke, the director, repeatedly stated that sexual harassment and discrimination are two different problems, with different consequences, and hence require different solutions. Employers should not always be liable for coworker harassment and the Brussels directive was too "over-prescriptive." Although its leadership acknowledged the importance of the issue, UNICE argued that member states rather than the EU should address it. UNICE also viewed sexual harassment in the context of bullying and stated that preventive aspects were already covered through the European Directive on Health and Safety at Work (UNICE 2002).

Diamantopoulou argued that the soft-law measures had not sufficed to promote significant legal changes in member states, the most obvious examples being Greece and Portugal. The fact that most member states had already passed laws served to legitimate the issue at the EU level; national governments' increased awareness of the issue further helped the cause.

Most important, advocates promoting stricter legal measures were helped by the 1997 Treaty of Amsterdam, whose Article 13 expands EU powers to tackle discrimination generally and whose Article 141 specifically prohibits gender discrimination in the labor market. In addition to establishing a firmer basis for EU intervention against discrimination, the treaty explicitly sought the elimination of gender inequality.

The gender equality TAN's work during the 1990s paid off: transnational expertise became crucial for policy-makers to convince member states to act. Opponents still tried to de-legitimize the issue of sexual harassment by ridiculing and trivializing the subject itself, but, as Helfferich stated: "These arguments didn't work any more" (interview, June 2003). Drawing on transnational expertise, policy advocates could refer to the new EU study, which indicated that sexual harassment occurred across Europe: 40–60 percent of working women suffered from harassment, deterioration of working conditions, and risk of dismissal (European Commission 1999). These results helped establish the link between sexual harassment and sex discrimination. In addition, the fact that many countries had already defined such harassment as sex discrimination legitimated its framing as such at the EU level.

Several national trade unions opposed the new law, arguing that the problem was under control and should be addressed through collective bargaining agreements at the national and local levels. But union ambivalence did not play an important role because national unions have significantly less power at the EU level. Most important, the "friendly" unions within the European Trade Union Confederation prevailed, and the confederation as a whole ultimately supported the directive. The women's unit in this organization participated in the gender equality TAN and helped construct this support, for example organizing seminars on sexual harassment.

The European Women's Lobby and the European Trade Union Confederation then collaborated to intensify their impact. In a joint letter to the Commissioner, they called for establishing a definition of sexual harassment as sex discrimination and obliging employers to take preventive steps. In preparation for the Treaty of Amsterdam, the two organizations had already established an alliance to promote gender equality (Helfferich and Kolb 2001).[34]

But overall in this phase of EU policy formulation, there were neither coordinated protests nor lobbying activities from TAN advocates for sexual harassment policy. Only a few press releases or position papers were issued by women's groups and labor organizations, including one joint press release from the European Women's Lobby and the European Trade Union Confederation in 2002. This low level of mobilization was perhaps due to an expectation that the directive would pass, in particular because of Commissioner Diamantopoulou's support, and within the European Women's Lobby the issue itself was not controversial.

Thus, several factors contributed to the passage of the 2002 Equal Treatment Directive. Despite its shortcomings, adding sexual harassment represented a major success. Individual policy-makers can make a

---

[34] *www.etuc.org* and *www.ewl.org*.

difference and draw on the groundwork laid by TANs since the 1980s in creating transnational expertise: introducing an alternative discourse; sharing professional and legal knowledge about developments in EU member states; and sponsoring empirical studies documenting sexual harassment as a compelling social problem.

Conclusion

As in the United States, advocates used existing gender equality laws to argue for European Community action against sexual harassment. The 2002 Equal Treatment Directive updates to the original 1976 Directive define sexual harassment as sex discrimination. The possibility of revising this existing law provided a policy window for advocates promoting change. Unlike the situation in the United States, in the EU the inclusion of sexual harassment did not represent the outcome of lawsuits before the ECJ. Rather, the 2002 Equal Treatment Directive reflected the twenty years of incremental policy change and the continuous efforts of the TAN on gender equality to effect changes in member states and in the EU. These changes were the consequence of a ping-pong effect, with activism and policy measures occurring at both the member states level and the supranational level, jumping back and forth. The ECJ, so far, has not played any role in these legal reforms.

The EU's path to change was shaped by bureaucratic policy-making structures. In this process, transnational expertise was crucial to convince fifteen member states that the EU needed a binding directive against sexual harassment. As at the US federal level, where lobby groups can influence policy change, the European Commission provided gender-minded activists with an avenue for promoting change. Yet, the TAN on gender equality did not merely use existing political opportunities but also helped shape EU gender politics. It has created opportunities for advocates by establishing a firmer legal foundation for gender equality politics. For example, the inclusion of gender equality in the Treaty of Amsterdam proved crucial in the revision process of the 2002 Equal Treatment Directive, and national gender equality bodies were important in implementing laws in the member states. These developments encouraged the ping-pong effect.

The EU-wide debate about the politics of sexual harassment and potential remedies for it was deeply influenced by the US debates and controversies during the 1990s. As a supranational actor, the EU served as an important catalyst in recognizing the issue and crafting a European response. EU soft-law measures provided various policy models and gave member states room to devise their own laws. The 2002 Equal Treatment Directive requires the now twenty-five member states to adopt new laws or modify existing ones, in particular to define sexual harassment as sex discrimination. Beyond this basic agreement, however, it is likely that the variation in legal interpretations and approaches for enforcement – not only between the United States and Europe but also among EU member states – will continue.

Can these laws make a difference in the member states? Will employers adopt workplace policies, and do these laws offer relief and compensation to victims of sexual harassment? Mazur critically states that the Spanish and French measures are "symbolic politics in their style and profile" (2002: 5). The problem remains in implementation and enforcement, especially in countries where institutional bodies such as the EEOC do not exist and employer sanctions are limited. Yet, by defining sexual harassment as sex discrimination, the 2002 Equal Treatment Directive provides the potential for improvements in implementation and enforcement of all anti-discrimination laws. One concern is that member states will not take sufficient steps; in this sense, the work of transnational advocacy networks has not yet ended. Implementation is a political process in which TANs need to take an active part. Thus, much depends on how TANs manage to use the directive's provisions and transnational expertise to effect legal changes in the member states.

These waves of incremental policy change also have an important function in raising awareness and mobilizing women in the member states. They contribute to changing not only policy-makers' attitudes but also women's perceptions that sexual harassment is something they need not live with. Feminist protest on sexual harassment has occasionally arisen, in particular in universities. For example, at the University of Bari, the Italian women's organization Giraffa (Research and Resistance Group Against Female Folly) mobilized around the case of a seventy-year-old professor who asked a student in his office "whether she believed in free love and had a boyfriend." The professor then "suddenly grabbed hold of her and kissed her on the lips" (*Guardian*, July 16, 1998: 106). In France, students protested sexual harassment by professors at the École des Hautes Études en Sciences Sociales and other universities (Saguy 2003). With the EU law on their side, feminist activists will be able to demand that these laws be implemented and employers and institutions held responsible to enforce them.

Because the path for policy change in most member states was parliamentary – based on consensus between parties, sometimes with the strong influence of unions – specific national factors still shape the politics of sexual harassment in the member states. The case of Germany illustrates how feminists and equality offices used the EU soft-law measures and benefited from the transnational expertise the EU created. But it also reveals the weakness of enforcement mechanisms and demonstrates the limits of the soft-law approach in "encouraging" member states to take action against sexual harassment.

The ultimate question will be whether the 2002 Equal Treatment Directive, which clarifies and solidifies the point that laws against sexual harassment should be gender-specific and tied to sex discrimination, will ensure that sexual harassment does not get subsumed or ignored. On the positive side, employees who experience sexual harassment can challenge national court rulings now in the European Court of Justice if they believe that employers and judges have not taken their complaints seriously.

4 The political path of adoption: feminists and the German state

In 1999, the story of a twenty-two-year-old policewoman, Silvia B. from Bavaria, stirred debates among the German public about the plight of women entering male-dominated workplaces. She worked in a police unit with a reputation for hostility toward women. According to her parents, Silvia B. repeatedly endured harassment by her supervisor, who insulted her by calling her *Bauerntrampel* (country bumpkin, yokel) and harassed her with descriptions of sexual intercourse. She complained about the supervisor's behavior, but the situation must have felt hopeless. She took her life on February 14, 1999 (Musall and Ulrich 1999).

Silvia B. was not the first young woman police officer to suffer from sexual harassment, nor was she the first to commit suicide. Instead of calling what happened to her sexual harassment, however, the media, the police, and later the judges discussed the case as mobbing – systematic and recurrent harassment and insult. When her parents filed a lawsuit against her direct supervisor for the costs of her burial and infliction of pain, the case went through several courts. Finally, in 2002, the highest court[1] decided that only the Bavarian state as the employer, not the individual harasser, was liable. The court left no doubt that the supervisor's behavior, including the *anstößigen Beleidigungen* (immoral offenses), was due to his basic position of hostility against women. But the judgment did not mention sexual harassment, again interpreting the supervisor's behavior as mobbing. This concept includes both sexual and nonsexual harassment and can happen to anyone regardless of his or her sex; it made invisible the violence and hostility Silvia B. encountered as a woman in a predominately male organization.

There is no German law that actually defines mobbing, though there is German and European law against sexual harassment. The 1994 German Federal Employee Protection Law defines sexual harassment

---

[1] Bundesgerichtshof (BGH), Decision August 1, 2002. III ZR 277/01, first decisions in Oberlandesgericht München and Landesgericht München I.

as the violation of dignity, but the courts did not even mention this law. Perhaps the judges thought not only that the law against sexual harassment was too weak but that even the notion *sexuelle Belästigung* (the direct translation of the English "sexual harassment") was too trivial for the offenses that led to Silvia's death. The term *Belästigung* is more frequently used to talk about a *lästige Fliege* (an irritating, annoying fly) that gets on one's nerves but does not drive one mad. In law, *Belästigung* (harassment) is also used for disturbances by noise or smells. It is more likely that the judges were not aware of this law nor felt that it was applicable, since the law has been a well-kept secret in Germany.

Legal and policy changes regarding workplace sexual harassment developed more slowly in Germany than in the United States, and the resulting law so far has been modest at best. The 1994 law was adopted more than ten years after the first national debate on sexual harassment. German law, like US civil rights law, assigned responsibility primarily to employers. The German approach, however, considered sexual harassment a breach of the working contract between employers and employees, not a violation of a civil right. The 1994 law was also more focused on the workplace than the French and Spanish sexual harassment laws, which seek to punish the perpetrators and consider the problem one of sexual violence. The 1994 German law treats sexual harassment as a workplace issue, but it does not define the problem as one of sex discrimination, despite the fact that the law was passed as an amendment to the 1994 law on gender equality.

The 1994 law disappointed feminist advocates and fell behind EU soft-law measures in several aspects. Sexual harassment was not conceptualized as a problem of gender equality, and only intentional, recognizable forms of harassment were prohibited. Legal redress for individuals remained weak, and the law lacked effective implementation and enforcement mechanisms because it did not stipulate penalties for employers or compensation for victims. It would take another ten years for policy-makers to discuss a bill that defines sexual harassment as sex discrimination. As a result, victims, employers, unions, attorneys, and judges are often either unaware of the law or reluctant to use or apply it. In labor courts, victims have been awarded meager compensation – a few hundred to a few thousand Euros – in only three cases (Pflüger and Baer 2005). The German *Bundesarbeitsgericht* (BAG) (Highest Federal Labor Court) has never ruled on a victim's case of sexual harassment. Almost 80 percent of the sexual harassment lawsuits that labor court judges rule on are those of male plaintiffs who had been accused of sexual harassment and then challenged their employer over what they perceived as unfair dismissal (Pflüger and Baer 2005).

Germany was slower than the United States to tackle the problem of sexual harassment because the path by which change occurred was a statutory–corporatist route rather than a legal one. West German feminists first protested against sexual harassment in the parliament, not in courts. These feminists embarked on the "march through the institutions," raising public awareness by politicizing the issue and struggling to convince state institutions, lawmakers, and unions to take action. The fact that the statutory–corporatist channel was monopolized by male-dominated political parties, unions, and employers steeped in traditional gender ideologies created substantial obstacles to change in sexual harassment policy. As in other EU member states, the most significant legal changes were compromises between political parties, state officials, unions, and employers, because creating statutory law means that a bill has to gain the majority votes of the political parties. This process took longer than in the United States, where court rulings took only a few years. Furthermore, the consensus process watered down feminist demands for an anti-discrimination law and marginalized feminist discourse and frames.

Nationally specific constellations of labor and gender politics have also limited the influence of feminists on policy outcomes and shaped a uniquely German approach reflecting traditions of collective social rights over individual legal rights. Strikingly, the politics of sexual harassment have attracted surprisingly little attention from feminists, unions, policymakers, and courts in Germany – in contrast, for example, to abortion rights (Ferree et al. 2002). Sexual harassment in the workplace has not been a high national political priority; nor did these legal developments generate much public debate. Both state officials and political parties have been reluctant to take on the issue because the basic idea is that the state should intervene only if employers and unions cannot handle issues themselves. With calls by businesses for deregulation of labor markets and labor laws in general, supporters for stricter sexual harassment law that would increase employers' liabilities have been in a difficult position.

The legal system did not offer the kinds of avenues found in the United States, because the German continental system relies on judges' interpretations of statutory law, and even the labor courts have limited power to set precedent. The feminist movement did not take up the possibilities for legal change through the labor courts, because Germany lacked an enforceable anti-discrimination law. Very few women have been willing to seek justice in the courts, given their mistrust of the legal system, or their discouragement by attorneys who have been unwilling to take on these cases because of the difficulty of winning sexual harassment lawsuits ("he said–she said" situations), especially under weak laws and with the meager compensation.

In the face of these adverse political opportunity structures, including lack of strong allies along with difficult economic and political situations, and institutional impediments, external impulses and outside pressures were necessary for German policy-makers to pass sexual harassment laws. The inspirations originally came through the transnational spread of (feminist) concepts, policy ideas, and debates from the United States and later also from within the EU. The EU has been a catalyst for anti-discrimination laws, laws on gender equality in general and sexual harassment in the workplace in particular, for example by promoting institutional changes and using increasing force to push German governments to take sexual harassment and discrimination in general more seriously. Furthermore, through several rounds of supranational measures, the EU pushed German policy-makers to put gender equality laws on the agenda, including the latest anti-discrimination law, in 2005. Germany, as all other EU member states, was required to transpose the 2002 EU Equal Treatment Directive with a deadline of October 2005. The European integration process created opportunities for German gender equality politics in the workplace, especially through the promotion of and strengthening of "state feminism," that is, equality offices for women. Women in these gender equality agencies, *femocrats*, became the crucial allies for advocates of sexual harassment laws because neither labor unions nor the autonomous woman's movement would take on the issues.

This chapter proceeds chronologically from the first mobilization of women around sexual harassment in the West German parliament in the 1980s to the response of German policy-makers to the EU measures and US debates with the 1994 Employee Protection Law, to the latest efforts of advocates and policy-makers to comply with the anti-discrimination EU Directives.

The scandal in the West German Green party

Ironically, the parliament was not just the main site for struggles over definitions of sexual harassment, responsibilities of employers, and the rights of victims; incidents in a parliamentary office brought sexual harassment onto the national agenda in West Germany. The first public debate concerning sexual harassment involved a scandal in the newly elected 1983 West German parliament. Foreshadowing US party politics, West German media attention focused on a politician's transgressions. In 1983 the newly founded Green party first entered the *Bundestag* (German parliament), having won more than 5 percent of the votes.

Though overall no more than 10 percent of the members of parliament were women, the Green party entered parliament with 35.7 percent women representatives. This promising start also raised expectations within the party, explicitly dedicated to feminist issues.

In the summer of 1983, three women staffers accused parliamentarian Klaus Hecker of sexual harassment. According to their accounts the scenario was similar in the three cases: Hecker would unexpectedly compliment them and then physically attack them. He used intimate physical behavior including touching their breasts. Afterward he would initiate an intimate discussion in which he explained that he was very sad, because he liked the woman so much and did not know how to deal with the situation, since it seemed as if they could not go on (Jansen 1984: 135–40). The women named this behavior *sexuelle Belästigung* because, as Plogstedt recalls (interview, 1999), "One of the harassment victims had been to the United States, so she knew what one calls this." They did not file a lawsuit against Hecker or the Green party. They wrote a letter to the party leadership entitled "*Friede der Erotik, Kampf dem Sexismus*" (Peace for Eroticism, Fight Sexism), with the intention of generating a broader discussion of the party's internal gender culture.

The media treated the issue as scandalous behavior of the Green party. The letter was leaked to the *Bild Zeitung*, a daily tabloid, and the case became known as *der Grüne Busengrapscher* (the Green Breast Groper). Sarah Jansen, one of the three women, pointed to the irony that the *Bild Zeitung*, otherwise known for blatant sexism and hostility to feminism, had printed this feminist complaint letter (Jansen 1984: 138). *Bild Zeitung* conveniently eliminated a sentence in which the women explained that they did not mention names because "sexism is such a widespread behavior that we do not want to link this to one perpetrator only" (138, translation by the author).

The media consensus against reporting on "personal" issues of public figures broke down in this case because the mainstream media wanted to ruin the reputation of the Green party politician (Plogstedt and Bode 1984: 11). By contrast, former chancellor Helmut Kohl's long-term affair with his secretary was suppressed in the German media for decades. *Bild Zeitung* was not concerned with the social problem of sexual harassment; the article was meant to discredit challengers to mainstream politics.

The Green party leadership drew an important conclusion from this incident. In a contentious week-long debate they decided that Hecker could no longer represent the party, which stood for the liberation of women, "because the political and human situation of women demands such a decision" (Plogstedt and Bode, 1984: 7, translation by the author). The incident triggered widespread interest by newspapers and magazines, mostly focusing on the sexual elements rather than questions of gender equality. *Der Spiegel* ran a cover story on *Sex im Büro* (Sex in the Office), emphasizing the pleasant, positive aspects of interpersonal relationships and encounters in office culture.

The scandal triggered the first study and book-length publication on sexual harassment. Dr. Sibylle Plogstedt, a journalist and sociologist and cofounder of the feminist Berlin magazine *Courage*, became the first feminist activist and expert on sexual harassment, and driving force behind this study. She approached the women involved in the complaint. Like US feminists, Plogstedt and her coauthor Kathleen Bode were aware of the power of "naming" and establishing legitimacy for a political issue via documentation. With funding from the Green party, Plogstedt worked with Infas, a widely recognized German survey institute, which in 1983 conducted the first survey on sexual harassment. The resulting book was entitled *Übergriffe: Sexuelle Belästigung in Büros und Betrieben: Eine Dokumentation der Grünen Frauen im Bundestag* (*Sexual Harassment in Offices and Enterprises: A Documentation of Green Women in the Federal Parliament* 1984, Reinbek: Rowohlt).

This 1983 Infas survey of 388 respondents showed that 25 percent of the women had experienced sexual harassment. The most common physical forms ranged from unwanted slapping of the behind (51 percent), to touching of the breast (43 percent), touching of genitals (17 percent), and unwanted kisses (13 percent); 4 percent had been forced to touch the man's genitals and 4 percent had been forced to have sexual intercourse (Plogstedt and Bode 1984: 94). The researchers did not report verbal harassment, arguing that everyone would agree that women often heard jokes and sexual remarks. Women told of their feelings of shame, anger, fear, and disgust in stories collected from workplaces, unions, political parties, institutions, universities, and schools. There were several examples of women who successfully confronted and defended themselves, some of whom outlined the perpetrator's behavior in a letter to the harasser, a tactic adopted directly from the United States (Plogstedt and Bode 1984: 141).

The survey not only documented the prevalence of sexual harassment (similar to the strategies of US feminists) but also investigated how employers, unions, political parties, and state offices dealt with the issue. It revealed that none of these actors and institutions was aware of the issue, and most denied that there was a problem at all. Unions were surprisingly insensitive and did not consider sexual harassment a relevant issue. In interviews, union leaders responded that there were no cases of women being harassed in the workplace or within the unions (Plogstedt and Bode 1984: 26). Most significant, even women's groups in unions did not perceive the issue as important, and felt that they had "better things to do" (27, translation by the author).

Institutional actors had basically ignored sexual harassment as an issue for working women, not surprising since labor market politics were dominated by concerns of unions and employers. West German gender politics had from the 1950s been shaped by the male breadwinner ideal, and women were viewed primarily as wives and mothers, dependent on their husbands' earnings. The famous three Ks – *Kinder, Küche, und Kirche* (children, kitchen, and church) – constituted the ideal life for women (Moeller 1993). Policy-makers did not work to create equal access for women to the labor market. In fact, tax laws and family benefits discouraged the employment of mothers (Lewis 1992; Ostner 1993, 1994; Ferree 1995b).

Unions

Plogstedt and Bode saw the trade unions, the main political actors to promote workers' rights, as the key ally and strategic target for change in dealing with sexual harassment. With the study in hand, Plogstedt approached the *Deutscher Gewerkschaftsbund* (DGB) (German Confederation of Trade Unions) for support for publication. Given the study's findings about the lack of understanding and acknowledgment of the problem, it is not surprising that the discussion on whether the DGB should provide funding was controversial.

Maria Kathman, a functionary in IG Metall (Union of Automobile Workers and Machinists) and a strong supporter for measures against sexual harassment, remembers the DGB debate as "hair-raising," including laughter, ridicule, and disbelief on the part of the male stewards (Kathmann, interview, 1999). There were seven men and two women in the room. Finally, one woman asked the men to think of their own daughters and how they could be harassed. This seemed to convince them to take the issue seriously enough to help fund the publication. References to international examples, such as International Trade Union meetings and the new US EEOC guidelines, also helped the advocates legitimate the issue. Nevertheless, Plogstedt continued to encounter great reluctance from union officials: "Often enough, we had to continue to push the issue with them. They already asked us, 'Why do you always want to make this public?'" (Plogstedt, interview, 1999).

Some union women's groups slowly began to put sexual harassment on the agenda. In 1985, the women's conference of the DGB discussed the issue for the first time, deciding that research and education were necessary and that women should receive support from the unions for legal action. IG Metall and ÖTV (Union for Public Services, Transportation and Traffic) began to mobilize around the issue, with two nationwide informational and awareness tours. An exhibition, *Seximus am Arbeitsplatz* (Sexism in the Workplace), organized by women in the ÖTV Berlin, traveled through Germany in 1986. An exhibition organized by union men from the ÖTV Hannover with the title "Mach meinen Kumpel nicht an!" (Don't come on to my buddy) showed solidarity across gender lines. Ironically, "Kumpel" (buddy) is a masculine term.

Women unionists contributed to raising awareness by addressing sexual harassment in public discussions. They organized seminars for women and integrated the issue into seminars for union stewards and works councils. Because union women encountered, great disbelief some unions, like the Deutsche Angestellten-Gewerkschaft (DAG) (Trade Union of German Employees) in Hamburg, conducted surveys among their members to document the prevalence of sexual harassment.

Because unions play a major role in supporting members' legal actions, the issue of union support for harassed women's lawsuits was crucial. Women unionists demanded there be union policies on how to handle such cases. IG Metall was the first to establish policies that ensured legal counsel and support for union members who chose to file sexual harassment suits against their employer (Plogstedt and Bode 1984; Plogstedt 1987). But the right to counsel does not apply if the perpetrator is a union member (Hamacher 1993; Kathmann, interview, 1999). This undercuts unions' seriousness about sexual harassment in their own organizations.

The DGB was also involved in changing rules about unemployment insurance. Benefits are typically delayed several months after an employee hands in their notice. In 1985, based on lobbying by women unionists, the *Bundesanstalt für Arbeit* (Federal Institution for Labor) added an exception for persons who left their workplace because of sexual harassment. Victims could thus receive benefits immediately. This is the equivalent to the "good cause" rule in the United States, where not all states make an exception for sexual harassment. Hence, the German (welfare) system of social insurance responded in a traditional way to a new problem.[2] This approach to sexual harassment protects workers from the social risk (poverty) associated with losing their job, but not from the risk itself. Furthermore, this system holds neither the

---

[2] See, for example, George Steinmetz (1993) for the historical origins of these German policies.

perpetrator nor the employer responsible, but instead the financial costs and burdens of sexual harassment are shared by society through the insurance. With the broader coverage of healthcare, the costs for victims' sick leave are also carried by the solidarity of the healthcare insurance system, to which employers and employees contribute equally.

Despite this groundwork, sexual harassment did not become a priority at the national level in the 1980s. The national unions did not support new regulations, holding that existing works council grievance procedures were sufficient to take care of the issue (Augstein, interview, 1999; Kathmann 1993; Kathmann, interview, 1999). Moreover, sexual harassment had to compete with issues perceived by union leadership as more pressing, such as the fight against dismantling the social security network and traditional issues such as higher wages and shorter working hours. What union women did achieve was that by the early 1990s male unionists would no longer state in public that sexual harassment was not a union issue (Kathmann, interview, 1999). And when public debate about psychological stressors in workplaces broadened the issue to include nonsexual harassment by colleagues and bosses, the unions came on board. Indeed, they have been strong promoters of collective agreements on policies of "fairness in the workplace" and mobbing.

Autonomous feminist movement

One might expect the autonomous feminist movement to be the most obvious ally for the Green party women to demand new politics on sexual harassment. Elman (1996) and Weldon (2002) argue that the existence of autonomously organized women's groups is an important factor to explain state responsiveness to violence against women. Elman finds, for example, that Sweden responded with delayed and weaker measures against sexual harassment than the United States, because Sweden lacked independent women's groups which organized around the issue.

In contrast to the United States, however, the German movement was not actively involved in promoting legal changes. The mere presence of anti-violence movements does not explain state responsiveness to sexual harassment. The ideology of autonomy and the lack of networks between women within unions and parties constituted a barrier for articulating successful feminist strategies for legal change. The West German feminist anti-violence movement had done much to prepare discussions on sexual harassment by providing feminist discourse on violence, but they neither organized around nor engaged in policy discussions on the issue in the 1980s and 1990s. Plogstedt explained why she did not seek out the women's movement: "We couldn't just send the women from the companies to the shelter. The institutions within the autonomous movement were not sufficient" (Plogstedt 1999).

In the early 1980s, the West German radical feminist movement consisted of loosely connected, locally organized groups whose strength was to establish women's centers and to build a rich "project" culture (Ferree 1987; Schenk 1981). Sexual harassment would certainly have fitted the agenda of the autonomous women's movement as an issue of violence. West German feminists had begun to organize around body issues, with the pro-choice movement giving rise to women's mobilization. Sexual self-determination, pervasive sexism in all its forms, and violence against women were key issues for the autonomous movement (Hagemann-White 1998). But the strategy of the shelter projects in the 1970s and 1980s was to build a counter-culture of women-only spaces, not to embark on the "march through the institutions." The movement was oriented toward transforming society by creating alternatives for women in abusive relationships and providing shelters and consciousness raising as a space for empowerment, but not demanding that institutions acknowledge sexual harassment.

These grassroots projects sought funding from the state while simultaneously adhering to an ideology of anti-institutional politics. This orientation prevented them from taking on workplace issues. In the 1970s and 1980s, neither unions nor state agencies were perceived as political allies for the anti-violence movement, and feminist-identified women did not build networks or coalitions with established political and institutional actors. Even though rape crisis hotlines dealt with violence against women in the workplace, anti-violence advocates generally perceived sexual harassment as a "workplace issue" for unions (Degen, interview, 1999). Promoting workers' rights would have required entering the workplace institutional domain. Thus, the perceived ideological gap between women's movements and unions hampered building the networks, alliances, and coalitions necessary to address the issue of sexual harassment effectively. Plogstedt was an exceptional activist since she was herself this bridge between the feminist movements and the unions (Degen, interview, 1999).

During the 1980s, the anti-violence movement emphasized issues such as (sexual) abuse of children and domestic violence against women (Hagemann-White 1998). The focus on the domestic realm was more in tune with the movement's preference for a "difference-oriented," autonomous strategy of separatism, anti-institutionalism, and distrust of legal means. It allowed for noninstitutional strategies, including building autonomous shelters and creating their own workplaces there; they had escaped "patriarchal" workplaces and saw their own work as providing shelter for women and children (Degen, interview, 1999; Hagemann-White, interview, 1999). The movement was "too autonomous" to push for legal and policy reforms.

These organizational, structural, and institutional factors explain why a broad-based feminist strategy around sexual harassment was lacking in Germany, even though issues of sexual violence against women and children were politically prominent. The autonomous feminist movement did, however, open new ways to conceptualize interpersonal dynamics between women and men, and created alternative discourses around sexuality, violence, and the abuse of power in general, built much on the US and UK discussions. The anti-violence movement certainly contributed to awareness about issues of violence both among women of the Green party and in the unions. Plogstedt together with Bode drew on feminist analysis of violence by analyzing sexual harassment as abuse of power and comparing it to domestic violence. The women's spaces created by the shelter movement and feminist movement in the 1970s were crucial in identifying domestic violence, rape, and sexual harassment as social problems. Feminist magazines such as *Courage* and *Emma* published articles about women who experienced harassment in the workplace.[3]

Much of the impetus for feminist actors to take note of sexual harassment came from the United States. Besides Green party women who gave the behavior the German name *sexuelle Belästigung* and Plogstedt and Bode, academics were also familiar with US feminist discourse on sexual harassment. For example, when Dagmar Schulz returned from the United States, during a women's summer school in Berlin in 1982 she prompted the first discussion about relationships between university professors and students, probing the difficulty of "consensuality" in the context of unequal power relations (Schultz and Mueller 1984). Sociology professor Ursula Mueller, who was later involved in the first nationwide study on sexual harassment, first heard about the issue at a conference in California (Mueller, interview, 1999). Sociologist Renate Sadrozinski, editor of the second influential book, *Grenzverletzungen: Sexuelle Belästigung im Arbeitsalltag* (*The Violations of Boundaries: Sexual Harassment in the Everyday Workplace*, 1993, Frankfurt: Fischer), lived in the United States for many years.

---

[3] *Emma* published three articles on sexual harassment before 1983, including a 1978 story "Der Wichser" ("The Wanker"). The total number of articles on "sexual harassment" between 1977 and 1998 was thirty (Frauenmultimediaturm, Cologne). The feminist magazine *Courage* had also previously covered incidents of sexual harassment, including Runge's 1977 open letter.

A second, unexpected US influence, the Senate Anita Hill/Clarence Thomas hearings, stimulated both debate and publications. Feminists wrote books that drew extensively on experiences combating sexual harassment abroad. *Tatort Arbeitsplatz: Sexuelle Belästigung von Frauen* (*Scene of the Crime–Workplace Sexual Harassment of Women*, Gerhart et al. 1992, Munich: Frauenoffensive) covered developments in the United States and France. The chapter "*Es ist nicht alles Gold, was gläntz*" (All that glitters is not gold) gave a critical review of the US legal situation. The book also included the European Community recommendation on sexual harassment.

It is striking as well that several German feminists involved in the politics of sexual harassment lived in other countries. Thus, the German feminist approaches to conceptualizing and defining sexual harassment were influenced by exchanges of ideas across national borders in Europe and the United States. West German feminists primarily view sexual harassment as the violation of intimate, personal space, following Sadrozinski's conceptualization; these influences contributed alternative discourses, such as boundary violations, crime, or sex discrimination, which later served German advocates by providing a language to legitimate sexual harassment as a policy issue. Union women and state officials translated them into their particular institutional context.

The anti-institutionalist stance of West German feminists was in part a realistic estimation of the limited opportunities to "work through the system." Through the 1980s, gender workplace issues, and violence against women in general, remained a low priority, and the party constellation at the federal level remained inhospitable. The ruling parties preferred to maintain the status quo of the male breadwinner model, or at best to modify it. West German gender politics have been dominated by the definition of women as mothers, so workplace gender policies have focused on flexible time, part-time work, and extensive parental leave policies, ostensibly to promote reconciliation of family and work issues.

Political Parties

Chancellor Kohl's government prioritized the homemaker model for women. Most workplace policies focused on women as mothers: long-term parental leave policies encouraged primary caregivers to stay home with children for up to three years (Morgan and Zippel 2003). The women's chapter of the CDU, highly skeptical of mothers' employment, successfully demanded caregiving leave benefits, with the argument that stay-at-home mothers had to be treated equally to working women.

When the Green party scandal broke out, the CDU/CSU had just formed a coalition with the liberal FDP. The FDP has been supportive of an anti-discrimination law, but individual liberalism is a weak political force in Germany and, as a small coalition partner (with less than 10 percent in elections), the FDP did not push a law against sexual harassment. The minor role of the FDP in German politics reflects the fact that liberalism in Germany is fairly weak, in contrast to the United States.

The Green party from its inception had been the party most open to feminist demands, with equal representation the rule at all levels. It put pressure on other political parties to take the representation of women and women's issues more seriously. Yet, in the aftermath of the scandal, the party did not adopt internal guidelines or policy against sexual harassment in the workplace. Many saw the call for measures against sexual harassment as reintroducing moral codes for everyday socio-sexual interactions. As former activists of the student movement, they believed that the sexual liberation of the 1960s had overcome the traditional problems of awkward (sexual) interactions between women and men.

Feminists in the party challenged this highly masculinist view of sexual liberation by pointing out that women's sexual self-determination had not been achieved, as witnessed in rapes, sexual assaults, and pervasive sexual objectification of women in the media. But the predominant view was that sexual harassment is not about politics because it is private behavior between two individuals, and a "cultural" rather than an organizational problem. The party, with its leftist hesitancy to criminalize individual behavior in interpersonal conflicts or to use legal measures to promote cultural change, was critical of a legal approach. The concern was that the state and employers would reintroduce "moral" codes to stifle the newly won, "uncomplicated" social and sexual interactions between women and men. Nonetheless, the Green party did become a strong supporter for a broader anti-discrimination law and put forward a parliamentary proposal for such a law, explicitly mentioning sexual harassment, in 1986 (BT-Dr.10/6137 October 9, 1986). The proposal did not stimulate much debate, because the Green party did not come to power until 1999.

The Social Democratic Party (SPD) was the obvious ally, since it traditionally has had the closest ties to the unions. However, although members of the women's caucus (*Arbeitsgemeinschaft Sozialdemokratischer Frauen*) have been strong supporters of an anti-discrimination law (Kodre and Müller 2003), advocates have had difficulty convincing the party to prioritize women workers' concerns – a reflection of male-dominated membership and leadership. Sexual harassment advocates did slowly work through party channels, and the party brought forward a draft law in 1992. But the party was in opposition between 1982 and 1999.

Thus, in the 1980s, the Federal political landscape did not offer strong allies for Plogstedt and the other activists. Party women and men who might have supported their cause had a difficult time convincing the mostly male-dominated leadership that working women's issues and issues of sexual violence should be taken seriously and warranted legal measures. Domestic political forces were slow to embrace the issue. This situation was no different from that in the United States, but West German activists did not use litigation as a strategy.

West German feminists and the courts

The intention of the Green women was to "raise awareness, to initiate a discussion within the party, and at least to prevent sexual harassment in their own workplace" (Plogstedt and Bode 1984: 7). Their goal was institutional change, and their hope was that a political process would change the working culture in the party. Their political strategy was in part successful, since the issue reached the party leadership, which took the issue seriously and asked Klaus Hecker to step down. So why did they not take their case to the courts?

The most important reason was that, unlike American attorneys and activists, who had the Civil Rights Act of 1964 to work with, Plogstedt and Bode needed to demand an anti-discrimination law for new and effective "protection of the harassed." West German labor laws are more extensive than US laws and the German constitution includes a passage establishing the equality of women and men. But the law provides little opportunity for individuals to challenge discrimination in the workplace. The labor laws protect workers against unfair dismissal, but the Green women were not dismissed, so the labor court would have given them little recourse. Prominent feminist labor lawyer Dr. Barbara Degen showed that various existing laws might have been used to reinterpret this incident, first and foremost the law that places responsibility on employers to ensure employee personal freedom (Holzbecher et al. 1990). The law is useful for reminding employers of their obligations, but it does not specify sanctions for failing to do so. Furthermore, interpretation and expansion of this and other laws were in the hands of judges who lacked awareness and sensibility on sexual harassment in particular.

Without a clear legal basis to tie sexual harassment to sex discrimination, the path through the courts was difficult for harassed women, attorneys, and activists. There was no law against *quid pro quo*, demanding sexual favors by a supervisor. Few women took their employers to court. Courts tended to consider the issues "private" (Degen

1991; Baer 1995), viewing even physical attacks as minor incidents, especially if women did not lose their jobs. A woman dismissed because of sexual harassment could use the stronger laws against unfair dismissal. But given that sexual harassment was not prohibited, the issue did not even come up at trial, since attorneys and judges wanted to avoid embarrassment for the victims. The only exception was when teenage female trainees filed suits against their employers. Then the labor laws were seen as more protective and judges more sympathetic to the victims, who were viewed as innocent girls (Degen 1991; Baer 1995).

The most problematic aspect of litigation as a strategy, however, was that existing laws provided little opportunity to frame gender inequality beyond the individual case. Testimonies of several women would strengthen cases against perpetrators because courts tend to believe a group more than an individual. But West German law does not yet allow class-action suits. An early case in which such a suit might have led to a dramatically different outcome illustrates the barriers women faced in confronting an employer collectively. In 1977, Annelie Runge, a union member who worked in public relations in an association (*Verband*), filed a lawsuit against her employer (Runge 1984: 131). Her boss had a pattern of demanding sexual favors from unmarried women who worked for him in return for salary increases and better positions. Women who did not comply were dismissed. Runge and four colleagues complained to the executive meeting and read an "open letter to a boss," but the supervisor was merely reprimanded. The women went public and the *Frankfurter Rundschau* newspaper and the feminist magazine *Courage* printed the letter. The association dismissed Runge, the only one who had signed the letter with her name.

With the help of the union, Runge filed an unfair dismissal lawsuit. As she recalls, the trial was very difficult: "All were moving on uncertain ground: the judge, the union steward, and the lawyers for the defense. It was one word against the other. My colleagues were not heard" (Runge 1984: 133). Without the possibility of a class-action suit, these women did not have the option to go through the trial as a group. The exhausting trial ended in a settlement: Runge's dismissal was revoked and her salary and remaining vacation money were restored. The trial and the media attention surrounding it took an enormous personal toll: for four months she received obscene phone calls.

Runge would also have found it difficult to win her case in the civil courts, because of the limited notion of violence. Verbal affronts did not constitute a "good cause." In rape and sexual assault cases, perpetrators were found guilty only if the attorney general could prove the perpetrator had used force. Merely to say no was not sufficient. The widely publicized case of a gynecologist who was raped by two colleagues during her night shift in a Berlin hospital, and who lost her case in court, demonstrates the difficulties of seeking justice through the legal system (Goy 1986). In a now familiar story, the men's attorneys put the woman on trial rather than the two defendants. Lack of awareness about violence against women, and judges' ignorance in particular, made it difficult to use these laws. Without rape shield laws and other important legal reforms, women did not expect the courts to be sympathetic to their situation.

Some legal reforms on violence against women began to be passed during the 1990s, including rape shield laws and the outlawing of rape within marriage, which came about only in 1998. If a strong law against sexual harassment had been in place, the woman doctor could have demanded a safe workplace environment independent of the court ruling. And the employer could have taken steps against the two men to prevent future sexual assaults.

The few cases in which employers indeed took steps against perpetrators were cases of men who had been fired because of sexual harassment and who challenged their employers' sanctions. In 1986, the year the US Supreme Court ruled that sexual harassment constitutes sex discrimination, a case of sexual harassment came before the West German *Bundesarbeitsgericht* (Highest Federal Labor Court). The court ruled in favor of an employer, stating that sexual advances toward subordinates could constitute grounds for dismissal of supervisors. This case strengthened the right of employers to dismiss perpetrators. This court, however, has never ruled on a case brought by a harassed person.

In short, West German feminists before 1994 did not have litigation in their repertoire of actions for social and political change. It is important to point out, however, that differences in legal systems do not fully explain why feminists did not use the judicial route. The German labor law system has some similarities with the US common law system. Lawyers can base a case on previous rulings, and judges frequently take these precedents into account. Courts have taken an active role in norm setting in the areas of strike laws, unfair dismissal laws, and mobbing. For example, the highest labor court in Thuringia provided a definition of mobbing, and ruled in a precedent-setting case that employers are responsible for protecting employees against mobbing.[4] Yet, so far, neither the Federal Labor Court nor the highest German state labor courts have been active in setting guidelines and norms for employer responsibilities toward victims of harassment.

---

[4] Landesarbeitsgericht Thuringia, April 10, 2001, 6 Sa 403/00.

Using the courts has in fact been a strategy of labor unions, for example to expand strike laws and individual workplace rights, including equality of part-time work. The unions have supported several suits by harassment victims who challenged their employers, but more often they have supported alleged perpetrators in cases of dismissals. In addition, men not women have sought justice in the German courts. Precedent-setting cases at the EU level were brought by German men who felt unjustly treated by positive action laws for women. In the most prominent Kalanke case, the European Court of Justice ruled that law of the city-state Bremen violated Kalanke's rights under the EU's equal treatment directive for women and men in 1995. An employee of the city of Bremen, Eckhard Kalanke, had not received a promotion but a woman with the same credentials had. The Bremen positive action law for women stated that if an equally qualified woman and man apply for the same position, the woman needs to be hired or promoted. The European Court of Justice ruled that Bremen's law would need to allow for case-by-case consideration.

As with sex discrimination law in general, labor courts have applied existing labor law most often to protect men against sanctions by their employers, and strong preexisting laws for women's rights have been lacking. So individual women could not base cases on strong anti-discrimination legislation or expand existing law successfully. And neither feminists nor unions could use litigation strategies to hold employers accountable in cases of sexual harassment. Therefore German labor courts have not played an active role in shaping laws, despite their potential. Without a civil rights tradition or class-action suits, activists concerned with sexual harassment did not use the courts. Legal changes would have to come through the parliament.

Neither the autonomous feminist movement nor the unions – the most obvious vehicle for addressing women's and workers' rights – put sexual harassment on the political agenda in West Germany. Instead, Green party feminists and Plogstedt thrust the issue onto the agenda of the Green party, the public, and the unions. Plogstedt's efforts to get unions involved as coalition partners were part of a broader political strategy. She represented a minority position in the feminist movement, questioning its strong autonomy stance. In 1983, she proposed a more broad-based women's movement and asked for a discussion of feminists' role within it (cited in Ferree 1987: 185). The issue of sexual harassment was an appropriate target for her political vision of broadening the feminist movement.

Plogstedt's strategy was correct in the German context: in contrast to violence against women, around which feminists created a new policy field, sexual harassment needed to be situated in the existing policy field of workplace regulation. This is particularly true since the avenues for change in workplace regulations in Germany are the employers and unions, with little place for "outside" organizations. Sexual harassment needed to become an issue for "institutionalized feminism" – women in parties, unions, universities, and the state. Consequently, no single-issue political groups or organizations emerged that specifically addressed sexual harassment, as in the United States, France, or the Netherlands. Thus, West Germany lacked both a legal and an organizational base for a revolution of sexual harassment law. With the hesitancy of unions and the relative weakness of women in institutions, the external influence of US and EU developments became increasingly important factors to catalyze the legal changes in Germany.

The 1994 Federal Employee Protection Law

The EU model of anti-discrimination laws, based on liberal individualism, has been the basis for profound institutional and political challenges to traditional gender politics in Germany. EU influence has systematically challenged German policy-makers to consider issues that women experience as women rather than as mothers. The European integration process and European directives since the 1970s kept the issue of women's rights as workers and workplace gender equality on the German agenda. For example, the state has had to address equal pay and discrimination in hiring, promotion, and working conditions. The first West German Gender Equality Law (1980), called the European Community Adaptation Law, was passed only because the European Court of Justice threatened sanctions should Germany not adopt the 1975 and 1976 directives. Nevertheless, West Germany's compliance with EU measures on gender equality was at best patchy (Kodre and Müller 2003), and German sexual harassment law also lagged behind the EU soft-law measures.

However, EU gender politics have changed institutional arrangements in Germany. There had been internal demands for offices for women's affairs, but it was the EU asking to have a contact in the federal offices that would be responsible for monitoring and enforcing EU measures that influenced the creation of West German gender equality offices in the 1980s (Hoskyns 1996; Ferree 1995a; von Wahl 1999; Berghahn 1995). While these offices were created at local and state levels already in the 1980s, only in 1994 did the Federal government pass a law to implement EU legislation and institutionalize gender equality offices throughout the public sector. This 1994 Second Federal Gender Equality

Law established these offices of "state feminism" that became a new institutional vehicle to promote gender equality in the labor market, and these offices were the key actors for promoting policy change regarding sexual harassment in the 1990s. The reform of this 1994 Second Gender Equality Law provided the policy window for advocates to push for a Federal law against sexual harassment.

It took eleven years after the first public debates on sexual harassment, four years after the European Council recommendation, and more than fourteen years after the US EEOC guidelines for German federal policy-makers to respond to sexual harassment. In 1994 the German parliament, led by the coalition of Christian Democrats and Liberals and overcoming the opposition of the Social Democrats and Greens, passed the Federal Law for the Protection of Employees, the first specific law against sexual harassment in private and public workplaces as an amendment to the 1994 Second Gender Equality Law.

The 1994 Second Gender Equality Law provided the opportunity for advocates to define sexual harassment as the responsibility of employers. While this broader law applies to the public sector only, the sexual harassment amendment covers all employers regardless of size. It provides a definition of sexual harassment and states that in the workplace it constitutes a violation of the labor contract. Individuals have the right to bring a complaint and employers are required to appoint an office for complaints. Employers have the responsibility to create a workplace environment that discourages sexual harassment, and public employers are required to take preventive measures. This law had important symbolic power and thus became an important tool for advocates in the workplace. Yet, it did little to strengthen the rights of victims because it did not go much beyond existing laws and jurisprudence.

For feminist advocates the 1994 Federal Employee Protection Law was disappointing. For instance, it does not explicitly define sexual harassment as sex discrimination, and does not put sexual harassment in the context of gender equality. Instead, it is intended to "create a climate at work which is respectful of the personal integrity and the dignity of all employees" (Drucksache 12/5468 p. 21). In fact, the 1994 law defined sexual harassment more narrowly than several *Länder* (state) laws already passed, and women in the city-state of Bremen worried that their law might have to be weakened in order to comply with the new law (Buhr and Klein-Schonnefeld 1996).

The German definition is also more limited than the 1991 European Council recommendation: only intentional, sexually motivated behaviors constitute sexual harassment. This means that the law does not follow the logic of discrimination law, which focuses on the outcomes for victims rather than the intentions of the perpetrators. Nor does it recognize a victim's subjective experience of sexual harassment, as the US and European Community definitions do. Finally, perpetrators are granted what critics call a one-time mistake, since only recognizably rejected behaviors fall under this law. Hence the law privileges the perspective of the perpetrator. German policy-makers copied the notion of dignity from the European Community recommendations, but the final version is weaker than the European model. The weakest point is that the law does not specify any enforcement mechanisms, nor does it empower state agencies to intervene on behalf of victims. For example, no state office has the right to impose sanctions against employers who violate this law. Not surprisingly, most employers ignore it (Pflüger and Baer 2005).

Why did the ruling Christian and Liberal parties, usually on the side of employers, take action in 1994? Several factors had radically altered the political opportunity structure which both led to the passage of the 1994 law and explain why the law offered very modest advances for victims of sexual harassment. First, the early impetus for public debates on sexual harassment came from the US Hill/Thomas hearings, which also raised interest among institutionalized actors. Second, German unification dramatically changed the political landscape, and altered government norms and ideals of women's employment. German policy-makers, even in the CDU/CSU, began to accept that the employment of women was not going to go away. Finally, the EU was a major catalyst in several areas, initiating research, providing policy models, and changing institutional constellations of gender equality politics. The politicization and new legal developments around sexual harassment coincided with these new developments in Germany.

The 1994 Employee Protection Law was not a reaction to popular demand or to a vibrant, broad social movement. The impetus for the second public debate on sexual harassment, after the scandal in the Green party in the early 1980s, was a foreign import, as the US Hill/Thomas hearings brought the issue again into mainstream media. Like French reports, German media described the hearings in such a way as to suggest that sexual harassment was entirely an "American" problem. But journalists also began to report more broadly on sexual harassment and to ask about the situation in Germany. The American hearings coincided with the German Ministry of Women's newly released study and the European Council recommendations. Thus not only did sexual harassment gain media attention in Germany, but the German study and the European policy created more legitimacy for the issue as a problem and gave it a national and European context – sexual harassment might indeed affect German women.

The German reception of the Hill/Thomas hearings meant that policy-makers tried to avoid any perception that they intended to create an American situation (*Amerikanische Verhältnisse*), in which women could sue their employer over dirty jokes or flirtation and the eroticization of the workplace would be criminalized. The US model was studied intensively as activists, experts, and policy-makers attempted to define a specifically German approach to the issue. For example, the most common definition of sexual harassment became the violation of boundaries, of intimate personal space, rather than the US frame of sex discrimination.

Unification

There was national media attention, but political conditions were less than suitable for creating consensus for gender equality laws. The German political climate of the early 1990s was difficult for drawing attention to working conditions for women and demanding more state regulation in workplaces. The political landscape had changed dramatically, because of increasing European integration, but most important, because of the collapse of the East German Democratic Republic (GDR). After the Berlin Wall fell in November 1989, the unification process took political center stage. The eleven West and five East *Länder* (states) were joined in the new Federal Republic of Germany. In 1990, in the first common election, both East and West Germans confirmed the coalition of Christian and Liberal parties under the leadership of Chancellor Kohl. Germany, like the United States, is a federal state, so the sixteen *Länder* have autonomy in several policy areas, such as education and public employment, and to some extent also in gender equality laws.

In the unification process, abortion rights not anti-discrimination measures took center stage (Ferree et al. 2002; Young 1999). In the context of economic integration and fiscal constraints for the economic monetary union, the main political mantra became a neo-liberal market orientation. Demands for state intervention in the labor market in the form of regulations were suspect. The major workplace problem for politicians, however, was the skyrocketing unemployment, which hit East Germans, but West Germans soon afterward. For East German women, with previous employment rates of over 90 percent, the political and economic transformation had severe economic consequences (Trappe 1995, 1996). Childcare disappeared and a disproportionate number of women lost their jobs. Managers (often from the West) decided that married men with children should be given preference, since mothers should be at home to take care of their family. Thus, the formerly more equal status of East German working women diminished with the reintroduction of the male breadwinner ideology (Kolinsky and Nickel 2003; Rosenfeld, Trappe, and Gornick 2004; Trappe 1995).

Keeping jobs was East German women's main concern, preempting discussions about rights such as working conditions. According to an East German gender advocate, the precarious employment situation not surprisingly prompted women to say, "I'd rather have a workplace in which I am being harassed than none." Women felt that they did not have a problem with sexual harassment, not because it did not happen but because they knew how to deal with it. In the public hearing on the 1994 Employee Protection Law one woman explained: "I can't actually corroborate sexual harassment in the East. Maybe women there are more courageous, and put up more of a fight. The issue is not as precarious and known at our place" (Lähner 1993). Christina Schenk, a West German Green parliamentarian, also placed the problem implicitly with West German women who fight back less.[5] Still, she emphasized the context of gender workplace culture in the former East Germany. In the parliamentary debate about the Federal Employee Protection Law, she made clear that job security might be an important factor when considering East–West differences:

Therefore we can assume that the prevalence of the problem of sexual harassment in the workplace in the East was less than in the West. The topic was more a taboo than here; there were never public discussions about it. Yet, in discussions with East German women, it becomes clear that gender relations in East Germany were less hierarchical than in the West. Women were taken more seriously, especially in the workplace, and in general were seen as equal colleagues. Women had the necessary self-confidence to keep a potential harasser in reasonable limits. It is important, that the fear about losing one's workplace practically didn't exist.

When the most pressing needs are jobs and access to the labor market, the politicization of working conditions becomes secondary. There were concerns that measures against sexual harassment could backfire against women's employment in general. In a precarious economic situation with weak laws against sex discrimination in hiring and firing, employers might opt not to hire or continue to employ women if laws required them

---

[5] Page 9482 in the Sitzungsprotokoll, Deutscher Bundestag, Drucksache, 12/111, October 9, 1992 (translation by the author).

to take action regarding sexual harassment. A typical employer response was, "If I have the responsibility to protect women, and to monitor the guys' behavior, then I just won't hire them" (Degen, interview, 1999). High unemployment also makes women more vulnerable to coercion and accepting imposed working conditions. An East German gender equality advocate stated: "In the old times, East German men would have never dared." She referred to an employer who explained during a job interview that he expected the female applicant to have sex with him if she wanted the job.

Employers were vehemently opposed to the proposed law, arguing that existing laws were sufficient to protect employees. The German *Fürsorgepflicht* (duty of care) law outlines employers' obligation to provide for the general welfare of employees. Further laws would only increase costs and lead to overregulation of the workplace. In a Federal hearing in 1993, the representative of the *Bundesvereinigung der Deutschen Arbeitgeberverbände* (BDA) (Federal Association of German Employers) gave lip service to the severity of the problem, beginning his statement: "Without wanting to trivialize the problem . . ." He recognized sexual harassment as a societal problem, but argued that legal instruments were not suited to combat it (Drucksache. Protokoll. November 11, 1993, p. 345). He suggested that the best prevention would be personnel management (*Personalführung*) to deal with the problem and apply conflict-resolution strategies.

In addition, the BDA argued vehemently against the introduction of a quasi-legal regulatory commission, as suggested by the SPD, because a commission would lead to an undesirable "*Verbürokratisierung des Arbeitslebens*" (over-bureaucratization of the world of work) and affect the character of *betrieblicher Rechtsprechung* (organizational jurisprudence) (Drucksache. Protokoll. November 11, 1993, Anhörung, p. 345). Nevertheless, by the early 1990s sexual harassment had a name and employers were careful not to publicly dismiss its importance. This change of awareness reflected public discussions and media reporting on the issue. It occurred in part because of the US debates and because of the sensitivity and awareness programs by state feminists and women within unions, which had created alternative discourses and expertise that could less easily be dismissed by opponents of legal measures.

State feminists

Despite employers' resistance at the federal level, *femocrats* at the state and local level had successfully initiated policy measures. Before the 1994 Federal Employee Protection Law, policy changes occurred in progressive cities and some *Länder*. In the 1980s and early 1990s, a number of cities and towns, including Hamburg, Berlin, Munich, and Stuttgart, created offices for women. Sexual harassment became defined as an issue within the framework of *Frauenförderung* (equal opportunity policies for women). One of the first cities to put sexual harassment on the agenda was Wiesbaden in Hesse. In 1987, its gender equality office published a brochure with the title "Leave me alone! Sexual Harassment in the Workplace." Among the first cities to pass specific *Dienstvereinbarungen* (collective bargaining agreements) on sexual harassment were Cologne and Bremen in 1993 and Freiburg and Heilbronn in 1994. In some cities, for example in Stuttgart in 1991, mayors issued *Dienstanweisungen* (executive orders) to prohibit sexual harassment and establish procedures for dealing with it.

Six of the sixteen *Länder* parliaments passed laws on sexual harassment in the early 1990s as part of equality laws for the public sector, though they were largely ignored even in the public-sector workplaces. The two earliest, Berlin and Hesse, are known for progressive gender equality politics, especially under the red–green (SPD and Green party) coalition governments. Berlin's 1990 anti-discrimination law legally defined sexual harassment. In 1993, Hesse updated its 1989 gender equality law to include a definition of sexual harassment. Two East German *Länder*, Mecklenburg-Vorpommern and Saxony, and two West German *Länder*, Lower Saxony and Schleswig-Holstein, passed laws in the same year as the 1994 Federal Employee Protection Law. The city-state Bremen established an office responsible solely for issues of sexual harassment called *Arbeitsstelle gegen sexuelle Diskriminierung und Gewalt am Ausbildungs- und Erwerbsplatz* (Office against Sexual Discrimination and Violence in Educational Settings and Workplaces) in 1994. Hence, rather than being top-down, the German process of policy adoption was a bottom-up process. The developments at the city and state levels served to create legitimacy for a federal law against sexual harassment.

Creating expertise on sexual harassment

National-level expertise on sexual harassment was also crucial for the passage of the Federal Employee Protection Law, and the gender equality offices were important in creating and bundling feminist informed knowledge about sexual harassment. The impact of transnational networks of experts was crucial here. Michael Rubenstein requested information about the issue from all member states for the first EU-wide study in 1986. When the recently created German Federal Ministry for Women was contacted, no information was available. So minister Rita Süßmuth commissioned the first nationwide comprehensive research study on sexual harassment. Süßmuth, a professor for education, and previously director of *Institut für Frauenforschung* (Center for Research on Women) in Hannover, had a record of progressive gender politics. Though a member of the CDU, she was a strong supporter of women's rights, had a strong pro-choice, pro-equality stance, was a major figure in challenging conservative notions of gender in her party and nationwide, and, considered sexual harassment an important issue (Augstein, interview, 1999). Thus, the initiation of federal policy development emerged under the rule of a conservative/liberal party, albeit through the initiation of a ministry with "progressive" leadership.

The nationwide study by Holzbecher et al. (1990) captured media attention. It documented the pervasiveness of sexual harassment and the harm done to women and included a report about the legal situation by Dr. Barbara Degen. She noted that existing laws could be applied to sexual harassment but were insufficient. The research institute *Soziale Forschungsstelle Dortmund* (Office for Social Research), which later conducted the important mobbing study, was chosen to survey women's experiences with sexual harassment because of its close affiliation with the unions. The survey found that 75 percent of women had experienced sexual harassment, but they did not dare report it, for they lost their jobs or were transferred if they filed official complaints (Holzbecher et al. 1990). The results of the study, in which Mueller also participated, were supported by a previous study commissioned by the women's office of the city-state of Hamburg on the prevalence of sexual harassment (Schneble and Domsch 1990).

An expert in labor law, Klaus Bertelsmann, had worked for the Hamburg equality office since 1979, the first labor lawyer to specialize in sexual harassment. He was interested in discrimination issues, and with Prof. Dr. Heide Pfarr, a law professor and expert for women's workplace rights, coauthored the first legal analysis on *Diskriminierung im Erwebsleben* (Discrimination in the Workplace) in 1989. He remembers that the inspiration to work on sexual harassment came from the United States. He had traveled there in 1986 to learn about the US model, visiting EEOC offices in New York and Washington. In his first article about sexual harassment (1987), he drew on the US model to define harassment, translating the ideas into the context of German labor law. Bertelsmann had close ties with the left-wing movement, unions, and feminists working on the issue. Plogstedt collaborated with him in the first publication on sexual harassment as an issue for unions (Plogstedt and Bertelsmann 1987; DGB 1987).

Bertelsmann was also the link with the European Community networks. He supplied the information on the West German laws for the Rubenstein report and participated in the EU TAN networks of legal experts (Bertelsmann, interview, 1999). He remembers the importance of this European network for his work: "This was truly a lot of fun, especially when again keeping an eye on which ideas one can take from other countries and then somehow transpose here."

Thus, the early legal assessments and psychological–sociological treatments on the issue of sexual harassment were initiated and funded by women's offices in state agencies in West Germany. The impetus for these studies came from the EU measures and the early legal models from the United States, because the EU basically copied the EEOC guidelines. Legal experts then translated these models into their national contexts, but state offices were also crucial to fund research and help the TAN to accumulate expertise and knowledge in this policy field, which is dominated by taboos, myths, and stereotypes.

Even with this expertise available, however, the new minister of women, Dr. Angelika Merkel, who held office from 1991 to 1994, and who was elected as the first woman German Chancellor in 2005, took a position against state intervention. In line with a socially conservative, corporatist understanding of sexual harassment as an issue between unions and employers, not the state, the ministry recommended collective agreements between employers and works councils to initiate policies at the company level. In 1991, the ministry sent a letter, the European Commission Code of Practice, and a sample of a policy on sexual harassment to employer associations and unions.

The ministry had for several years promised a broad reform of the 1980 first Federal Gender Equality Law to adjust it to recent ECJ rulings. The process was slow. Merkel finally initiated the drafting of the 1994 Employee Protection Law as part of the reform of the gender equality law. Merkel and her successor Claudia Nolte (1994–1998) were more conservative on equality issues than Süßmuth; for example, both were pro-life, reflecting the party line of the Christian parties. As women from the former East Germany, however, they continued Süßmuth's support of women's employment, since they took it for granted.

The ruling party coalition of the Christian Democratic and the Bavarian Christian Socialist party showed little support for a strong gender equality law. The women's unit within the CDU, for example, placed highest priority on recognizing the work of housewives and women's work in the voluntary sector. Merkel could have used the new constitution for the unified Germany, which mandated the state's responsibility to promote gender equality, as a base for a strong gender equality law. Instead, she argued that specific measures for positive action were not necessary because the constitution already covered the issue.

Important challenges came from the oppositional parties, as both the Greens and the SPD pushed for the recognition of sexual harassment. In 1986 the Green party had brought to parliament a proposal for a broad anti-discrimination law that mentioned sexual harassment. The proposal did not lead anywhere. The SPD drafted a law on sexual harassment and put the issue on the parliamentary agenda in 1992 (Drucksache 12/2096). Hanna Wolf, SPD parliamentarian and initiator of this draft, remembers that the impetus came from both developments in the *Länder* and women in unions (Wolf, interview, 1999). Sexual harassment was on the agenda in two working groups, the group on gender equality in the SPD, founded in 1990, and the group on "special topics." In the gender equality group, chair Ilse Jans from Bremen and Marlies Dobberthien from Hamburg were both from city-states with progressive *Länder* laws that included definitions of sexual harassment. In the second working group, women within unions advocated for dealing with the issue. The SPD proposal for the law was more encompassing than the government proposal would be; both were discussed in the parliament in 1992 and 1993.

Because the sexual harassment law was appended to the package of the Federal Equality Law, the law itself did not generate much public attention. Questions about quotas for women employees, the ambivalent role of part-time work, and compensation in discrimination cases received more attention in parliamentary commissions and plenary discussions. Neither sexual harassment nor the 1994 Second Gender Equality Law was perceived as an important political issue. Male parliamentarians did not even show up at the 1992 parliamentary debates about the SPD proposal and the 1994 discussions on the CDU proposal. So these debates took place in a very unusual setting: the majority of speakers and parliamentarians present were women, even though 79.5 percent of parliamentarians at that time were men. This might explain the consensus of the speakers that sexual harassment was a devastating problem for women in the workplace. Many speakers told stories of individual women's experiences with harassment, and referred to the studies noted above to show how widespread the issue was as a societal problem.

The influence of European integration

What role did "Europeanization" play in the first German law against sexual harassment? Kodre and Müller argue that advocates for the

Second Gender Equality Law missed the opportunity to draw on EU norms and laws. They analyze parliamentary debates and publications on positive action for women and find that "Equal opportunities issues and controversies were discussed exclusively within a domestic framework" (2003: 104).

By contrast, policy-makers, politicians, and experts used European Community developments extensively to legitimize the issue and demand a German law against sexual harassment. This is especially surprising because the EU measures were merely soft laws and thus nonbinding. Several examples of the parliamentary debates and drafts for laws by the SPD and government illustrate how national-level actors used the supranational developments to make their case.

The first SPD proposal for a law against sexual harassment, in 1992, mentions the European Community Code of Conduct on the first page. Hanna Wolf (SPD), who introduced the proposal, felt strongly about the definition and argued that it should be based on "what women feel" (Wolf, interview, 1999). In parliament, she defended the subjective, victim-centered definition of sexual harassment by referring to the Community soft-law measures: "Whether behavior constitutes sexual harassment should be judged from the perspective of the affected women. This is in line with the decision of the Council of the European Community on sexual harassment in the workplace. If one tried to use an objective catalogue with criteria, one would use a male perspective, which unfortunately happens still today" (PlPr.12/111 page 9478, October 9, 1992).

In the parliamentary debates leading to the passage of the 1994 Second Gender Equality Law, several politicians used the European Community regulations to legitimize the issue of sexual harassment. Minister for women Merkel opened her speech by justifying adding sexual harassment to the Federal Gender Equality Law in the following way: "With the law for the protection of all employees . . . from sexual harassment, the government complies with the European Community legal recommendation" (Bundesministerin Dr. Angelika Merkel BTPlPr. 12/179 p. 15435, September 30, 1993). To justify employers' responsibility to prevent harassment from occurring, both the SPD draft and the government proposal referred to the EU calls for prevention, along with examples of British and French legal ways to handle sexual harassment.

Thus, politicians and bureaucrats used the European context strategically to legitimize the issue of sexual harassment in proposals for the national law and parliamentary debates. Just as experts used transnational expertise, so policy-makers used European community models. In fact, the administrator who drafted the government proposal copied the notion of violation of dignity directly from the EU documents. Thus, the TAN provided legal concepts, frameworks, and models for state intervention and collective bargaining.

What is striking in these parliamentary debates is politicians' caution about mentioning the United States. Very few speakers drew on US discussions or studies. The European models provided a counterweight to American policies and created a moderate "European" way of handling sexual harassment in Germany. Renate Augstein, chair of the unit (*Referat*) for violence against women in the ministry of women, remembers: "The European Union was in this regard a support, so that we could claim that this is now increasingly an issue in Europe. [Sexual harassment] is not just a story in the United States, but is also gradually coming up as an issue in Europe. And look, the EU is making this an issue, and is addressing it. So we're in good company" (Augstein, interview, 1999). Hence, European discourse on sexual harassment was important in legitimizing national advocates for sexual harassment. In addition, the impetus for the first federal study on sexual harassment, as well as for the establishment of the gender equality offices throughout the public sector, came from the European community.

National economic conditions and gender and party politics certainly shaped the final form of the 1994 Employee Protection Law. The new law provided a lowest common denominator among the government, employers, and unions under the CDU/CSU and Liberal parties. As Dr. Margret Funke-Schmitt-Rink, a member of the liberal FDP party, described the outcome: "It was a long road with difficult confrontations both within and between the coalition parties and the ministries. The result is a compromise. In many places, the draft lacks sharp teeth. Often, it is not precise, and there are too few binding regulations" (BTPlPr. 12/179 pp.15437, September 30, 1993).

This German statutory–corporatist route to pass a law based on the consensus building in parliament brought about a very different sexual harassment law than the US route. While the US legal reforms were the outcome of court decisions, the 1994 Employee Protection Law was invented by male administrators and modified by party politicians to reach a political consensus, setting minimum expectations for responsibilities of employers and rights of harassed individuals. The negotiations took place between male-dominated political parties, state administrators, unions, and employers' associations. When US judges ruled, they faced victims of sexual harassment, they listened to the testimony and first-hand experience of women with sexual harassment, heard about the consequences that sexual harassment had for these victims, listened to psychological experts, and heard legal arguments by attorneys who interpreted these women's experiences. Given how emotional the issue of sexual harassment is, the embarrassment, but also then the power to talk about the incidents from the women's perspective, the US laws reflect the sympathy the judges had with these victims.

By contrast, in the German debates about the 1994 Employee Protection Law, only in one official public hearing did feminist legal experts speak out. The decision-makers did not hear any victims telling their story, nor did they hear psychologists explaining what sexual harassment does to victims. The feminist and pro-feminist politicians did bring a women's voice into the debate, but during the parliamentary debate, the majority of male parliamentarians, who would later vote for the weak law, were missing. Not surprisingly, the whole process of getting the majority of votes within mostly male-dominated political parties in parliament watered down feminist visions and demands.

For example, the Greens, SPD, and unions supported a subjective definition of sexual harassment from the victim's perspective. As representative Konrad Weiss (Berlin), Bündnis 90/Die Grünen, put it: "That which should be seen as harassment can, according to our understanding, be only a subjective definition." By contrast, CDU Federal Minister Merkel explained that the proposed (and later passed) law had the goal to be objective: "The law defines the notion of sexual harassment on the basis of objective criteria" (BTPlPr. 12/179, September 30, 1993, p.15435). Hanna Wolf, who had put forward the 1992 SPD proposal, criticized this government proposal in the parliament: "Sexual harassment in your [Minister Merkel] draft is not defined from the perspective of the woman. What you call objective means, in practice, a male perspective" (BTPlPr. 12/179 September 30, 1993, p. 15446).

Both the Green and the SPD proposals, supported by the unions, used explicitly feminist discourses to define sexual harassment as sex discrimination. Interestingly, the 1992 internal policy issued by the Federal Minister for Women, which served as a model for other employers and unions, was closer to the SPD proposal and the European recommendations, and used a more subjective victim's view: "Sexual behavior that is unwanted by the affected person and which serves to degrade her as a person." It also clearly defined the issue as sex discrimination.[6]

It is striking that the unit for "equality," not the unit for "violence against women," was responsible for drafting the 1994 Employee Protection Law, presumably because it was an amendment to the 1994 Second Federal Gender Equality Law for which the unit for equality

---

[6] Grundsätze zum Schutz vor sexueller Belästigung am Arbeitsplatz, February 10, 1992.

was in charge. Because the issue touched on workplace regulations, the Federal Ministry of Labor and Social Affairs was also involved. Conservative voices came from other federal ministries, concerned that they would be required to implement the law themselves as public employers and worried more about men being falsely accused than about those who experience harassment. Very few women were ministry heads, and the conservative voices won.

In addition, under the Christian and Liberal parties, employers' concerns about increasing costs and overregulation of the workplace led to a very moderate law regarding workplace requirements for internal complaint procedures and prevention and enforcement mechanisms. The SPD draft called for a commission to handle complaints in every workplace, to be chaired by a woman and with at least 50 percent women. The FDP was vehemently opposed to complaint procedures and commissions. As Dr. Margret Funke-Schmitt-Rink (FDP) argued: "The FDP wants the equality law, but one has to ask, if so much bureaucracy is really necessary, for the instruments of women's equality plans and women's advocates to work" (BTPlPr. 12/179 p. 15437, September 30). The CDU argued that mid-size enterprises would not be able to fill these commissions and would be overburdened with such a proposal. Minister Merkel's proposal did not suggest new complaint procedures. The final law requires employers to appoint an office in which complaints can be filed, without further specification.

It is hard to tell what the law would have looked like if the SPD and the Green party had been in power in the early 1990s. The Green party's entry brought sexual harassment onto the West German agenda in 1983, and sixteen years later the party was for the first time in a coalition government with the SPD. Yet since the 1999 elections the governing SPD–Green coalition has not strengthened the law itself. The coalition did pass several legal reforms that aid sexual harassment victims: for example, the burden of proof was eased, damage awards for victims were raised, and works councils now have quotas for women. But in the first four years the government did little to promote workplace gender equality, despite the fact that the anti-discrimination law had been the cornerstone of the negotiations to form the coalition, and even though the Green party had promoted an anti-discrimination law since the 1980s. Chancellor Schroeder tabled a discussion of a gender equality law for the private sector that would have required creation of equality offices, explaining that voluntary commitment by private businesses was sufficient. In fact, it was twenty years after Dr. Plogstedt's vision before an encompassing anti-discrimination law was seriously discussed in the parliament. It was again external influences, renewed EU pressure in the form of the 2002 Equal Treatment Directive, that put the issue back on the government agenda.

New impulses from the European Union: the German anti-discrimination law

In 2004, the issue of compliance to EU anti-discrimination laws once again brought sexual harassment onto the agenda of German policy-makers. The EU again became an important catalyst for passing equality laws, putting pressure on Germany to implement the EU measures. A member of the Green party explained: "Without the EU Directives, we would not be having this discussion [on an anti-discrimination law]." In fact, since the EU now required regulations on sexual harassment and the definition of sexual harassment as sex discrimination, the issue itself has generated surprisingly little debate within the coalition.

The EU had passed three directives on equal treatment: (1) Directive 2000/43/EC, which covers race and ethnicity; (2) Directive 2000/78/EC, which covers religion or belief, disability, age, or sexual orientation; and (3) Directive 2002/73/EC, on equal treatment of women and men, which focuses on gender and sexual harassment. Member states had until 2003 to implement the first two directives and until October 2005 to translate the gender equality directive into national law.

The political climate at the beginning of the twenty-first century was no more receptive for adopting a sexual harassment law than it had been in the early 1990s. The continuing economic crises, high unemployment, and other long-term costs of unification have not been successfully confronted by the German government's reform agenda. The government has been very hesitant to impose more regulations in the workplace and in fact has justified reforms that allow employers more flexibility. Consequently, the 2001 proposal for an anti-discrimination law was tabled, and the government (the SPD/Green coalition) asked for an extension, arguing that it would work to pass an encompassing anti-discrimination law. Yet, the EU Commission began an infringement procedure against Germany, threatening sanctions if Germany did not take steps to incorporate the EU anti-discrimination directives into national law in January 2005 keeping up pressure on Germany to take action.

Several aspects of the debates about this anti-discrimination law to cover both sexual and gender harassment were reminiscent of the intro-duction of the Federal Employee Protection Law. There was still reluc-tance to use law to effect social and cultural changes. On the one hand, the pro-business advocates and German employers still insisted that the existing law against sexual harassment was sufficient and no further steps were necessary. On the other hand, the Green and leftist political forces have been reluctant to bring back regulations into the workplace that were reminiscent of traditional German paternalism in labor regulations. Bestowing employers with control over what is perceived as the "private" sphere of employees rings warning bells because of the specific German history of state–employer relations. On the one hand, employers had powers through the paternalistic *Betriebsordnung* (work rules) during the Nazi period, on the other hand, after World War II, the East German secret police extended its power into the labor force through police informants.[7]

Advocates for stronger laws against sexual harassment now faced a difficult choice: to demand a separate law on gender equality and sexual harassment, or to advocate a law encompassing them along with discrimination based on sex, race, ethnicity, religion, and sexual orientation. The obvious concern was that sexual harassment might disappear in a laundry list of very different discrimination issues. Yet this might be an advantage for advocates for a strong sexual harassment law if contentious debates could thus be kept to a minimum, and surprisingly little discussion against sexual harassment came about during the negotiations.

The decision was to work on one law because the implementation and enforcement mechanisms would be similar. The issue of sexual harassment itself did not attract much attention; the debate was more generally how to introduce class-action suits and how organizations could file on behalf of victims, neither of which the German legal system had accommodation for. Several practical issues of implementation and enforcement were also contentious. The question was whether gender equality offices, established as offices for women's affairs, would now also be charged to enforce and implement measures against the ethnic, religious, or sexual orientation discrimination of men.

The new proposal improves the definition of sexual harassment: the German premise of intentionality had to give way to the EU directive's clear definition of sexual harassment as sex discrimination. The addition of gender harassment gave policy-makers the opportunity to go beyond American law to what American feminists like Vicky Schultz have been calling for: to clearly prohibit harassment that has to do not with sexuality but with gender–targeted at women. The 2005 window of opportunity seemed ripe to strengthen the German law: the German parliament began to debate the new anti-discrimination law, with almost a third of

[7] Thanks to Susanne Baer who pointed out this historical meaning (personal communication March 1, 2005).

women politicians, and the ruling parties, the SPD and Greens, a government that has made an effort to adopt legal reforms concerning violence against women. Yet, the proposal was stalled in the *Bundesrat* before the elections in 2005.

Conclusion

Legal and policy changes regarding workplace sexual harassment developed more slowly in Germany than in the United States. Gender equality politics and the German system of workers' relations shaped the emergence of the issue. During the 1970s and 1980s, advocates for policy change faced state and political actors' lack of awareness and had little support. In the 1980s, a political scandal generated media attention and promoted some awareness. The Green party's entrance into politics provided an opportunity for feminists to politicize the issue in unexpected ways: the media used the issue to emphasize a scandal about the Green party itself rather than about sexually harassing behavior as a problem of gender equality in the workplace. Neither the anti-violence and feminist movement nor labor unions strongly supported legal change. Nor could existing laws simply be expanded. Because the labor courts did not take an active role, politics were the main stage on which advocates had to win allies. The path through the parliament took a long time, and the law finally passed only because of external influence. US debates on sexual harassment had created an ambivalent awareness about the issue, since Germans did not want to adopt the US model. Thus, the European integration process was critical to change the adverse political opportunity structure.

In the specific German socially conservative, neocorporatist institutional context, in which unions and employers dominated labor relations, the introduction in the 1990s of new institutional actors – femocrats – dramatically changed gender politics in the workplace (Gottfried and O'Reilly 2002; Ferree 1995a). The institutionalization of state offices for women coincided with the politicization of sexual harassment. These gender equality offices were crucial for addressing sexual harassment in the workplace as a social, political, and legal issue. Gender equality officers played a central role in the politicization and institutionalization of sexual harassment by organizing and coordinating a variety of feminist actors across the anti-violence movement, unions, and other groups. They were able to bridge the ideological and organizational gap between the feminist movement, which considered the issue a workplace problem, and the labor movement, which considered it a feminist, women's issue.

These gender equality offices were also able to draw on the TAN to establish useful networks with the Europe-wide policy community. They drew on the West German feminist anti-violence movement for alternative discourses to discuss sexual harassment. They also used the EU soft-law measures and benefited from the transnational expertise the EU had created. They promoted studies, created legal expertise, and used the transnational expertise to draft legal proposals.

The 1994 Employee Protection Law resulted from the success of institutional actors, state offices for gender equality, in turning sexual harassment into a legitimate policy issue. That the law did not meet the expectations and hopes of advocates reflects the constraints of power of the federal office. Bureaucrats can put issues on the agenda, but they have little power to push through their definitions and ideas. Their role in creating a policy consensus is circumscribed by powerful ministries and party mechanisms. Their limited enforcement and implementation powers compared with the EEOC will become even more apparent in the following chapter.

Because unification and unemployment have continued to be the dominating political concerns since the early 1990s, state regulation of workplaces has been an even harder sell. The 1994 Employee Protection Law was created through the consensus between parties under the CDU/CSU/FDP ruling party coalition. Not surprisingly, employers' concerns had a stronger impact than those of workers, represented through the unions, or concerns of women, represented through gender equality offices. By contrast, in 2005, the government was obliged to comply with the binding EU law, which promised to finally bring into German labor law the EU victim-centered definition of sexual harassment as sex discrimination, including more meaningful implementation and enforcement mechanisms. Without the EU as a catalyst for sexual harassment laws and for promoting gender equality in the workplace in general, there would be no hope for an effective German anti-discrimination law in the early twenty-first century. At the time of writing, however, the bill is held up in the arbitration commission. With the coalition government of CDU/CSU and SPD under the leadership of Chancellor Angela Merkel after the election in September 2005, the future of the bill is uncertain.

5   "Good behavior versus mobbing": employer
     practices in Germany and the United States[1]

Because my study of German employer practices has been discussed on
the internet, I received emails from several American women in Germany who experienced sexual harassment on the job there and sought
my advice because they did not know where else to turn. One woman
was shocked when she found male colleagues (including her supervisor)
surfing pornographic websites together. She had experience working in
male-dominated environments, but she quickly became aware of different
cultural norms of acceptable and unacceptable behaviors even in male-
dominated organizations.

Not only American women but anyone working in a German business
would be unlikely to know their rights and where to turn. This is because
even though sexual harassment is now illegal in Germany, as in most
other European Union countries, employers have taken little action
against it. The politics of sexual harassment is *politics as usual* in
Germany. Women have not used the law to hold employers or harassers
responsible in court. Public-sector employers have gender equality officers, and the problem falls into their area, but most private-sector
employers do not. Some public employers and a very few private ones
have adopted broader, union-negotiated, general anti-mobbing policies
that include sexual harassment. In larger workplaces works councils can
act on behalf of employees in workplace conflicts. There are, however,
no state offices to file complaints and few services specifically for victims,
though an industry for victims of mobbing has emerged, including
hotlines, attorneys, coaches, and psychologists, as well as consultants
for employers and unions. This situation has led to little awareness
around sexual harassment and victims remain stigmatized, while it is
easier to be recognized as a victim of mobbing.

By contrast, the politics of sexual harassment in the United States
creates *politics of fear*. Employers are told to fear expensive lawsuits by

[1] Some ideas in this chapter have been published previously in *Policy Studies Review*
(Zippel 2003).

women, and men are told to protect themselves against allegations, leaving a lurking concern that any word or sidestep can lead to unemployment or even the court room. Many employers have adopted zero-tolerance policies and internal complaint procedures, and an industry for victims and employers has emerged including consultants, attorneys, and women's organizations.

The first question this chapter asks is what explains the difference in the dynamics of implementation of sexual harassment laws in the United States and Germany. In particular, why have employers responded to different degrees with workplace policies, procedures, and prevention efforts? The short answer is that the United States and Germany have embarked on very different institutional pathways to implement and enforce the laws. Implementation is a *political process* in which employers translate laws into organizational practices. A second important question is what difference these trajectories make in the workplace. How do employers address, construct, and talk about sexual harassment? This chapter examines the intended and unintended consequences of these policies regarding improving the situation of victims, empowering women, and changing gender cultures at work.

The US legal–regulatory route has been more effective in employer compliance, but it fundamentally relies on individuals to complain to their employers, and if employers do not act, to complain to state EEOC offices and to go to court if necessary. The German statutory–corporatist route has led to fewer anti-harassment programs; the issue is addressed as a collective one rather than as a problem of individuals. Neither outcome has satisfied feminist goals because both have turned a radical feminist issue into a gender-neutral problem – "bad behavior" in the United States and "mobbing" in Germany. While US employees are being sent to "charm school," German employees learn about sexual harassment (if at all) as part of general violations of workers' dignity.

There is an important difference though. Germans continue to value flirtation at work and German employers avoid discussing the potential problems of (consensual) intimate relationships at work. By contrast, some US employers explicitly discourage or prohibit *any* sexual relationships, even consensual, between supervisors and subordinates or among coworkers, justifying these measures as preventing sexual harassment. Underlying these difficult, complex issues are the inherent contradictions in feminist calls to protect women from violence by men and to empower women to sexual self-determination.

The underlying dynamics and routes for implementation and enforcement shape the politics of sexual harassment in the workplace profoundly. Different sets of actors are in charge of interpreting laws and translating them into practice. US human resource personnel, more specifically equal employment opportunity or affirmative action offices, have the responsibility to implement Title VII of the Civil Rights Act of 1964, and therefore apply general anti-discrimination laws; these offices have become the main organizational units for sexual harassment. German human resource personnel, together with works councils, have shaped policy approaches by collective agreements, resulting in broad, non-gender-specific anti-mobbing policies that subsume sexual harassment as a violation of workers' dignity. Even public-sector gender equality offices ostensibly created for gender-specific issues include sexual harassment in broader training programs against mobbing.

In both countries the basic idea is that complaints should be handled in the workplace, with the courts as the last resort; yet, the driving force of the implementation process varies greatly. The US legal–regulatory route means that the EEOC and courts have a central place. They can pressure employers to comply with the laws, provide "guidance" to employers on how to interpret and comply with the laws, and courts can sanction noncompliant employers more severely than German labor courts can. US sexual harassment politics are unique because they built on and expanded the institutional litigation/legal infrastructure of civil rights law. At the core is the basic idea of legal enforcement – individuals will claim their civil rights through individual legal redress. US employers then share the belief that they need to take at least symbolic steps to combat sexual harassment in the workplace to prevent expensive lawsuits, even though the risks are exaggerated, since million-dollar damage awards are rare.

By contrast, the German implementation process is merely driven by the political will of employers and unions, instead of legal enforcement or state regulation. In the statutory–corporatist path to implement sexual harassment law, German labor courts and state agencies play a more limited role; neither state agencies nor labor courts have been active in enforcement and implementation of laws, leaving individual employers and unions to negotiate policies and prevention measures. Employers and unions are expected to handle workplace issues with minimal state intervention, for example no state agency equivalent to the EEOC exists so far. Not surprisingly, few employers have taken action.

Instead, the German system of social insurance, presumably carried by all employees and employers based on the principle of solidarity, covers the financial risks of sexual harassment victims. Health and unemployment insurance, financed by employers' and employees' contributions, is expected to cover (mental) health-related costs as well as the loss of a job. This collective solution of distributing the costs among all employees and employers has an important drawback: it does not help victims hold employers or perpetrators responsible, nor does it get to the problem of sexual harassment itself.

Both routes for implementation and enforcement are influenced by legal mandates and industrial relations constraining the role of feminists in these processes. Some innovative employers adopted measures before laws required them to do so, which points to the agency of individual complainants and informal women's groups within organizations, who brought the issue onto the agenda of employers. In both countries, feminist advocates initiated employers' responses, but there is no official role for informal or formal women's organizations in implementation and enforcement in either country. Even in the German public sector, where gender equality offices existed, these offices had little to do with the negotiations between works councils/unions and employers. Hence, gender relations have shaped processes in both countries, as feminists and those representing victims' interests were shut out of the formal process of policy design.

Feminists have had to find different sets of allies in these two different routes. While US women's main allies were the human resource management, EEOC office, and courts, in Germany sexual harassment advocates primarily worked with unions and works councils. Finally, these different routes for implementation have trade-offs for employer responses to sexual harassment and for pursuing gender equality and changes in workplace culture more generally. Before discussing the advantages and disadvantages of these routes, this chapter compares the legal mandates, paths for change within organizations, and dynamic processes of implementation and enforcement.

Workplace policies and awareness programs

Along several dimensions, US employers have become more cautious than German ones about workplace sexual harassment and thus have taken more extensive measures to combat it. Many US employers covered by the Civil Rights Act of 1964[2] or by state-level fair employment laws followed case law developments and adopted policy approaches that emphasize individual rights and internal redress, defining sexual harassment as sex discrimination. A new employee on the first day of work is likely to receive a copy of the company's policy on sexual harassment. The policy may also be publicized via brochures or newslet-

---

[2] That is, with more than fifty employees or any government contracts.

ters, bulletin boards, or the internet. Employers may, for example, inform employees that surfing pornographic websites is against policy. Supervisors or colleagues may recommend leaving doors open, especially during meetings between men and women. Employers with policies that discourage or prohibit consensual relationships will warn employees accordingly.

Less frequently, employees are required to participate in a training program organized by the EEO office. The instructor may be a human resource professional, attorney, or legal consultant. The training will familiarize employees with sexual harassment law, company rules about what is considered sexual harassment, the rights of victims, and the responsibilities of supervisors. The information will include where within the company complaints can be filed, what the complaint procedures are, and what sanctions can be imposed on perpetrators. Group-based approaches of team-building and general sensitivity training programs are the exception, however.

By contrast, German employers have by and large ignored the 1994 *Bundesbeschäftigtenschutzgesetz* (Federal Employee Protection Law), and employees most likely have never heard from their employer about their legal rights regarding sexual harassment (Pflüger and Baer 2005).[3] Both employers and unions have redefined sexual harassment as an issue of mobbing, and use an underlying group-based, collective orientation to training and broader awareness. Very large corporations and public-sector employers have responded to some degree to the 1994 law. These employers together with works councils have adopted *Betriebsvereinbarungen* (collective agreements) that subsume sexual harassment as an unfair workplace practice alongside non-gender-specific discrimination and mobbing. The employee will have to look through the anti-mobbing policies for a definition of sexual harassment.

It is very unlikely that the employee will participate in an information seminar. By law, public (but not private) employers are required to conduct training, but actually doing so is the exception. The sporadic training efforts that do exist are voluntary, usually group-oriented, focusing on mobbing with perhaps a few comments about sexual harassment. The trainer is most likely a "coach," a self-employed consultant with a pedagogical or social work background, or a gender equality

---

[3] Almut Pflüger and Susanne Baer (2005) find that there is a significant implementation deficit of the 1994 law. In a comprehensive study, commissioned by the Ministry of Women and completed in 2002 but released only in February 2005, they surveyed 1,000 employers and the jurisprudence of the labor courts since 1994, including interviews with judges, lawyers, and unions.

officer. The program will focus on awareness around group dynamics, psychological health, and social rather than legal aspects of mobbing. In rare cases, gender equality advocates have initiated assertiveness programs for women, especially in the public sector. Unions may offer training programs on mobbing for shop stewards, but mandatory programs on sexual harassment for supervisors do not exist.

The main difference in workers' representation is that only the US public sector has a significant degree of unionization. In the United States in the 1990s only around 14 percent of wage and salaried workers were members of unions – less than 10 percent of private-sector employees but 38 percent of public-sector employees, the latter similar to the overall German rate of 35 percent. Women make up 30–40 percent of union membership in both countries (US Department of Labor Bureau of Labor statistics 2000, Statistisches Bundesamt 1998). Rates of unionization have declined in Germany, but the system of works councils, based on the legal right of worker representation, is firmly institutionalized. Employers with fifty or more employees must comply with the *Betriebsverfassungsgesetz* (BetrVG), the law that constitutes workplace regulations, to allow the establishment of *Betriebsräte* (works councils), empowered to represent workers' interests on the company level. Works councils have a say in personnel decisions and by law may challenge unfair dismissals. Similar to these works councils in the private sector, there are *Personalräte* (employees' representatives) in the public sector. But fewer than one quarter of elected worker representatives are women (BMFSFJ 1998: 142). In both countries, scandals and lawsuits involving male perpetrators who were shop stewards or union officers have drawn attention to the fact that sexual harassment is a pervasive problem in any male-dominated organization, even those that supposedly represent all employees' interests.

The innovators – in pursuit of gender equality

In both countries, within workplace organizations activism around sexual harassment emerged. Because of the countries' different paths for change, however, activists' (discursive) strategies and their supporters varied. Most importantly feminists were successful with different frames, because of preexisting laws and different institutional structures they encountered. As we will see, they would find different allies in their struggle against sexual harassment.

In some pioneering organizations in both countries, management took action before the (case) law required them to do so. The first innovative US employers adopted internal policies and grievance procedures in the late 1970s (Baker 2001: 334). These were usually public-sector employers and cities, universities, and colleges, not private employers (Edelman 1992). A survey of the federal Office of Personnel Management revealed that most federal offices had adopted policy statements before the 1980 EEOC guidelines (sixty-two of seventy-three; see Baker 2001: 334).

Similarly, though ten years later, some German public employers and companies took measures against sexual harassment before federal laws were passed. The first awareness programs against sexual harassment in the workplace, organized by gender advocates, took place in the late 1980s, in Cologne and Berlin, for example. In a few cities, such as Stuttgart in 1991, the mayor issued a regulation against sexual harassment (*Dienstanweisung*), and a few companies followed.

Feminists were key actors in initiating these organizational changes in both countries. Informal female employee groups included union members and sometimes progressive administrators or human resource management staff. In universities and colleges, staff from women students' offices and rape/sexual assault centers, and sometimes faculty joined networks and demanded that employers take steps against harassment.

Employers in both the United States and Germany needed to be convinced that the problem existed and they were responsible for it. The resistance of many employers manifested itself in a manner similar to that in the legal and political realm – laughter, ridicule, and disbelief. The most common response was that sexual harassment was not a problem, or that if it was, it did not exist in this workplace or company. Other responses included trivializing the impact on victims, blaming victims, or considering sexual harassment unfortunate but merely private behavior between individuals for which employers should not be responsible.

With no laws that explicitly prohibited sexual harassment, feminist actors had to find arguments to overcome traditional views. Individual cases of women who had experienced sexual harassment were powerful in several ways. Breaking a taboo by naming the problem can turn the shame of the victim into the embarrassment of the perpetrator or institution. Individual women who had sought help mobilized informal women's groups in workplaces. Outrage usually grew, not only over the fact that sexual harassment took place in their own workplace but over how the situation was mishandled by the administration. Often supervisors either did not act at all or retaliated against the women as whistle-blowers. Individual cases might be interpreted ambiguously by women as well as men, but these situations nevertheless had the potential to create solidarity among women and their allies. Some institutional activists used these cases strategically to create awareness in the leadership and to demand action beyond solutions to specific situations. Individual incidents helped draw attention to the pervasiveness of the problem, refuting the argument that sexual harassment either did not exist at all or did not exist in this organization. These cases also illustrated institutions' failure to resolve the problem.

Because these women's groups usually did not have a formal position in workplace organizations, they worked informally through talks behind closed doors or in hallways. They also held meetings for women employees and conducted surveys to document how widespread the problem was (Maenz 1994). They could not use legal pressure; their strength came through the potential embarrassment for the employer of going public with the accusations, for example by getting local newspapers involved. Employers, concerned with reputation, were eager to appease these activists (Hawkesworth 1997; Katzenstein 1998).

In Germany, this mobilization of women in workplaces against sexual harassment coincided with the creation of gender equality offices in the public sector and a few large corporations. The first offices for women were created in the late 1970s in progressive city states and *Länder*, and were in place in most states by the early 1990s (Ferree 1995a; von Wahl 1999). The 1994 Federal Second Gender Equality Law mandated for public-sector employers only the establishment of these offices. In several progressive states these advocates are elected by all women employees; in others they are appointed by the administration's leadership. Their resources and powers vary greatly between the states. It is important to note that, in contrast to the United States, neither private nor public employers have offices for general anti-discrimination or "diversity" efforts, in part because Germany has lacked an effective anti-discrimination law. Public-sector employers might have separate advocates for foreigners, but these German offices for gender equality were created primarily for positive action for women, not for minority men.

These offices of femocrats – institutionalized feminism – became central actors for a number of reasons. First, some of these advocates decided to take on the issue to raise their own profiles. Their job description was often vague, which allowed them to come up with their own agenda. The issue of sexual harassment brought high visibility because of controversies around it – one employee called it a *heisses Eisen* (hot potato). Other measures of *Frauenförderung* (positive actions for women), such as child care, equality of part-time workers, and parental leave policies, were difficult to handle, especially for small, often underfinanced, understaffed offices. Sexual harassment allowed these advocates to adopt a feminist, radical agenda and establish their office. They could promote more substantive changes than, say, creating women's parking spaces, despite not being powerful enough to change pay scales.

Second, some of these offices used the issue strategically to reach constituencies of women in and outside city/town administration. Internally, these advocates brought together informal women's working groups as across-hierarchy networks that could establish an alternative path of communication to the established works councils. The issue served an important goal of gender equality advocates: to create local networks among state administrators, union women, and women in the anti-violence movement.

Finally, gender equality offices were perceived by both women and men as responsible for handling sexual harassment complaints. These newly created offices, not the works councils, have been the obvious preferred units to provide support for complainants. In the federal ministries, only 12 percent of complaints were filed with works councils and 27 percent with personnel offices; almost two-thirds were filed with women's equality offices (BMFSFJ 2000).[4] When the US debates on sexual correctness reached Germany in the early 1990s, these offices had to take a position not just about their role vis-à-vis sexual harassment but about the kinds of measures they would take. One advocate remembers: "Men who had wondered all along what our job was, now thought they had found the answer: we were going to be the protector of moral standards." This dynamic of bureaucratic, administrative EEO/AA offices to expand their institutional capacity has been well documented in the US case, both within state institutions and in the workplace (Edelman 1992, 2004; Pedriana and Stryker 2004; Dobbin 1998).

Because the issue was "new," employers on both sides of the Atlantic needed expertise. They frequently hired outside consultants to help design workplace policies and procedures as well as awareness programs. The first sexual harassment experts were mostly feminist-identified women, and expertise generated by women was without competition in the professional field. A German legal expert put it: "We women own the issue" (Degen 1999). Many US experts were activists who made a career as consultants, including Susan Webb, Mary Langelan, Freada Klein, and members of feminist organizations such as the Alliance Against Sexual Coercion, 9 to 5, and Working Women United Institute. In Germany, where feminist groups did not address the issue, a very small group of consultants were called on by word of mouth. Some consultants, including Dr. Barbara Degen and Ute Wellner, were legal experts; others,

---

[4] See also Almut Pflüger and Susanne Baer (2005) for similar findings.

such as Heike Maenz, Bärbel Meschkutat, or Dr. Sibylle Plogstedt, a sociologist known for her publications, had social work, psychology, or sociological training. They drew on US and EU publications, but they also created a nationally based network of sexual harassment experts.

Much of the expertise came through the unions, as some women began to specialize in sexual harassment and give advice to individual members or local unions. Finally, a few offices specifically created to combat sexual harassment became centers for information, for example the German *Arbeitsstelle gegen sexuelle Diskriminierung und Gewalt am Ausbildungs- und Erwerbsarbeitsplatz* (office against sexual discrimination and violence in vocational training and the workplace) in Bremen.

Gender-specific discourses

The arguments these experts used to convince employers to adopt measures were strongly influenced by feminist discourses. The dominant feminist perspectives, fairly similar in Germany and the United States, defined it as a gender-specific issue, rooted in gender inequality, which means not only that sexual harassment is a women's issue but that women are harassed because they are women. On both sides of the Atlantic feminists with roots in the anti-violence movement defined sexual harassment as an abuse of power and sexual exploitation of women (Farley 1978; MacKinnon 1979; Backhouse and Cohen 1981: 36ff, see German definitions; Plogstedt and Degen 1992: 17; Sadrozinski ed. 1993: 32ff).

Yet, despite a common frame of violence, different feminist frames became dominant in US and German workplace organizations because of the different gender politics in institutional arrangements. In the absence of strong anti-discrimination laws as a discursive opportunity structure, German gender equality advocates referred to sexual harassment in the workplace primarily as an issue of sexual self-determination, closely linked to the violence against women frame. For example, policies explicitly prohibited "sexualized violence," while brochures and manuals referred exclusively to sexual harassment that happens to women by men. In Mannheim, an early German city policy exclusively protects female, not male, victims in the context of *Frauenförderung* (affirmative action for women).

German feminists have drawn on the constitutionally guaranteed freedoms of the person, including the right of sexual self-determination, and implicitly use the constitutional right to dignity. Sexual harassment is thus defined as violation of boundaries, which resonates with women's experience of intrusiveness, shame, and personal insult. This notion allows a range of behavior and situations to be covered. Several West German interviewees defined sexual harassment most broadly as

"Everything which oversteps the boundaries which women set."

"Every form of violation of boundaries in personal contact through words, touches, or creation of the environment through sexualized communication and interaction."

"Every behavior, verbal or physical, which is unwanted by a person, and where the personal boundary is transgressed."

"Everything that violates the personal space, for example also calendars and pictures of naked persons."

In contrast to these definitions that include verbal as well as physical forms of harassment, an East German woman preferred a narrower definition: "In my personal definition I don't go as far as posters, verbal forms, or phone calls. I understand only physical assault, everything else we can handle. I do not want to build up hysteria." By drawing on a more narrow definition of sexual harassment as physical violence, this advocate used a more limited definition than the German law of 1994.

By contrast, US advocates drew the strategic parallel to race discrimination, based on legal discourse on sex discrimination as their discursive opportunity structure. The legal–regulatory route for change enabled feminists here to mobilize not only civil rights laws but also the infrastructure of implementation within organizations. Sex discrimination soon became the dominant frame to define sexual harassment in both policy discourse and workplaces (Cahill 2001; Saguy 2003; Bernstein 1994; Marshall 2001; Baker 2001). Feminists already in the early phase, for example Working Women United Institute, Alliance Against Sexual Coercion, and 9 to 5, clearly drew on the legal frame of the 1964 Civil Rights Act. Sexual harassment defined as the violation of individual rights to equal treatment resonates with cultural understanding of equality as sameness: the solution to sexual harassment is to treat women the same as men.

This frame also resonated quickly with employers because of the twofold parallel to hostile environments for blacks. First, women should no longer be segregated, for example excluded from male-dominated jobs, and should be treated the same as men (not being harassed). Second, they should have the same working conditions, which means that supervisors cannot impose sexual demands on women if they do not do so on men. Of course this rationale assumes that men treat each other fairly and equally and that employees conform to heterosexual norms in workplaces, two assumptions that have limited the applicability of the sex-discrimination frame.

Because of the Civil Rights Act orientation toward "market" metaphors, the implied goal is to create a fair chance for every individual to compete for jobs, promotion, and so on. In this view sexual harassment is "wrong" because it creates unequal working conditions for those who are harassed. For example, if a supervisor demands sexual favors from a subordinate, this subordinate is evaluated under a different standard than other subordinates.

The injustice frames of sexual harassment as sex discrimination (United States) and as violation of women's self-determination (Germany) have an important similarity: they contextualize sexual harassment as a gendered issue so that it can be addressed as a problem of gender inequality and abuse of power. Similar to arguments and discourses about sexual assault and rape in both the US and German antiviolence movements, this move also shifted attention to issues previously considered "private." Instead of blaming individual women for being harassed, the frames help direct the view onto the perpetrators and onto a whole range of "causes" for sexual harassment, including cultural, social, institutional, and organizational factors.

This gendered frame of sexual harassment then allowed feminists to point out that not only is the gender of the harasser and harassed significant but also that of those involved in handling complaints. Harassed women prefer to confide in women and within organizations certain offices also carry gendered meanings – offices can have a reputation of being women-friendly or hostile toward women. Hence, feminists in Germany argued, for example, that women would not turn to works councils because of their reputation of representing men's but not women's interests (gender equality officers, interviews, 1999).

Both frames resonated with existing laws and focused on holding employers accountable for allowing harassment to happen in the workplace. German employers could be held to their duty to guarantee constitutional laws about personal freedoms in the workplace, while Title VII made US employers liable for equal treatment. This US notion of equality came out of the legal system and civil rights litigation. Feminists in the United States could tie sexual harassment to a comparatively stronger legal framework of anti-discrimination. By contrast, the respective German concept of "employee protection" has lacked implementation and enforcement mechanisms, because of assumptions of the statutory–corporatist route for change.

In practice, framing sexual harassment as sex discrimination meant that in the United States, the EEO/AA offices became the obvious agents to take on the issue, whereas the German corporatist route presumes that works councils and human resource management together handle sexual harassment. With the establishment of (public-sector) gender equality offices in Germany, however, new institutionalized actors have come onto the terrain of workplace regulations, and as we will see, not only women have perceived these offices as the obvious ones to handle these issues. Yet, without a legal mandate, only a few private-sector employers have established these offices, leaving the issue to works councils and human resource management.

The two frames imply different solutions to sexual harassment, however, because they imply different notions of gender equality. In the United States women should receive the same treatment as men; in Germany women should be treated with respect and men should be prevented from overstepping women's boundaries. The discrimination frame in its simplest interpretation requires just that women be treated the same as men. The violation of dignity and sexual self-determination frame, however, implies the empowerment of women to choose whether to enter into personal and sexual relations with men in the workplace.

Feminists believed that creating awareness was crucial to any improvement of the situation. Feminist notions were centered on empowering women to stand up and confront sexual harassers. With awareness training the hope also was to change traditional views of employers, managers, and others in supervisory positions so they would stop ignoring the problem or blaming victims and instead take preventive action. Some employers were responsive to the notion that awareness was crucial to stop harassment and help women affected by it. American outside consultants and German gender advocates began training programs that were surprisingly "feminist" in their orientation and content. For example, in both countries the first government and union training manuals, which would serve as models for others, strongly reflected the feminist conceptualization of sexual harassment as a form of violence against women and abuse of gender and hierarchical power. They also suggested readings of feminist writers and scholars (Baker 2001: 336; Sadrozinski 1991). Several early programs were women-only seminars structured around feminist principles of empowerment and using consciousness raising and assertiveness training (Meschkutat et al. 1993; Meschkutat, interview, 2003). Some trainers also conducted programs for leadership in which they explained the responsibility of supervisors to prevent harassment by setting new norms of behavior (Wellner, interview, 1999; Maenz, interview, 1999; Degen, interview, 1999).

These pioneering workplace organizations adopted measures as a reaction to feminist outcries over the ways organizations had previously dealt with complaints. Feminist discourse was the only alternative to traditional views. Feminists together with employers developed a range of innovative measures, focusing on creating awareness within organizations and experimenting with new procedures to ensure that complaints would be taken seriously. Some of these became standards that US courts have enforced, including internal grievance procedures. Informal women's groups have continued an important role in initiating and, as we will see later, revising policies, and have developed a watchdog function, holding employers accountable for implementing rules. By contrast, the isolated German initiatives to combat sexual harassment did not become "mainstream," because neither state offices nor the legal system pushed for the implementation of the law against sexual harassment.

Impact of the law on implementation

Even with the Federal Employee Protection Law of 1994, the German statutory–corporatist route to address sexual harassment has led to private employers' non-responsiveness, and German practices have remained "politics as usual," ignoring both harassment and legal obligations and responsibilities. By contrast, the US dynamics of the legal–regulatory route have created a "politics of fear" around sexual harassment. The 1986 US Supreme Court decision in *Meritor Savings Bank v. Vinson* and case law on sexual harassment more generally speaking, as well as the nationwide debates around the high-profile cases such as the senate hearings of Anita Hill and Clarence Thomas, spurred several waves of policy implementation, revisions, and refinements. Consultants and attorneys advised companies to take sexual harassment seriously, and most US employers covered by the Civil Rights Act had adopted some measures by the late 1990s.

By contrast, the law has had little effect on German employer practice. Few employers have adopted policies and educational programs. Even the early innovators have not developed serious, continuous efforts to educate employees about harassment. Despite the fact that the 1994 law requires public-sector employers to have programs in place, in 1999 many training and awareness programs had already ceased to exist. I was told by several interviewees that seminars were no longer offered because of lack of employee interest. The 1994 law gave increased impetus to introduce or update information on the issue, but in the late 1990s these educational and awareness efforts dwindled.

One explanation is that participation in training programs is not mandatory. According to public officials I interviewed, "interest" in the seminars was not very high and few participants turned up. The problem is obvious. If prevention efforts are based on voluntary partici-pation, and the "interest" of participants determines the frequency with which seminars are held, it is not surprising that efforts have fallen short. Furthermore, those who would need the training most because of their ignorance of sexual harassment are unlikely to participate voluntarily.

Moreover, the voluntary nature of these workshops provides hurdles for women to get information on sexual harassment. In order to sign up, women may have to get permission from their supervisors, a difficult action if they have been harassed by the supervisor. Ridicule and stigma can discourage women from participation. Therefore, organizers instead offer women's or mobbing seminars, which are far less stigmatized.

Despite the difference in employers' responses in the two countries, however, there is an interesting similarity in how sexual harassment has been discussed. In both countries in workplace organizations, sexual harassment has been transformed from a radical feminist issue into a mainstream one. The legal developments gave activists a strong original stance by giving legitimacy to demands that employers take action, but in neither country are feminists any longer key players, because the institutionalization process has brought other actors onto the scene. Feminist notions, expertise, and discourse have increasingly been replaced with an emerging professionalized human resource discourse that focuses on ethically "good," appropriate behavior in the United States and local union and works council language about mobbing in Germany. Both discourses are gender neutral, as we will see.

Legal requirements for employers, or what does compliance mean?

Why have more US than German employers responded to sexual harassment? Employers operate in different institutional contexts and therefore interpret legal mandates differently. US employers certainly carry higher financial risks for noncompliance than German employers do, because potential sanctions are much higher than in Germany. These risks, however, also do not exist out of the institutional context of enforcement agencies. In line with the legal–regulatory route, US courts and state institutions have actively worked to force employers to comply. US employers today operate in a legal environment, a concept Edelman uses (1992), in which they share the belief that they need to take at least symbolic steps to combat sexual harassment in the workplace to prevent expensive lawsuits, though consultants seem to have built this mentality of risk prevention by exaggerating the legal threat (Dobbin and Kelly 2004).

In line with the German statutory–corporatist route, neither German state agencies nor labor courts have been active in enforcement and implementation of sexual harassment laws. Policy-makers decided that there should be no meaningful sanctions for employers for noncompliance with the 1994 Employee Protection Law, for example there are no punitive damages for employers. This means that the driving force in the German implementation process is political will of individual employers and unions to negotiate policies and prevention measures.

The legal context for employers' actions is determined by the requirements of laws and other workplace regulations. In both countries employers are required to take measures against sexual harassment, but the laws have left much leeway to employers to figure out how to protect employees' dignity in Germany, and to protect them from being discriminated against in the United States. In both countries the basic idea is that sexual harassment complaints should be handled in the workplace, with the courts being the last resort. But there are some important differences regarding how employers can be held legally accountable, especially regarding assumptions about the dynamics and process with which sexual harassment laws will be implemented.

The behaviors German and US employers are supposed to be concerned about are generally similar. Sexual harassment according to the US definition is any "unwanted attention of a sexual nature." The 1994 German law prohibits "sexually motivated behavior that intentionally violates the dignity of a person." The US notion is stronger because it takes the subjective perspective of women who experience "unwanted" attention; the German law emphasizes the perpetrator's perspective because only "recognizably rejected" behavior constitutes harassment. This is an important difference, but less crucial for workplace organizations than in the courts. Many employers have used broader definitions of sexual harassment in their policies beyond the legal definitions. For example, the German automobile company Volkswagen uses a subjective definition of what constitutes sexual harassment, while US workplace policies have used an inclusive standard of conduct of a sexual nature that makes an employee uncomfortable.

The 1964 Civil Rights Act did not explicitly define how employers should comply with the laws; in fact, it left a great deal of ambiguity (Edelman, Uggen, and Erlanger 1999; Dobbin and Kelly 2004; Kelly and Dobbin 1998; Edelman 1992; Dobbin and Sutton 1998). This meant that not lawmakers but the EEOC and the courts have defined employers' responsibilities. In the workplace, human resource managers and legal consultants have interpreted case law and EEOC guidelines. The EEOC 1980 guidelines clearly put responsibility with employers:

(f) Prevention is the best tool for the elimination of sexual harassment. An employer should take all steps necessary to prevent sexual harassment from occurring, such as affirmatively raising the subject, expressing strong disapproval, developing appropriate sanctions, informing employees of their right to raise and how to raise the issue of harassment under Title VII, and developing methods to sensitize all concerned. (1980, § 1604.11)

Because of the case law system, the enforcement mechanism works through the courts, and lawyers and human resource managers advise employers on how to take action. Following the 1986 Supreme Court *Meritor v. Savings Bank* decision, more employers adopted policy statements and training programs. As Dobbin and Kelly (2005) point out, human resource managers diffused this model of compliance by making two arguments: on the one hand, they tried to convince public employers to adopt policies with the argument that they should improve working conditions for their women employees; on the other hand, they made cost-benefit arguments to private-sector employers, telling these employers that they needed to adopt measures to shield themselves from lawsuits.

Following this line of argument, employers have implemented the laws in order to minimize the risk of (legal) costs associated with suits by employees. The EEOC (1990) elaborated further on these preventive measures and added that employers should have policies and internal grievance procedures, and should train employees regarding their rights and procedures.

Court judgments have taken individual cases as the basis for setting standards. This individual–liberal model is based on individuals' right to complain and to challenge in court employers who do not take adequate action. In practice this means that employers have designed internal complaint procedures. Civil rights legislation has transformed workplaces into quasi-legal organizations where employers hold court (Edelman and Suchmann 1999). In the process of policy creation or revision policies, the leading guides are lawyers.

By the end of the 1990s, most employers covered by the Civil Rights Act had refined and enhanced their policies, especially following the increased awareness brought about by high-profile cases. Only in 1998 did the Supreme Court decide that employers could limit their liability by having a policy and internal grievance procedures in place. The Supreme Court developed this concept of "affirmative defense" in *Faragher v. City of Boca Raton* and *Burlington Industries Inc. v. Ellerth*.[5] These decisions have given employers clear incentives to implement policies and procedures, because employers can use their preventive efforts to limit their liability. These decisions have now not only established a

---

[5] 111F. 3d 1530 (1998); 123F.3d 490 (1998).

standard for all employers, placing even more emphasis on in-house procedures, but gone a step farther. The courts now expect victims to use the procedures, which some have argued can be disadvantageous for victims. Martha Chamallas (2004) argues: "In practice, the affirmative defense has proven to be of great value to employers, often resulting in defense victories on summary judgment. In many cases, employers are able to assert the affirmative defense and defeat the claims of employees who have been subjected to even the most severe forms of harassment, largely because those employees have failed to pursue formal complaints through their employers' internal grievance procedures." (309)

German law does not require employers to issue policy statements against sexual harassment, but the lawmakers were surprisingly more explicit than US lawmakers about requiring employers to designate an office responsible for sexual harassment – most often personnel management, human resources, or gender equality. The German law does not specify the procedures with which employers should handle sexual harassment complaints, given that general grievance procedures exist with the German system of works councils in any organizations over fifty employees. Since the 2000 Public Sector Gender Equality Law, gender equality officers have been designated to be involved in sexual harassment complaints, but their powers are left to be defined by the workplaces. For the public sector only, the 1994 Employee Protection Law obliges public-sector employers to conduct training programs. Yet, there are no meaningful fines or sanctions that a state agency or courts can impose on employers if the employers do not comply with these laws. Given this weakness in the law, not surprisingly few women victims have taken their employers to labor courts.

In both countries, activist feminists have used the laws strategically, demanding task forces or working groups to formulate policies and programs. Because of the nature of the phenomenon of sexual harassment the struggles in workplace organizations have mostly occurred at this discursive level, so sexual harassment law strengthened their case. The German law also strengthened feminist demands that employers take action. Because management frequently learned about the law first from women's advocates and women's groups, these groups contributed to the law's translation and interpretation into the context of their workplace. Some activists turned employers' ignorance into an advantage and bolstered their case by purposely exaggerating employers' legal responsibilities. A German woman's advocate (1999) states: "They [the employers] didn't know about the law, we told them. We told them that they are responsible and that the law required them to take action." In the United States, even within universities, which have frequently had active informal women's groups, compliance and legal threat arguments were more convincing than calls for the equality of women and men (Zippel 1994). Hawksworth (1997) observes that university administrators were ultimately more convinced by arguments of legal liability than by arguments about the necessity to improve women's equality in the workplace. Feminists used the fact that sexual harassment was prohibited by law to legitimate their demands for employers to take action. Any law, even one lacking teeth, carries symbolic value and helps legitimate sexual harassment as a serious issue that requires employers' attention. As Mary F. Katzenstein (1998), who studied US women in the military and the Catholic Church, puts it: "It's one thing to complain about sex discrimination – it is another to complain because it is illegal" (5).

Enforcement by state agencies and the courts

A more traditional policy analysis needs to examine how laws are enforced, not just how they are used for mobilization. What sanctions do employers fear if they do not comply? What happens if a German public employer does not conduct awareness programs or a US employer fails to communicate policy to employees? Who holds employers accountable for measures against sexual harassment?

In both cases, only judges can impose sanctions on employers. But the possibilities of and focus on individual legal redress are greater in the United States than in Germany. Using the implementation and enforcement infrastructure of the Civil Rights Act, victims can file an individual complaint with the EEOC and state agencies about the harasser, supervisor, or employer, holding them responsible for the harassment endured.

German official agencies have few monitoring and enforcement tools. In the German system of statutory–corporatist route, there is no equivalent to the EEOC. Unlike the United States, Germany has no history of civil rights litigation and with no effective anti-discrimination law in place, no governmental agency is there to enforce gender equality laws. Most importantly, government offices have no powers to pursue or investigate individual victims' reports against private employers. The public gender equality offices, though they implement gender equality and sexual harassment laws, have little power to investigate individual reports and none to impose sanctions.

However, these gender equality offices have an important potential to be resource centers and generate expertise; for example, the Federal Ministry of Women has commissioned several studies and informational brochures on sexual harassment (see Degen 2002; Holzbecher et al.

1990; Pflüger and Baer 2005). The Federal office in practice provides referrals to experts, and consults victims, unions, and employers. But this ministry merely recommends that employers adopt policies and training programs – it cannot force them to do so. The only recourse outside the workplace in Germany is the courts, not state agencies or the EEOC as an intermediate step. This interpretation of a minimalist state so far has been in line with the corporatist route: the state trusts employers and unions to enact workplace regulation, and creates, thereby, in fact a more cozy climate for employers in which they can ignore laws. This is in contrast to the US liberal welfare state which has increased its enforcement powers and with the EEOC and the courts is more interventionist, holding employers liable.

Hence, the dynamics of implementing and enforcing policies vary greatly between the two countries. While German government agencies have taken no initiative to enforce the law, US EEO agencies have taken a more active role (Pedriana and Stryker 2004; Kelly and Dobbin 1998; Edelman 1992). But the US dynamic relies mostly on individual challenges to employers in the courts, and so brings victims into the center (Mink 2000). These different dynamics both constrain and shape the roles for individuals, activists, employers, and unions to carry the burden of sexual harassment and/or to participate in effecting social change.

Employers in both countries certainly try to avoid lawsuits because they cause embarrassment, create negative publicity, and damage the company's reputation. But US employers have more incentives than German ones to comply at least symbolically with the laws. This is because the financial risks involved in court settlements and awards are very different. US courts have played a major role in enforcement because individual women and some men have taken their employers to court. The US legal system allows for greater compensation and with the Civil Rights Act of 1991 for punitive damages depending on the size of employers. When courts have ruled in favor of victims they have made monetary awards and/or imposed sanctions on employers, in a few cases imposing damages in the million-dollar range. Juliano and Schwab (2001) found an average award of $80,000 in sexual harassment cases. Out of sixty-nine jury judgments that Sunstein and Shih (2004) analyzed, only four judgments included more than million-dollar punitive awards – these were rulings against AT&T (1993), Atlantic City Police Department (1996), Wal-Mart stores (1995, 1997), and Riviera Beach Associates (1994). Sunstein and Shih[6] argue that the awards in sexual

---

[6] The total average jury award was $981,292 and the median was $138,241. The range of punitive damages is especially striking: when courts awarded punitive damages the

harassment cases are not systematically excessive; they found relatively low median awards with $50,000 for compensatory and punitive damages, but rulings are inconsistent: "plaintiffs with similar injuries, and perpetrators who engage in similar acts, are treated differently" (2004: 338). While juries awarded on average slightly higher damages in *quid pro quo* cases, the Civil Rights Act of 1991 had a negative effect on the jury awards, because it caps compensatory and punitive damages (Sunstein and Shih 2004: 338).

This inconsistency makes sexual harassment cases unpredictable for all parties involved, raising also questions about fairness vis-à-vis victims and employers (Sunstein and Shih 2004). Some advocates argue that employers should not be able to foresee the potential costs attached to their non-responsiveness or mishandling of sexual harassment complaints, because if they knew the price attached, they could calculate the costs associated with allowing an alleged harasser to continue, and hence the deterrent function of the sanctions would disappear. Many judgments have included demanding training programs, so in these situations the courts have also taken an "educational" role. For example, in 1999 Ford agreed to spend $10 million on a three-year internal training and awareness program.[7]

By contrast, even when German labor courts have sided with harassed women, and in one case a man, so far there has been only insignificant financial compensation. Since the 1994 law was passed, only nine victims harassment had asked labor courts to award damages for infliction of pain (Pflüger and Baer 2005). Of these nine cases, only in three did the courts make awards against male perpetrators. In the first case, the perpetrator had to pay €500 for grabbing the woman's breast in front of a witness.[8] The second perpetrator paid €3,000 to a woman he had grabbed by the breast and between the legs.[9] In the third case, the male victim received the highest sum of €3,750 for harassment.[10]

Given the difficulty of pursuing sexual harassment lawsuits, women in Germany have few expectations about solutions the courts might bring them. Financial compensation in labor courts is no more than back pay, with a maximum of six months. Not surprisingly, few attorneys special-

---

average was $1,439,484, but the median was $63,410, which means that half of the victims received less than $63,410 (Sunstein and Shih 2004: 338–42).

[7] "EEOC and Ford Sign Multi-Million Dollar Settlement of Sexual Harassment Case." Press release, 1999, *http://www.eeoc.gov/press/9-7-99.html*

[8] ArbG Bonn, 03.02.95, 2 Ca 1136/94.

[9] LArbG Berlin, 20.11.00, 18 Sa 583/00; ArbG Berlin 10.12.99, 36 Ca 36555/98.

[10] ArbG Hamburg, 26.04.00, 6 Ca 525/99.

ize in sexual harassment cases and the number of lawsuits brought by harassed women against employers has been negligible. Since the passage of the 1994 law, only twenty-one victims had filed labor court sexual harassment lawsuits against their employers (Pflüger and Baer 2005). In rare cases of sexual assault and rape at work, judges in civil courts have awarded increasingly higher damages to victims, though the maximum was €25,000 (Goy 1996).

In fact, the overwhelming majority of sexual harassment cases in German labor courts are brought by male alleged harassers. Since 1994, eighty-five (or 77 percent) of the sexual harassment labor court judgments had been filed by alleged male perpetrators. Only twenty-one judgments on sexual harassment dealt with women who took their employer to court because of sexual harassment.[11] German laws about sanctions or dismissal are relatively strong, and these men have made use of the courts to challenge employers after having sanctions imposed on them. In a twisted way the law has been more important in helping employers impose sanctions on harassers than in helping women hold their employers responsible (Degen 1999). But this gender imbalance demonstrates the entitlement men feel about not losing their jobs over "insignificant" behavior and their expectation that judges will side with them. Basically, the gendered outcomes of the German route of statutory–corporatism are visible here: German sexual harassment laws have not served to expand victims' individual legal redress vis-à-vis employers, yet the traditional stronger laws against (unfair) dismissal continue to serve to protect the alleged perpetrators, not the victims.

In general, lawsuits are important because they can generate publicity, serve to mobilize advocates and supporters, and influence public perception. Advocates for policies against sexual harassment have used both the law and lawsuits to make a case that employers should act. They strategically exaggerated the "legal threat" of the Civil Rights Act even before courts imposed high damage awards and before the 1998 Supreme Court affirmative defense ruling. The weight of the argument that managers should comply with the law because of risk of a lawsuit certainly has more potential threat in the United States than in Germany.

In the United States this portrayal of sexual harassment as "high risk" has strengthened the rule of legal consultants and human resources

---

[11] Since 1994, according to Pflüger and Baer (2005) fewer than 300 cases of sexual harassment have been filed with labor courts. Of those, around 111 cases ended with a judgment (so the full information was available). Of these 111 cases, 21 were filed by women (19 percent), 85 by men (77 percent) and 4 by employers (4 percent). These cases include lower and appellate (state-level) labor courts.

professionals. Feminist groups have done much to initiate policy innovation, but not in a formalized process. Employers do not have to listen to them or adopt their arguments. What counts is the judicial interpretation. Interestingly, however, management consultants have tended to exaggerate the dangers of an ever expanding case law and have recommended that employers should adopt broad sweeping employer policies to ban a far wider range of behaviors than what courts would in practice consider sexual harassment to be (Edelman et al. 2001).

This threat of legal costs has brought another enforcement mechanism onto the field in the United States: larger companies have corporate insurance to cover the costs of lawsuits should they arise. Insurance agencies have become concerned with minimizing their risk of paying legal fees and settlements. They are holding employers increasingly accountable for measurable goals of implementing sexual harassment laws and demanding that companies do everything possible to prevent these legal costs. They interpret case law very cautiously and fuel the perception of the legal threat.

Enforcement and implementation through courts and state agencies have thus pushed employers to take sexual harassment seriously in the United States, while German courts and state offices have few effective ways to pressure employers to take the law seriously. Not surprisingly, the group of employers who have responded neither to women's groups nor to laws is larger in Germany than in the United States, since they would respond only to direct enforcement and sanctions imposed by state agencies or courts.

Dynamics of adopting policies in the workplace

Not only legal and state institutions but also systems of workplace regulation and institutional arrangements within workplace organizations have shaped the underlying dynamics of change. The dynamic has been a top-down process in the United States and a bottom-up process in Germany. In both cases, however, feminists have been shut out of the process when it comes to "compliance" with the law.

Policy adoption in the United States is a top-down process for two main reasons: it is dominated by legal compliance, and workplace organizations lack effective systems of worker representation. Professional human resource managers or EEO/AA offices have taken the lead in interpreting sexual harassment laws in organizational contexts and creating policies and procedures, because few companies are unionized and women's interests have no formal representation. In a unionized organization, specific grievance procedures, for example the right to be represented by stewards, would be negotiated for members.

Unlike German gender equality offices, whose primary mission is to promote gender equality, US human resource and EEO/AA offices were created to implement the Civil Rights Act of 1964. They are responsible not only for women but for all groups protected against discrimination. Sexual harassment in their eyes is only one of many forms of discriminatory action. For example, one trainer drew the explicit comparison between sexually harassing remarks and jokes and comments that men who are bold might endure. The solution to sexual harassment in the simplistic form of the discrimination framework (without a gendered interpretation) is to ensure that men and women receive the same treatment.

In Germany, with little state or court enforcement, it has been left up to the political will of actors in workplace organizations to develop policy approaches and negotiate grievance procedures. Unlike in the United States, where management can dictate policies, at least for non-unionized employees, in the German bottom-up process democratically elected employee representatives participate in the creation of these measures. Worker representatives have negotiated with human resource offices over what the specific policies and procedures should look like. Any employer with more than fifty employees must allow the creation of works councils, which are involved in personnel decisions and have the right to help employees file grievances, creating a consensus-oriented process and decisions based on compromise.

Despite their potential to effect "democratic," bottom-up changes, works councils have so far taken little initiative to use the law to promote more equal gender culture in the workplace. Rather, at the local level, women's offices have taken the lead to initiate, organize, and mobilize women's interests. The networks these femocrats have built may include individual women in works councils, but works councils themselves have had to undergo a process of awareness raising on issues of sexual harassment. Thus the negotiation process is profoundly shaped by gender politics. We can observe a bottom-up process, in which communal public workplaces have been at the forefront of introducing policy measures against sexual harassment.

When we compare policy outcomes, this more democratic process, based on consensus of management and employee representatives, is a mixed blessing. German employers did not pass policies that prohibit consensual relationships or severely restrict employee job security through zero-tolerance policies. But women's interests were marginalized

Table 5.1. *Agencies of implementation and enforcement of sexual harassment policies*

	Workplace level	State offices
United States		Federal Equal Employment Opportunity Commission State fair practices employment offices
Private employers	EEO/AA offices	
Public employers	EEO/AA offices	
Germany		Federal Ministry of Women *Länder* gender equality offices (without any enforcement powers)
Private employers	Human resources, works' councils & few gender equality offices	
Public employers	Human resources, works' councils & gender equality offices	

because the vast majority of works council members are men. These male-dominated organizations, with no experience or expertise in implementing discrimination laws, are in charge of holding employers accountable for measures against sexual harassment (see Table 5.1).

Unions and sexual harassment

The problem with the corporatist model of implementation is that it assumes that employers and unions will negotiate the issues. Even with the 1994 law in place, German unions were hesitant to encourage local unions and works councils to promote the issue in the workplace. The ways in which unions have handled the issue of sexual harassment goes beyond the fact that sexual harassment was trivialized and considered a "women's issue" of less political relevance (Hamacher 1993). The hesitation of unions to embrace the issue of sexual harassment is related to the fact that sexual harassment does not fit smoothly into the institutionalized forms of workplace relations. It constitutes a structural problem of a conflict of interest for systems of workers' representation when sexual harassment occurs among union members. The system of dispute resolution in the workplace and workers' representation both in the United States and in Germany is based on the idea of a confrontation between employees and employers.

Therefore, if an employer or a supervisor who is not a union member is accused of sexual harassment, women have been able to gather legal counsel and support from unions, because these conflicts fit into the logic of workplace regulation. As Silke Roth puts it: "Criticizing employers and mobilizing sexual harassment prevention at the workplace fostered union solidarity by emphasizing the conflict between workers and employers" (2003: 148).

Individual cases of sexual harassment cross cut the dualistic notion of interests between employers and employees. Gender, rather than class, is the line for conflict. In cases of sexual harassment, class, race, sexual orientation, and other lines of conflict can intersect. If union members bring forth allegations against other union members, there is a conflict of interest for the union, since shop stewards have to represent union members if they are accused of sexual harassment. The American Federation of State, County and Municipal Employees (AFSCME), for example, advises shop stewards to assign two union representatives in these cases, one for the woman who files a complaint and one for the man accused of harassment, and to call upon outside support to handle these cases. This conflict of interest is also reflected in the fact that IG Metall and other unions in Germany have a policy that they will not give legal counsel if a woman member files a lawsuit against another union member. Thus, sexual harassment among colleagues creates conflicts that can be resolved only inadequately in the traditional system of workers' representation.

Not surprisingly, then, women union members who raised the issue encountered strong resistance, sometimes from other women. Women in US unions had similar experiences (Reese and Lindenberg 1999). A woman steward of a German teachers' union recalls:

And that was the first major dispute, when I made it an issue in the union at the state level. When I was later then vice chair of the union at the state level and made the law for the protection of employees a topic . . . There were counter-arguments: 'This is a problem on the construction sites, but not here among us!' And this was an argument from women, from full-time union women. 'We are coming from higher education.' . . . I made a press release on the issue, and I was afraid to get in trouble because of this press release. I was new in my position. And it turned out to be that way. There were resignations within the unions. There were wild letters. The chair was ok, he supported me. But internally, they put the issue down.

Defining sexual harassment as a class issue would justify sexual harassment as an issue for unions. Paradoxically, doing so here does not serve class solidarity but is used to dismiss the issue as irrelevant for the teachers' union, which in Germany sees itself as one of educated, middle-class employees. This is even more ironic as, according to popular myth, sexual harassment is an issue for middle-class women only, because working-class women know how to take jokes or fight back.

Here union women argued that sexual harassment does *not* happen to middle-class women, because educated middle-class men do not harass women.

Policy adoption and procedures to handle sexual harassment complaints depend not only on legal considerations but also on systems of worker representation. In both countries, informal/formal women's groups argued that the existing works councils or union stewards were ill-equipped to handle harassment cases. One reason was a frequently unacknowledged argument about the politics of gender within unions. Feminist activists perceived unions as bastions of male privilege and male bonding rather than as a "spearhead of women's liberation" (union woman and gender equality officer, interview, 1999).

When women have been harassed, they look for a sympathetic person and often prefer women to talk to. Given the notorious under-representation of women in German works councils, they would most likely find a male steward to whom to file a complaint. Hence, German gender equality offices (where they exist), not works councils, have been the preferred place for women to come and talk. Only in cases when the supervisor was the harasser have women turned to works councils (Pflüger and Baer 2005). Harassed women perceive works councils as more open to listening to and providing help for superior perpetrators in line with the tradition of workers' representation. About two-thirds of all complaints, however, are about coworker not supervisor harassment in Germany and works councils seem to lack legitimacy for handling these complaints among (unionized) coworkers (Pflüger and Baer 2005). Similarly in unionized US organizations, specific grievance procedures are negotiated for members, for example the right to be represented by stewards. But the reputation of shop stewards is that they are likely to support perpetrators' rights to stay in the workplace rather than victims' rights to redress.

According to German women in union leadership positions, it was also difficult to find union support for specific grievance procedures for cases of sexual harassment. In part, this is because these procedures were perceived as competing with union–employer negotiated grievance procedures. Unions in both countries tend to view equality officers or EEO/AA officers who handle complaints as competitors to collective representation of workers' interests.

Because feminists were critical of the ability of shop stewards/works councils to represent victims' interests, they attempted to circumvent them and demanded specific procedures against sexual harassment. Conflicts therefore arose between demands for specific procedures against sexual harassment and union-negotiated grievance procedures.

It is important to note that the positions unions take on the issue of sexual harassment and whether they promote or resist policies and grievance procedures are likely to vary according to a number of factors, such as the percentage of women in the union. The underlying issue, however, is that unions have no interest in creating alternative procedures for sexual harassment complaints, since they have an organizational interest in preserving their collectively negotiated grievance procedures as the dominant ones.

In the public sector in Germany, works councils play an even more important role than gender equality offices. As one gender equality advocate put it: "I don't have a seat at this table. The works councils are responsible to get the employer to agree to the collective bargaining agreements. Our office has nothing to do with it." Even though the 2000 law declared gender equality offices responsible for sexual harassment, they have no official, formal role in devising policies. Hence, despite the fact that for gender equality offices, sexual harassment clearly constitutes a gender issue in the context of "women-friendly" policies and measures, they had to seek works councils as allies. This coalition brought about a gender-neutral approach to sexual harassment.

Hence, though the workplace dynamics are different in the two countries, in neither system do advocates for victims' or women's rights have an official place. The next section discusses the consequences of the two dynamics for the ways sexual harassment is framed in workplace organizations, which in both countries have become increasingly gender-neutral.

The trade-offs of implementation paths

Discourses or framing of sexual harassment in the workplace

Though the US legal–regulatory route is more effective for creating employers' compliance with the Civil Rights Law, this does not mean that US employers address sexual harassment in a more feminist way than German employers have. As Rubenstein (interview, 2005) distinguishes: "The most effective way of implementing the law does not mean necessarily the best way to address the problem of sexual harassment." In fact, both German and US employers have embraced notions of sexual harassment that are void of feminist discourses of violence against women in the workplace and hence they lack a framework to address sexual harassment as unequal gender relations and the abuse of male power over women.

In both countries, legal consultants, human resource managers, and gender equality advocates have translated sexual harassment into a "workplace issue," primarily as an *organizational problem*. These actors have strategically used certain frames which resonated with management beyond the legal threat of failure to comply with the law. This professionalized discourse is void of any feminist analysis of sexual harassment as rooted in unequal gender relations. The focus shifts from the victim to the organization: sexual harassment does not merely harm the victim, it is bad for the organization, too. Simultaneously, it takes the responsibility off those who cause the harm, the perpetrators.

In the United States the general view that sexual harassment is *bad for business* seemed to catch on quickly in the early 1980s (Off Our Backs). Sexual harassment scandals have been perceived as damaging to the reputation of workplace organizations; measures against sexual harassment as polishing their image. Sexual harassment has been portrayed as costly for the organization in terms not only of potential legal costs but of loss of productivity. Research has documented how sexual harassment can increase costs associated with victims taking sick time and with higher employee turnover (when either the victim or the harasser leaves and must be replaced). More generally, sexual harassment is portrayed as affecting employee productivity, the idea being that employees are at work to work and not to think or talk about sex. Saguy (2003) also found that US managers used these bottom-line arguments to justify anti-sexual harassment programs. In this view, time spent surfing for pornographic images, downloading them, and using them to upset someone is lost as productive working time.

In Germany, consultants focused less on the potential costs involved but cast the issue as a management problem, assigning responsibility to supervisors. Sexual harassment is seen as a signal of a lack of leadership, which needs to be addressed by management because it is likely to have other negative impacts (consultants, interviews, 1999). In the German public sector, sexual harassment was discussed as an organizational problem, especially in the context of administrative reforms that took place in the 1990s. In the German private sector, flattening hierarchies and team work came into vogue in the 1990s and led to discussions about new forms of employee relations in general. In this context mobbing and sexual harassment became managerial issues that had little to do with gender equality per se.

The parallels of professionalized discourse on sexual harassment are even stronger in the frame of business ethics. Despite the difference in processes and legal frameworks, employers in the two countries have translated the sexual harassment laws in a very similar discourse of *business morals and ethics*. Though the emphasis is more on the actual problematic behavior than on the organizational frame, business morals are another way to use gender-neutral ways to frame sexual harassment. This notion of business ethics includes corporations' commitment to embrace principles of equality, diversity, and treatment of every employee with fairness, dignity, and respect.

Interestingly, these corporatist commitments do not, strictly speaking, reflect compliance with laws. There are no American laws that protect the personal right to dignity or respectful treatment of all workers in the workplace. Only workers who fall into a protected category under the Civil Rights Act of 1964 – women and minority men – have the rights. Similarly, while the German law clearly refers to violations of "dignity," there is no effective anti-discrimination law that would force employers to adhere to the rationale of "fairness" or equal treatment to prohibit harassment. Hence, in both countries, in implementing the sexual harassment laws, employers have adopted their own language, and address sexual harassment under the broader theme of ethical and moral behaviors in the workplace. In both cases the effect is that feminist frames of sexual harassment as violence against women disappear entirely, and the connection between sexual harassment and unequal gender relations becomes less visible. This fraught strategy trivializes any form of sexual harassment and paints male harassers as boorish, coarse, ill-mannered individuals, losing sight of the meaning that these actions carry for the individual woman and women in general. Their actions of erotizing and sexualizing women need to be considered in the societal context in which they appear. Perpetrators use sexual harassment as strategies to objectify women, to demean, offend, intimidate, scare, torment – in short, harass women as women.

EEO offices have defined sexual harassment in the context of diversity management, the US corporate mantra to change organizational cultures (Edelman et al. 2001). The idea is that diversity is profitable in its own right, because integrating minority men and women into the workplace takes advantage of "new" labor force developments, supposedly improves working conditions for everyone, and enhances creativity and productivity in the workplace. Several white male interviewees expressed their preference for working in mixed teams by sex (usually they will not mention race), because they do not like the dynamics that develop in exclusively male teams. Women, for example, are credited with improving the "social climate" at work.

After settlement of a sex discrimination case against the investment banking company Morgan Stanley in 2004, CEO Philip J. Purcell used this notion explicitly in his statement to the press: "We are proud of our commitment to diversity, and would like to thank the EEOC staff for working with us to conclude this matter in such a positive way."[12] This suit involved sexual harassment allegations and cost the company $54 million, including a mention on national newspaper front pages.

Furthermore, US employers tend to use a decontextualized, individualistic notion of sexual harassment even in the context of "diversity management." Sexual harassment is treated as a conflict between individuals; the proposed solution is curbing *bad behavior* by introducing more professional norms of workplace behavior. By contrast, the dominant frame in German workplaces is unfair treatment of employees with the group-based notion of mobbing.

In the United States, legal professionals and consultants have promoted standards for "appropriate behavior" and "don't do it" rules. An HR manager from a manufacturing employer explained: "We use two examples/mottos for our company: (1) We are a 'G' rated company in an 'R' rated world and (2) if it isn't appropriate for your three-year-old to hear, it doesn't belong in the workplace."[13] These standards have little to do with a feminist analysis of sexual harassment, where the problem lies not with sexual behaviors in the workplace but with the fact that men objectify women and use sexuality as a means of exerting power over them.

Because of the corporatist route of implementing sexual harassment laws, in Germany employers have embraced the non-gender-specific term mobbing, which describes the violation of personal rights (*Persönlichkeitsrechts*) through intimidation and degradation. Mobbing can happen to everybody, independent of a person's sex, race/ethnicity, age, sexual orientation, etc. No German law explicitly prohibits mobbing, but in 1997, the Federal German Labor Court[14] defined mobbing as "systematic hostility, harassment, and discrimination between employees or by supervisors." As recently as 2001 a state-level labor court defined mobbing as a violation of personal freedoms and health.[15] In these few years of case law building based on victims of mobbing taking their employers to the labor courts, judges have been more generous to victims of mobbing than to victims of sexual harassment, with significantly higher monetary awards – some awards on mobbing have been up to €50,000.

---

[12] Press release Morgan Stanley *http://www.morganstanley.com* (downloaded July 13, 2004).
[13] "How Employers Address Sexual Harassment," IOMA survey 2001, *HR Focus*, Vol. 78, Issue 12, pp. 3–6.
[14] Bundesarbeitsgericht (BAG) January 15, 1997, NZA 1997, pp. 781f.
[15] The LAG Thuringia ruled that mobbing can violate constitutional *allgemeine Persönlichkeitsrechte* (general personal freedoms), including Article 1 human dignity, and/or Article 2 personal freedoms, and/or health (LAG Thuringia: Decision April 10, 2001).

The comparison of mobbing and sexual harassment cases before court reveals important differences in the interpretation of these two phenomena. On the one hand, judges might perceive mobbing cases as more "clear cut" and acknowledge harm done to a greater extent, because they have greater sympathy with victims of mobbing – anyone can identify with being bullied, and any child at least has felt mistreated or treated in a demeaning way by groups of children or teachers (Degen, interview, 1999). Hence, the predominantly (male) judges can identify more easily with mobbing victims.

By contrast, judgments in cases of sexual harassment reveal sympathy with the (male) perpetrators. Several (male) judges have found excuses, tried to explain away sexually harassing behaviors, clearly using the perpetrator's view – not that of the victim. They have interpreted the pestering, frequent asking out, and all kinds of sexual advances by male perpetrators as "love that went wrong" (Pflüger and Baer 2005). While perpetrators of mobbing are seen as "bad guys" with mean intentions (to get rid of a person in the workplace), perpetrators of sexual harassment are given the benefit of the doubt, and are considered as "good guys" who in fact expressed their love and affection (even if in inappropriate ways), and certainly did not intentionally harm their victims, since they had positive emotions for them. Hence, while cultural patterns immediately help judges identify with the "underdog" and mobbing victims, sexual harassment victims do not enjoy the same taken-for-granted "victim" status. This is why laws that force judges to use the victim's not the perpetrator's perspective are so crucial in challenging societal and cultural norms of victim blaming.

Employers have interpreted these court rulings on mobbing as an indication of their responsibility to protect employees from mobbing. Even before these rulings, the notion of mobbing had replaced sexual harassment in both the media and workplaces, and unions and employers had negotiated and adopted anti-mobbing policies. Since the mid-1990s the implementation of sexual harassment measures in German workplaces, based on consensus models and collective bargaining agreements, has broadened sexual harassment to a non-gender-specific issue of abuses of power in workplaces. On the downside, from a feminist perspective, unions have created class rather than gender solidarity, and mobbing has been a convenient vehicle to avoid discussing gender conflicts in sexual harassment. More broadly speaking, discussions of mobbing has raised awareness of social–psychological stressors at work and victims of sexual harassment, too, have benefited from this development. Since sexual harassment frequently leads to forms of mobbing, once women reject and resist men's advances, women can at least now use mobbing to capture in words the retaliation they encounter, though without a gendered analysis, and without being able to name the behaviors "sexual harassment," women will have to be silent about the underlying problem of the mobbing they encounter.

After the 1994 law was passed, employers in a most surprising move went beyond their legal mandate. They adopted fairness or anti-mobbing policies, despite the fact that sexual harassment law referred only to violations of dignity through sexual behavior, and there was no law against mobbing. Volkswagen, known for being a progressive company, designed the model policy, which includes sexual harassment, in 1995 even before case law existed on mobbing. Similarly, larger companies including the Deutsche Telekom AG, Deutsche Bahn, Deutsche Bank, and several multinational corporations followed the VW model and adopted anti-mobbing policies.

The gendered institutional arrangements shaped the implementation process. Even if the gender equality offices took the initiative, passing these policies meant not only getting employers on their side but also collaborating with works councils. This was because of the gender politics in workplaces and the dynamic of the bottom-up process, in which works councils have been stronger than gender equality offices. Because implementation of measures in German workplaces is based on consensus models and collective bargaining, union definitions of sexual harassment mattered more than those of feminists.

Finally, another reason why mobbing has become a more popular term than sexual harassment in Germany is that even feminists have avoided a notion associated with US politics of sexual harassment. The German discourse on Jones's lawsuit against President Clinton undermined and de-legitimized advocates' attempts to create institutional responses to sexual harassment. One interviewee explained: "When we tried to bring the issue up in a meeting, one colleague asked us if we really wanted to adopt American puritan standards." Several gender equality officers and union women who conducted training programs were forced to explain how their approach was different from the American approach. Not surprisingly, the language of mobbing was a convenient way for feminists to avoid negative connotations of sexual harassment including those associated with American exaggerations.

Feminist frames in general have thus had to compete with gender-neutral organizational, business ethics, and mobbing frames. The gendered manifestations of sexual harassment disappear in these organizational and management frames. Neither harasser nor victim nor organization appears to be gendered when we talk about sexual harassment as diversity management, bad behavior, or mobbing. These frames not only de-gender the phenomenon of sexual harassment but, most interestingly, imply an overlap of employer and employee interests (Marshall 2001). Both organizations and women then have a stake in singling out and blaming harassers, rather than dealing with hierarchical structures or gender politics in workplace organizations that silence women. Hence, instead of embracing the goal of enhancing gender equality with more concrete feminist, gender-specific solutions, such as increasing women in positions of authority, employers focus on creating safe environments for women. But taking down pornographic images and sending men to "charm school" does not come near to what feminists intended when they portrayed sexual harassment in the context of gender inequality in the workplace.

Individual vs. collective rights

The dynamics of the implementation and enforcement process have very different logics in the United States and Germany, with important consequences for individuals affected by sexual harassment and also for the potential to change the gender culture in the workplace. The US model places individual victims at the center of the dynamics of change; the German model is oriented toward group-based approaches (Zippel 2003).

In the US system, in the absence of union representation in workplace organizations, organized women did not have to negotiate with existing workers' representation. The main enforcement of the US system remains individual legal redress: individuals need to step forward to file complaints with employers and to bring cases to state agencies and courts if employers do not take appropriate action. In the workplace, individual legal discourse is more prevalent than that of group-based, collective employee rights. Alternatives, such as informal complaints or "dispute resolution" through mediation, an approach promoted by the EEOC in the 1990s, still focus on resolving individual cases. In the absence of strong labor protection law employers can use measures against sexual harassment to erode (male) workers' rights. For example, zero-tolerance policies give little protection or internal redress to individuals, and thus diminish collective, group-based rights.

Instead of empowering victims to choose among multiple ways to deal with harassment, an unintended consequence of the focus on individuals is the "pressure to report" (Zippel 1994). The 1998 Supreme Court decisions have put even more pressure on victims to use internal procedures first. But employers' and victims' interests can be at odds: employers in general have an interest in solving issues of sexual harassment internally to shield their organizations from lawsuits.

"It's in the interest of the institution to have people file an official complaint because that's the one way you have to get a result. And to prevent a later, maybe upcoming complaint. What I talked about was protection of the institution, which doesn't really address the concerns of the individual." (Director of Dispute Resolution, interview, 1994)

As a result, training and awareness programs encourage individuals to report harassment.

There is a great deal of ambivalence for feminist administrators, who are aware of both the need for women to speak up, report, and complain about the behavior, and the risks associated with doing so. There is a risk of institutional re-victimization, retribution, and for complainants frequently the disappointment with the institutional response. Increasing numbers of retaliation claims have been reported to the EEOC: in 2004, 29 percent of cases filed under Title VII of the Civil Rights Act were complaints about retaliation, compared with only 15 percent in 1992.[16] Though complaining about harassment often has negative consequences for the victim, the underlying assumption of the US model is that organizational improvements in handling harassment can be achieved only if individuals come forward and use them (Reese and Lindenberg 1999). Thus the individual victim becomes responsible for effecting institutional change.

Paradoxically then, instead of an organizational openness for reporting, the pressure to report puts the burden on those most affected by harassment and exposes them to further risks. As a consequence, we now discuss and know more about why victims do not report than about why individuals harass or what organizational factors contribute to harassment. Making victims politically responsible for stopping the social problem ignores the socio-cultural factors that contribute to sexual harassment, such as status differences, gender power, and organizational hierarchies. One might ask how many individual women then will need to go through the grueling process of reporting harassers before harassment will stop.

Another consequence of the individualistic model focused on legal redress is that employers' responses to sexual harassment are primarily focused on avoiding lawsuits rather than addressing the causes of harassment. The precedent-setting court rulings have raised the expectation that employers should take preventive measures in the form of training

---

[16] http://www.eeoc.gov/stats/charges.html

and awareness programs. However, courts expect little beyond informing employees of their legal rights and the employer's policy. Thus, training programs emphasize individuals' rights and encourage victims to use internal procedures rather than filing lawsuits against the company.

We are making sure that people are well informed about the policy and the procedures. So there is on-going training that we provide. We have training programs that we actually offer for people so they can understand what the policy means, what it means for them personally. (Director of Dispute Resolution, interview, 1994)

Employers' training programs also focus on managers and supervisors because of legal liabilities for employers if the harasser has supervisory functions over the harassed person. In addition, supervisors are responsible for handling complaints and taking action and are seen as the key to setting and enforcing behavioral standards. One interviewee pointed out: "We have training programs for managers and supervisors, so they understand what their obligations are to make sure the climate is free of sexual harassment"(Director of Dispute Resolution, interview, 1994). Thus, training programs are oriented toward compliance with the law – and minimizing the costs for training. More expensive group-based interventions or training programs oriented toward teambuilding, say, are left to employers' discretion and constitute an exception rather than the rule.

In much the same way as consultants exaggerate the legal threat in order to convince employers to take action, instructors in training and awareness programs frequently use fear to win over hostile, resistant audiences. One strategy is to exaggerate the legal risk for supervisors if they fail to handle a complaint appropriately. A consultant explained: "At first the men don't listen, laugh, and think it's funny to be in a sexual harassment seminar. When I then explain to the supervisors that they too can be held accountable in the court they start listening." Most sexual harassment victims will in fact sue not the supervisor but the employer, so the cases are extremely rare, but consultants still use them to create fears among supervisors in order to encourage them to take the issue seriously.

Finally, sexual harassment pedagogy also works with the fear of false accusations. Trainers create emotions of fear strategically to handle uninterested audiences in mandatory awareness programs. The argument is to be on the "safe side," to convince "innocent" men to leave their doors open when speaking with women, and police their language and behavior vis-à-vis women. Raising awareness on sexual harassment primarily with fear of legal consequences or job loss has the advantage that audiences do take it as a serious legal threat. In this atmosphere, the simple message is to stop behavior that could be misinterpreted, such as joking, touching, or whistling. But operating with fear also has an important disadvantage: it recreates myths and stereotypes about women as untrustworthy, vengeful, and always ready to file a complaint about men's innocent behavior.

Training programs that focus on individual behavior tell men what not to do, how not to behave inappropriately. But the challenge is to encourage men to see and treat women as equals in the workplace. Feminist goals to create workplace cultures in which men and women enjoy positive, equal working relationships require an explicit awareness of gender and hierarchical power and organizational changes. These broader concerns have no room in one- or two-hour training sessions focused on individual legal redress, complaint procedures, and (re-) creating fears among men of being falsely accused by women.

By contrast, the German model relies on consensual, collective agreements between employers and unions that privilege solutions addressing sexual harassment as a group rather than an individual harm. Union women embraced this notion and explicitly demanded protecting women as a social right. One union woman explained:

"If we don't make politics around the issue, then each individual woman will have to see how she deals with it. But what are [union] organizations for: to have collective protection. And not that each individual woman will have to claim her rights. Naturally, individual rights are important. But there has to be a political shield of protection. This is typical for social rights. Otherwise they are not realized" (union leader, interview, 1999).

The German Federal ministry also financed an alternative project focused on gender-specific, group-based training, "structural mediation," initiated by Dr. Degen (Degen 2002). It is based on the assumption that changes in the broader workplace culture are necessary to combat sexual harassment. Women and men employees first discuss issues separately and then come together to develop group-based solutions to gender conflict. One of the most prominent issues for women was that they felt men did not respect women's expertise and would not take them seriously (Degen, interview, 1999).

The mobbing approach also emphasizes group dynamics that contribute to sexual harassment as a conflict in the workplace. Training programs that address sexual harassment as part of anti-mobbing seminars focus on group-based processes of discrimination and exclusion. Such seminars, with the advantage of a focus on teambuilding and cooperative leadership styles, have become an integral part of changes in workplace culture in general.

The negative side is that political will rather than strong incentives to comply with laws is the motor of implementation. Mobilization of women's pressure groups and alliance building with works councils is necessary to pressure employers to adopt policies. For this reason, the adoption process has been slower in Germany than in the United States.

In addition, individual redress for victims is weak. Legal threats and sanctions for noncompliance are less serious than in the United States, so employers have had little incentive to improve internal grievance structures. Works council structures represent individual employees' interests. The challenge is to reform these by increasing awareness and making them available for women who have been harassed. In the public sector, the expectation since the gender equality law of 2000 is that public-sector equality offices are to be "involved" in harassment cases. But they lack formal power to investigate or sanction. Moreover, because of their mandate to represent women's interests, some equality officers do not feel responsible for handling reports by men.

The most problematic aspect of having unions/works councils negotiate policy approaches, however, is the danger that concerns about mobbing will eradicate the gender dimension of sexual harassment. Power differentials based on unequal gender-relations are invisible when considering the gender-neutral group dynamics of mobbing. Concerns with workplace cultures of respect and dignity are prevalent, but challenging sexist language, pornographic images, and so forth as part of male-dominated workplace cultures is not generally considered mobbing.

Sexual favoritism

One of the most controversial aspects of employers' practices around sexual harassment in the United States has been how to deal with mutual, consensual relationships. Policies that discourage or prohibit sexual relationships in the workplace have existed in various forms in both countries, including, for example, laws that prohibited married women from becoming civil servants (in place in Germany until 1957), anti-fraternization policies that prohibit related employees from passing on favors, and so forth. What is new, however, is the notion that sexual favoritism is illegal. While 30 percent of US employers have adopted policies that discourage or prohibit any relationships, German collective agreements do not even mention this issue (Schultz 2003). The governments' stances vary greatly. The US EEOC warns employers against allowing supervisors to favor employees with whom they have a relationship; the German Federal Ministry of Women (BMFSFJ 1994) welcomes flirtation and acknowledges that the workplace can be the birthplace of future marriages.

Sexual favoritism in the workplace, which adversely affects the employment opportunities of third parties, may take the form of implicit "quid pro quo" harassment and/or "hostile work environment" harassment. (US EEOC 1990 Guidelines on Sexual Favoritism)[17]

It is not about prohibiting eroticism in the workplace . . . Will flirting in the workplace be forbidden in the future? The law does not assume a working world that is out of touch with life, in which women and men have forgotten to which sex they belong. But the law is supposed to protect those effectively, who are confronted with sexual harassment. Sexual innuendos have nothing to do with eroticism. Flirting, when it is wanted by a woman and a man, is not going to be prohibited in the workplace either. After all, many future marital partners meet in the workplace. (BMFSFJ 1994)

The US EEOC and the German Federal Ministry of Women take very different stances on sexual harassment and sexuality in the workplace. US consultants and employers explain that these policies are necessary to prevent sexual harassment from occurring, but Vicki Schultz (2003) argues US employers use laws against sexual harassment as an excuse to "sanitize" the workplace by narrowly focusing their policies to eliminate any sexual expression. The question, however, is why US but not German employers have been interested in this "neo-Taylorite project of suppressing employees' sexuality" (Schultz 2003). I agree with Schultz that "Puritanism" is not a sufficient explanation for the US employers' stance, but I argue that these approaches are the consequence of legal concepts, notions of gender equality, and the different dynamics of implementation in which German employers' policies have been created in more democratic, consensus-based ways.

Based on the equal treatment (gender sameness) rationale, the US EEOC guidelines interpret the Civil Rights Act to prohibit sexual favoritism (EEOC 1990). The issue is fairness and equal treatment, not of those exposed to harassment but of someone who might be negatively affected by flirtation or a consensual relationship between others. If a boss has an affair with an employee, then a third person, say a coworker of the employee, can file a complaint based on sexual favoritism. The argument is that the third person did not receive equal treatment if the employee involved in the relationship was preferred.

---

[17] *http://www.eeoc.gov/policy/docs/sexualfavor.html* (downloaded October 12, 2004).

Cases of sexual favoritism brought under the Civil Rights Act are extremely rare, but human resource consultants have argued that prohibiting all consensual relationships (even among colleagues) in the workplace is necessary to prevent harassment (Schultz 2003). There is no research to support this notion. Employers have simply followed consultants' views that such policies protect the organization from lawsuits that could emerge when consensual relationships turn sour. Managers and human resource personnel I interviewed justified the policies by referring to cases in which after the end of a consensual relationship a subordinate employee alleges being treated differently or being sexually harassed. In practice, these policies resonate with paternalistic understandings that women need to be protected from men's sexual advances. They do not challenge existing (unequal) gender relations or empower women in consensual relationships with men. Ultimately, they restrict rather than support women's right to sexual self-determination, because if employers have a policy against relationships, women will have to choose between their job and a romantic relationship with another employee.

By contrast, with the intention of avoiding any resemblance to the American model, the German Ministry of Women does not encourage employers to discourage flirtation or consensual relationships in the workplace; indeed it welcomes the gender difference expressed through eroticism, and flirtation is portrayed as a positive element. Since German law has defined sexual harassment as infringement of personal rights to dignity and not as a violation of equal treatment or the demand for the sameness of conditions of work, sexual harassment law does not offer any justification for complaints about sexual favoritism.

Neither unions nor women's groups have advocated prohibiting relationships among employees in the context of sexual harassment policies. No one at any of the workplace organizations where I conducted my interviews had even discussed discouraging consensual relationships. Because of the consensus-based process of designing policies against sexual harassment, unions had to agree with any policy that would limit relationships among employees, and neither employers nor unions put the issue on the agenda.

From a German perspective, formal rules to prohibit sexual relationships in companies are interpreted as an overreaction and stand for everything that is wrong with the American approach to sexual harassment. As a femocrat explains (gender equality officer, interview, 1999):

But it cannot be the answer, to fall into prudishness and in such a form of control, which again makes one fall into new authority and patterns of violence. It is a form of violence to prohibit people from falling in love with another. This can't be it. This is very American, and very weird. What I want is to create awareness about what happens, and this has a lot to do with the private lives of men and women.

The interviewee here formulates the right of employees to emotions, to intimate feelings, which in fact resonates with employees' taken-for-granted right to privacy, a concept that does not exist in the United States to the same extent.

This lack of concern in German discussions with coerciveness in relationships between supervisors and employees is surprising, given the complicated nature of consent in gender and other hierarchical relations. For example, Professor Ursula Mueller (interview, 1999) observed in discussions of sexual harassment policies in universities that this issue was depicted very differently by male faculty and female students: male faculty members were worried that policies like this would prevent them from engaging in serious relationships, women students were concerned with what they could do if a professor approached them.

The German ministry also fails to mention that employers indeed have informal and formal rules about consensual relationships. Multinational corporations in Germany tend to discourage but not prohibit relationships across hierarchies. In the public sector, specific workplaces such as the police prohibit placing couples in a workplace unit because of safety concerns. Courts have ruled that flirtation, adultery, and other relationships between civil servants are inappropriate. The Weberian ideal of the professional, impersonal civil servant is indeed more legally embedded in Germany than in the United States. According to the laws that guide the civil service, any behavior that can be seen as violating the *dignity of the office* can bring severe sanctions. But employers do little to educate their employees about the problematic nature of consensual workplace relationships in the context of sexual harassment. And the specific regulations for relationships across hierarchies were in place before sexual harassment became an issue – not responses to these concerns.

Conclusion

Policies that discourage and prohibit any sexual relationship in the workplace have existed in various forms in both countries; what is new is that US employers have adopted them in the name of protecting women from sexual harassment. The definition of sexual favoritism made it into the EEOC guidelines as a concession to conservative groups, who were concerned with moral questions about women sleeping their way up (Baker 2001). US feminists have been split on whether to endorse employers' projects to eradicate any sexuality from workplaces (Schultz 2003; MacKinnon 2004). Sexual harassment raises complicated issues about consensus and women's agency in hierarchical relationships and in gender relations in general, a longstanding concern in feminist (legal) debates. Feminists are in a bind when they argue, on the one hand, that institutions should help two-career couples by practicing partner hires, and on the other hand, endorse an institutional ethic that discourages any intimate relationships within organizations.

Within the workplace, the issue of sexual favoritism shows how employers have subverted the radical feminist call for women's sexual self-determination and turned sexual harassment laws into policies that in fact undermine self-determination and compromise feminist goals of empowering women to engage in consensual, equal partnerships with men. These policies – ostensibly created to protect women from men's sexual advances – have been adopted with the rationale to shield the organization from possible legal risks. Organizations here might follow the Weberian ideal of disembodied, professional, disconnected, emotionless individuals, but discussions about institutional ethics of gender relations reveal how gendered this Weberian ideal is in reality, revealing the gendered nature of organizations and bureaucracies themselves that feminists have long pointed out (Ferguson 1984; Acker 1990; Hearn and Parkin 2001).

By contrast, German employer policies have taken more into account the perspective of all employees. Despite the fact that German employers already had norms to curb consensual relationships in the workplace, employers did not use sexual harassment policies to extend them. Without the support of unions, which did not advocate these policies, employers would not have passed such regulations, since male-dominated unions are against giving employers the right to curb privacy in the name of protecting women against sexual harassment. Finally, German feminists and advocates were forced to take a stance on this issue, and some have chosen to distinguish themselves from the United States by being silent on how to deal with consensual relationships across hierarchies.

While politics of sexual harassment in the United States stand for an atmosphere of fear where men feel that the slightest misstep can lead to the courts or unemployment, German employers have largely ignored the problem. The politics of sexual harassment are more politics as usual. The fact that employers have ignored sexual harassment laws might be surprising given Germany's long-standing tradition of worker protection and representation. Yet, it is important to realize that the state has not been an ally in monitoring and enforcing the law against sexual harassment. German federal and state-level authorities, in concordance with a corporatist model of a state, as well as the courts, have been reluctant to interfere in what they see is best left to collective bargaining of employers and local unions. Thus, despite its administrative capacity, the state, even as itself an employer in the public sector, has made little effort to use a top-down implementation process.

In the United States, those covered by the Civil Rights Act of 1964 and state fair practice laws have adopted policies and procedures but few have adopted more costly training and sensitivity programs (Dobbin and Kelly 2004). In fact, the majority of employers have already gone through several revisions of their sexual harassment policies to reflect changes in case law. This process of creating policies has been dominated by employers' legal concerns, with employees having little say over how to create more gender equality in the workplace. Court decisions together with insurance companies have convinced most of the hold-outs to adopt some kind of policy statements.

Employers who have taken steps in either country frame sexual harassment in different ways. US employers send their male employees to "charm school" to teach appropriate, nonsexualized, "good" behavior in the workplace; employers in Germany worry about violations of dignity of all workers. These inclusions/exclusions have important consequences for creating fairer gender cultures in the workplace.

What is the process through which employers have adopted policies and other preventive measures? The dynamics highlighted here tell a complicated story. The dynamics of implementation of the laws have been shaped by actors, legal requirements, and institutional arrangements. In neither country have employers simply complied with the law. Hence the different laws alone do not explain employers' reactions to sexual harassment. The "legal threat" argument in the United States pushed employers to adopt risk-managing strategies beyond the legal mandates, but in Germany the argument seems to have had little potency.

Instead this comparison has demonstrated that in both countries implementation is a variable *political process* by which employers translate laws into organizational practices. Political implementation processes are influenced by legal mandates but also by industrial relations, which have important consequences for the politics of sexual harassment. Gender relations have shaped these processes in both countries, as feminists and those representing victims' interests were shut out of the policy design process. These processes have also been shaped by normative assumptions about gender and sexuality, gender power, in organizations (Hearn and Parkin 2001). Feminist advocates played an important role in initiating employers' responses, but there is no official role for informal or formal feminists in organizations in either country in implementation and enforcement. Hence, in Germany employers adopted policies with the participation of unions and works councils. This consensual process has led to broad, non-gender-specific anti-mobbing policies that subsume sexual harassment as a violation of workers' dignity.

Finally, legal frameworks did influence how actors have framed issues. When unions have been involved in negotiating collective bargaining agreements and new informal and formal rules in Germany, they have promoted the notion of guaranteeing the dignity of all workers. In the United States unions embraced the diversity discourse and were legally obliged to ensure their own organizations' adherence to anti-discrimination laws.

6 Social movements, institutions, and the politics of sexual harassment

The evolution of sexual harassment policies, beginning in the United States and spreading to the EU and its member states, demonstrates the important role of transnational movements and advocacy networks in promoting social change on a global scale. In this transnational effort, feminists have been able to draw on resources beyond their national borders. Alternative feminist discourses – including a range of viewpoints and sophisticated forms of transnational expertise based on social scientific and legal research – readily travel across national borders. The German case, however, demonstrates that the nation-state remains a key actor because institutional arrangements of legal systems, workplace regulation, and gender ideologies shape both feminist strategies and the (gender) politics of sexual harassment in general.

This book has compared the rise and development of the politics of sexual harassment in the United States, the EU, and Germany, focusing on cultural, social, political, and institutional contexts. The preceding chapters reveal how different trajectories and dynamics of change – from the origins of laws to their implementation in the workplace – have brought about very different politics.

Demonstrating how important a gender approach is for the comparative study of sexual harassment policy, this chapter discusses policy outcomes from a gendered perspective. Comparison of how feminist frames were translated into laws allows us to examine the links among frames, institutional arrangements, and political opportunities. Hence, this chapter addresses what this analysis tells us about how social movements affect policy change in general and feminist policy in particular. More broadly speaking, it examines the relationship between social movements and institutions. It focuses on several ways social movements are shaped by institutional arrangements and reciprocally influence institutional arrangements and political opportunity structures as well. Consequently, both movements and institutions shape the different routes of institutionalizing sexual harassment politics. Finally, the chapter draws some lessons from this transatlantic comparison for employers, feminists, and unions for shaping and reshaping the future of sexual harassment politics in the United States and the EU.

Although the story of sexual harassment in the United States is a national, domestic one, US debates have had an impact on politics worldwide, particularly in the EU. The transnational exchange of feminist ideas, discourses, and frames was crucial to the mobilization of actors advocating for policy changes in the EU and its member states, and the transnational movement against sexual harassment has continued to influence sexual harassment politics in the member states. In the United States, anti-discrimination laws are used to combat sexual harassment, but it is judges, not policy-makers, who decide how to hold employers accountable. Though the US model of individual legal redress did not fit easily into EU member states' politics of gender, the EU adopted the US model of sexual harassment as sex discrimination in its 2002 binding directive for the now twenty-five member states. The EU modified the US law by adding important components of sexual harassment as a "violation of dignity" and gender harassment. Member states have embarked on trajectories to combat unwanted sexual attention in the workplace different from those in the United States.

These trajectories tell us which institutional access routes activists have found and how advocates have shaped policy outcomes. Legal systems and industrial regulations mattered not only in policy origins but also in implementation and enforcement. The US legal–regulatory path is possible because important legal changes can occur through the courts without going through Congress. Feminists have used the European Court of Justice to effect EU gender equality law, but they did not use the litigation route for sexual harassment; instead, in the EU, the law came through the bureaucratic, administrative path to policy-making and a ping-pong path of incremental policy change between national and supranational levels of legislation. Because Germany has lacked strong anti-discrimination legislation and the women's movement repertoire has not included litigation strategies, only the establishment of feminist state actors, in the form of gender equality offices, put sexual harassment onto the agenda of cities, *Länder*, and, finally, the federal government (see Table 6.1).

While US courts and EOCs have implemented and enforced the law, the German state leaves employers and unions to negotiate measures. Without representation of women's interests in this statutory–corporatist route, sexual harassment was turned into a universal issue of workers' dignity in the context of German institutional arrangements dominated by socially conservative corporatist workplace regulations. The highly

Table 6.1. *Politics of sexual harassment in the United States and Germany*

	United States legal–regulatory route	Germany statutory–corporatist route
Route to legal reforms	Civil Rights Act of 1964 Court Decisions EEOC guideline 1980 Supreme Court 1986	Labor law Parliament enacts 1994 Federal Employee Protection Law
Legal definition	Sex Discrimination	Violation of dignity
Route for implementation and enforcement	Case law and state regulation	Political will of employers and unions: Collective agreements
Federal agency for enforcement	EEOC	Federal Ministry of Women has no investigative or enforcement powers
Company level	Policy statements Grievance procedures Some training	General grievance procedure Few anti-mobbing policies Few specific policies
Legal remedies	Individual or class-action charges filed with EEOC and law suits Max. award for civil rights lawsuits: $50,000 to $300,000	No state complaint office No punitive damages Very limited damages Award less than €3,700

decentralized, fragmented system of industrial relations in the United States meant that unions were less important allies than in Germany, especially at the federal level. With the declining labor movement, they have also played a less central role in shaping policies at the local level. As a consequence, legal changes pushed US employers to take sexual harassment more seriously and created a *politics of fear* surrounding it, while in the EU, particularly in Germany, weaker laws, coupled with lack of enforcement and implementation, allowed employers to give it only scant recognition and continue *politics as usual*.

Feminists were the initiators for these policy changes, and they were able to influence laws and policies to varying degrees. The EU, state agencies, and courts responded by translating feminist visions of sexual harassment in different ways into legal frameworks and employment policies. However, feminists on both sides of the Atlantic have been shut out in the implementation processes. So feminist principles of gender equality, women's sexual self-determination, and empowerment no longer define the politics of sexual harassment. It is now in the hands of management and unions, who have turned it into a gender-neutral issue. US employers consider sexual harassment primarily a problem of business ethics and the "bad behavior" of individuals. In Europe, unions persuaded employers to crusade against bullying, moral harassment, and mobbing, redefining the issue as a universal European project. Both processes could be interpreted as co-optations of feminist frames because they have de-gendered the problem (Stratigaki 2004). This examination, therefore, has raised broader questions about the processes that translate and transform a contentious feminist issue into laws, workplace policies, rules, regulations, and awareness programs, which comparative feminist policy studies have aimed to address.

The explanation for these differences offered in this book may be surprising for Europeans who believe that they are more sophisticated regarding sexual cultures than Americans, who are constrained by the Puritan tradition. Nor is there support here for American readers who believe that feminism has gone too far, or that a feminist agenda is at the heart of employer practices; for example, feminists have never seriously advocated that sending men to "charm school" would prevent sexual harassment. Instead, feminists challenged fundamental gender dynamics at work that serve to belittle, demote, and humiliate women in sexual and sexist ways.

The forerunner policy role of the United States will perhaps also surprise those who have the impression that European welfare states are paradises for working women. Several EU member states are more generous with public funding for child care, social services, family benefits, and longer paid parental leave, but US courts have been more responsive to the plight of sexually harassed women. Countries that have helped mothers combine work and family responsibilities have not been at the forefront of sexual self-determination in the workplace (see Elman 1996; Mazur 2003). Feminists did not demand major expenses; compared with child care, sexual harassment measures are cheap. Yet, the politics of sexual harassment occur on a difficult political terrain, on which feminists challenge and dismantle masculinist privileges and power to define norms and meanings of everyday sexual interactions. Combating sexual harassment means challenging organizational and institutional practices in the same institutions and organizations that advocates need as allies in effecting change – unions, courts, the state, and supranational institutions. Hence, they reveal state and organizational commitments to empowering women to resist these norms individually and collectively.

Because the politics of sexual harassment are about sexuality and gender relations in workplaces, this new field of gender policy should inspire scholars to test theories of gender and welfare states, social movements, and public policy. The findings of this study challenge feminist assumptions about the uniform "patriarchal" nature of states as unresponsive to women's issues. They also challenge our common rankings of women-friendly states. Institutions in the United States, the EU, and Germany vary in their responsiveness to feminist demands. We need to work more on integrated theories of social movements, institutional approaches, and legal and policy studies to explain the gendered nature of institutions and movements, and the dynamic relationships between them.

Gendered policy outcomes

How laws define sexual harassment matters; the frames they are built upon evoke different notions of what the problem of sexual harassment is about and how to solve it. People intuitively agree that sexual harassment has to do with gender, not only in defining the issue but also in finding legal and policy solutions. Furthermore, gender fundamentally structures any social process, and institutionalized practices give us gendered meanings. We have gendered ideas and concepts, as well as gendered notions about what constitutes sexual harassment. The institutions that deal with it are themselves gendered.

Gender plays a role in how we conceptualize sexual harassment, whether as miscommunication or as a reflection of deeply embedded unequal gender relations. US courts had a difficult time recognizing men as victims. Laws are gender-neutral, but they rest on underlying assumptions about gender relations and sexuality. Comparing politics reveals the deeply gendered nature of this issue. Comparing frames embedded in legal texts, court rulings, and employer practices illuminates how gender has shaped politics.

How we think about which situations and actions constitute "sexual harassment" is based on our assumptions of how women and men should behave, what "normal" interactions in the workplace should be, and whether sexual harassment is predominantly an expression of desire in an inappropriate context or of dominance fueled by abuse of power. Not surprisingly, the laws and policies parliaments, courts, and employers have designed are also fundamentally informed by assumptions about gender and sexuality.

Feminists originally defined sexual harassment as abuse of power by men over women, drawing on concepts of violence against women. Not surprisingly, this frame is not explicitly reflected in laws and workplace policies. In the United States and the EU, feminists were most successful in having some of their policy visions translated into laws. In a successful translation of feminist visions, US and EU laws define sexual harassment as "unwanted" behavior based on the subjective experience of victims rather than an "objective" standard. Finally, feminist arguments that women and men perceive sexual harassment differently found their way into the United States "reasonable women's standard," which can be used to acknowledge gender differences in perceptions, interpretations, and ways of dealing with sexual harassment.

The definition of sexual harassment in the 1994 German Federal Employee Protection Law has little to do with feminist discourses. As early as 1983, German feminists called for a broad anti-discrimination law to cover sexual harassment. However, federal policy-makers defined it instead as a non-gender-specific violation of dignity. Furthermore, the 1994 definition limits sexual harassment to behavior that is "intentionally designed to harass" and has to be "recognizably rejected by victims." Comparing the United States and EU "unwantedness" to the German "recognizably rejected" behavior illustrates how cultural notions of gender relations and sexuality are embedded in legal texts and highlights the key question of definitional power: Who has the say over what constitutes sexual harassment, and whose perspectives does the law privilege?

The German law means that asking for or demanding sex, showing pornographic images, making sexual overtures, or telling sexual jokes is not illegal per se. These behaviors are illegal only if someone "recognizably rejects" them. Not only is it incumbent on the victim to recognizably reject such behaviors, it is also necessary for courts to investigate how the victim communicated the rejection to the perpetrator. Therefore, the definition forces us to take the subjective perspective of the perpetrator rather than the victim on what constitutes sexual harassment. Furthermore, the German definition ignores the fact that many victims do not immediately resist harassment for a host of reasons, such as fear of repercussions or of losing their job.

But inherent in this German law is the cultural belief that women in general welcome flirtation, sexual overtures, and sexual advances by any men – as Fitzgerald (2004: 95) puts it, a "stubbornly androcentric view of female sexuality and men's right of access." In practice, men and women interpret situations differently, as Fitzgerald, drawing on US psychological research, explains: "Men routinely interpret women's behavior as inviting sexual overtures despite women's assertions that they want nothing of the sort." Not surprisingly, then, despite feminist experts on both sides of the Atlantic documenting the difficulties of resisting sexual harassment, German policy-makers adopted an androcentric viewpoint, privileging the perspective of men that sexual harassment is flirtation gone wrong. This formulation allows men to commit any form of sexual harassment at least once.

Feminist frames have by no means already entered "mainstream" US culture; judges continue to base their decisions on often unacknowledged understandings of gender and sexuality, which, as Fitzgerald (2004) points out, can lead to silencing or misinterpreting victims and their behavior. The US notion of "unwelcomeness" shows how an initially feminist, victim-centered perspective can be undermined in court. The definition is from the perspective of victims, but courts apply it the other way round when they examine women's behavior, inquire whether women used vulgar language, and examine what they wore in order to assess whether the behavior was welcomed. The main difference between these perspectives seems subtle but is crucial. As Fitzgerald puts it: "Interrogating unwelcomeness necessitates examining her perspective, whereas examining welcomeness implicates his" (2004: 95).

The assumption that "sexual advances by any man to any woman are by definition welcome until she proves otherwise" (Fitzgerald 2004: 95) underlies both the German formulation of "recognizable rejection" and US court rulings. However, the German legal definition allows men a one-time mistake, whereas attorneys for victims in the United States can more easily make a case that certain behaviors are unwelcome and unwanted in general. Nevertheless, its application in US courts has not always been consistent with these notions. This discontinuity also demonstrates the importance of continued struggle over meanings in implementation and enforcement. In addition, it reveals how important a gendered discourse on sexual harassment is to making visible how otherwise unspoken gendered notions of sexuality and power creep into interpretations of what constitutes sexual harassment.

At the workplace level, both US and German employers have adopted non-gender-specific frameworks for conceptualizing sexual harassment. Their predominant discourses have little to do with feminist theories. US employers have turned sexual harassment into "bad behavior." The German notion of mobbing equally lacks a clear link to unequal power. On both sides of the Atlantic, these conceptualizations are far from the

US and EU legal definitions that situate sexual harassment in the context of gender inequality.

How institutional arrangements shape movements

The movements against sexual harassment were born out of the second-wave women's movement, labor movements, and the civil rights movement, in training activists, shaping discourses, and developing strategies. The movements on both sides of the Atlantic have challenged existing cultural codes, the gendered culture in the workplace, and employer condoning of discriminatory, unfair practices, resulting in victims rather than perpetrators losing their jobs. They have used scientific knowledge and alternative discourses to alter recognition of sexual harassment as a problem. Their strategies have included creating public awareness and convincing unions, courts, policy-makers, and the state to take action.

The politics of sexual harassment are a prime example of the process of institutionalizing feminist politics, "moving feminist protest inside" of institutions (Katzenstein 1998). Feminists have embarked on a path of continued discursive battles inside institutions in which expertise and persuasion have been crucial, rather than choosing protest forms outside institutions that require drawing media attention and mobilizing large numbers of activists. The argument here is that feminists were more or less successful in Europe and the United States because feminist actors and advocates negotiated sexual harassment policies and laws in different institutional arrangements: different legal systems, constellations of industrial relations, and degrees of institutionalized gender politics.

Social movement theorists view these institutional arrangements as part of political opportunity structures, but have also most recently challenged this view of "structures" as too static (Goodwin and Jasper 2004). This research supports this critique by demonstrating how the political opportunity structures shaped the movements but social movements also began to shape these institutional arrangements. Finally, because ideas are so crucial to the politics of sexual harassment, we need to examine the different discursive opportunities feminists encountered (Ferree 2003).

Each institutional context has created a specific movement. The broadest movement developed in the United States, beginning with individual plaintiffs and their (feminist-identified or not) attorneys in the courts. Grassroots activists founded independent women's organizations that advocated for policy change and worked on creating public awareness. This movement brought radical feminist anti-rape activists and activists concerned with working women's issues together with women in "liberal" public interest law firms. Together they turned sexual harassment into a legitimate issue for policies. Together they achieved a legal revolution through the courts, aided by "friendly" politicians and administrators, for example in the EEOC. Today there is an industry of sexual harassment, including experts, consultants, attorneys, and women's organizations, offering advice to individuals and employers alike.

In the EU, advocates were located within the supranational administration and were able to connect with, augment, and draw on the contributions of a few feminist organizations concerned with the issue. French and UK activists used the European Community strategically to circumvent their nonresponsive national governments. These actors did not use the courts; policy change came through incremental change over almost twenty years until the 2002 EU binding directive. Europeanization of sexual harassment, or the evolution of EU regulation, has been a ping-pong process between the supranational and national levels. Keck and Sikkink's concept of the boomerang effect does not fully capture this interaction. Nevertheless, their concept of transnational advocacy networks is useful in unraveling the importance of networks that brought the concept of sexual harassment into the EU. Within the EU, the TAN on gender equality circulated the concept and various policy models. This TAN was created by the second-wave women's movement, which includes anti-violence advocates and international women's labor unions. The TAN was crucial because it connected the levels of policymaking and diverse, overlapping substantive issues. These advocates did not organize international protest activities or other traditional forms of social movement action. Instead, they helped create transnational expertise, knowledge, and professional legal discourses. This expertise helped advocates make their case and provided policy-makers with models at the national level. Activists now can mobilize on both the national and the supranational level and try to effect changes.

The West German movement began with a few women who protested sexual harassment in the German parliament. For the statutory–corporatist route for change in the German structure of workplace regulations, these activists built a strategic alliance with the unions to create awareness and needed to convince political parties to take on the issue. Not surprisingly, activists had an uphill battle to elicit support from male-dominated organizations that had problems internally with sexual harassment. Only with the newly created femocrats, the gender equality offices, did an institutional ally come onto the terrain. Without influences from the United States and the EU, even the weaker 1994 German law against sexual harassment would probably still not exist, nor would the parliament have debated a broad anti-discrimination law in 2005.

The lack of broader awareness and support for the issue of sexual harassment in Germany is even more apparent when we compare the three self-help books and one city office specifically addressing sexual harassment with the tremendous popular support for the movement against mobbing. The anti-mobbing industry includes offices and hot-lines organized by unions, churches, lawyers, experts, and research agencies. This broad acceptance of mobbing victims is in stark contrast to the continued distrust and stigmatization of victims of sexual harass-ment. Especially in East Germany, given the greater reluctance to iden-tify sexual harassment as a form of gendered injustice, the concept of mobbing does offer victims of sexual harassment a language to talk about psycho-social interpersonal and group dynamics. This ambivalent progress is best expressed by one activist (2004): "When women who have been sexually harassed say 'I have suffered mobbing,' we have lost the battle that we fought for: to make violence against women visible."

Hence, the movements themselves were shaped by the different polit-ical opportunity structures they encountered. The legal focus in the United States brought about an army of feminist legal scholars and ex-perts, whereas feminist legal discourse on sexual harassment is only emerging in Europe. German feminists did not perceive the courts as responsive, though the labor courts played the major role in creating laws against mobbing. Nor have women across Europe decided to challenge their national governments and take cases of sexual harassment to the European Court of Justice. This demonstrates that political opportunity structures do not exist unless activists interpret them as such.

Feminists' influence and the paths for change

The paths for change depended on the political and legal institutions in which the struggles took place. These routes also shaped the ways in which feminist ideas could influence the laws and the meanings of sexual harassment. As Mazur (2002) points out, feminist success means that feminists participate in policy debates and ensure that gender is taken into account. In practice, these routes gave different status to feminist expertise and to women who experienced sexual harassment. Only in the United States did decision-makers face victims. Because the most important steps to creating sexual harassment law occurred in the courts, judges made decisions with individual women in front of them. In the court room, lawyers could draw on feminist legal, social, and psychological expertise and feminist organizations' support in the form of amicus briefs.

In the EU, advocates achieved bureaucratic, incremental policy changes at the supranational level, building on continuous expansion of gender equality law. The European Commission was able to mobilize significant transnational feminist expertise. In the German case, the most important policy changes came through consensual compromise, mostly behind closed doors, and employers and unions lobbying the political parties did not consider individual stories or feminist expert testimony. When parliament debated the law, the audience was predominately female because most male parliamentarians did not even attend. Feminist discourses were lost in creating consensus about what sexual harassment means in male-dominated organizations and institutions.

In other words, when decision-makers shaped policies based on individual women's experiences and feminist expertise, they tended to be more victim-friendly. By contrast, when parliaments did not hear from victims or feminist experts, the laws tended to be more limited, reflecting how decision-makers identified with perpetrators and were more concerned with potentially falsely accused men who needed to be protected than with ensuring legal redress for victims.

Comparing these paths also highlights the important role of the institutional arrangements that shaped politics and reveals how dominant frames are "anchored institutionally," as Ferree's (2003) concept of discursive opportunities suggests. The 1964 Civil Rights Act constitutes an institutional anchor for feminist frames, as does the 1975 EC Directive on Equal Treatment. Using these strong existing laws, advocates built a case for legal and state intervention. By contrast, the German frame of violation of dignity refers symbolically to constitutional law but without effective legal enforcement.

Institutional arrangements are important in shaping the paths and successes of feminist policy-making. The frames feminists used to mobilize support "made sense" for individuals and movements because drawing on existing laws convinced policy-makers and judges. Social movements do not select frames to package an issue as if to sell in a supermarket (Oliver and Johnston 2000). Frames that become dominant must not merely resonate culturally; they must also have institutional anchors and fit into institutionalized gender equality policy logics (O'Connor, Orloff, and Shaver 1999). Here the institutional anchors were existing laws and court decisions, which created dominant ways to conceptualize gender equality in the United States and the EU, while Germany has lacked an enforceable anti-discrimination law despite the constitutional assurance of gender equality.

Transnational political opportunity structures

Advocates took advantage of policy windows to create or reform laws (Kingdon 1984). The media played a major role in diffusing the concept of sexual harassment and opening these windows of opportunities to raise awareness. Because of the explosive mixture of sex and power, media coverage of scandals reaches national and international audiences. Even if Anita Hill's allegations did not preclude Clarence Thomas's confirmation, her testimony created public awareness across North America and Europe. Many Americans and most Europeans heard the term sexual harassment for the first time during the Hill–Thomas hearings. In the United States, the scandal rejuvenated the anti-harassment movement; a new wave of activists working within institutions lobbied for legal reforms and revisions of workplace policies in the aftermath of the hearings. The incident created a policy opportunity window for promoting the passage of the Civil Rights Act of 1991, even under a Republican president. In the EU member states, the Hill–Thomas controversy, combined with the EU measures, provided impetus for legal changes but also the grounds for anti-American, anti-feminist media discourses (Möller 1999).

For EU member states, we need to add an international dimension to the concept of political opportunities. This includes transatlantic and transnational exchange, international media coverage of events, and the impact of EU measures on member states. In most member states, including Germany, reforms of existing gender equality laws provided openings to push for including sexual harassment; in others, reforms of penal codes and labor laws of health and safety were used to formulate the first legal definitions.

The reform of the EU 2002 Directive on Equal Treatment provides a transnational window of opportunity for advocates: most member states have to adopt or modify their laws. In this second round of reforms, policy outcomes and enforcement and implementation mechanisms will depend on national-level feminist advocates' ability to convince policy-makers to design meaningful laws and build institutional mechanisms to enforce them. The 1994 reform of the German Federal Gender Equality Law provided the first window of opportunity to pass a law against sexual harassment; the EU directives now provide the impetus to pass an inclusive anti-discrimination law.

Scandals can create public awareness, but they can also de-legitimize victims and de-politicize the issue. The reception of the Hill–Thomas hearings in EU member states was more than ambivalent, and European media continued to misrepresent US law by decontextualizing allegations and reporting selectively on court cases. Since Jones's "day in court" and former president Clinton's impeachment process, advocates in the United States, as in the EU, face greater difficulty demanding enforcement of sexual harassment laws (Mink 2000; MacKinnon 2004). Since the 1998 Supreme Court decisions, the EEOC has received fewer complaints, employers have relaxed enforcement of policies regarding consensual relationships, and courts have been more favorable to employers.

Movements changing institutional arrangements

Even institutional arrangements, which might seem to be the "structural" aspects of political opportunities, are less static than they appear, and social movements can influence them. Activists can build on the successes of previous social movements, effecting legal changes and creating new institutional arrangements. The US legal–regulatory route was possible only because of the 1964 Civil Rights Act. The civil rights movement also promoted newly institutionalized access for social movement activists: the EEOC and EEO and HR personnel modeled sexual harassment measures on anti-discrimination workplace policies with grievance policy procedures.

It is not surprising that women in "progressive" organizations and political entities first politicized sexual harassment. Claims to equality by these organizations had raised these women's expectations of equal and fair treatment. African American women in state civil rights agencies brought sexual harassment lawsuits during the 1970s, and Anita Hill's testimony was against the then director of the federal EEOC, the very agency in charge of enforcing anti-discrimination laws. Similarly, the women in the West German Green party in the early 1980s politicized sexual harassment when the party's entry into parliament opened a political space.

Advocates in Europe also built on existing sex equality laws and used political opportunity structures shaped by the women's movement. The European Community had responded to the second-wave women's movement by creating a women's policy agency. This Unit for Gender Equality under the Directorate of Employment and Social Affairs in the European Commission has been a central actor in promoting sexual harassment measures by helping to create transnational information, knowledge, and expertise, by diffusing policy models, and by promoting EU-level soft- and hard-law measures. In administration, individuals and politicians, including Evelyn Collins and Commissioner Anna Diamantopoulou, made a difference.

Furthermore, the Commission's gender equality unit aided the creation of the TAN, which helped strengthen the EU gender equality law through the Treaty of Amsterdam in 1997 (Helfferich and Kolb 2001). This in turn helped advocates make the case for including sexual harassment in the 2002 Equal Treatment Directive. Hence, at the EU level this office has been crucial for giving advocates and organizations access to the policy-making process.

The successes of feminists at the EU level have slowly trickled down to the member states. It is important to see that the EU has not merely added a supranational arena to the national political opportunity structures: EU gender equality politics have the potential to transform the very political landscape of gender equality politics in the member states (Roggeband and Verloo 1999; Hoskyns 1996; Liebert ed. 2003; Imig and Tarrow 2001). One important way has been to charge them with creating women's state agencies to monitor the implementation of EU sex equality law.

In Germany, this Federal Ministry of Women became the main actor in preparing the 1994 legislation. Nevertheless, the ministry had little influence over the debates through which political actors created consensus. In the end, the ministry was not able to provide access to the policy-making arena for feminist experts and advocates. As others have pointed out, this ministry has few resources and little power compared with the other ministries (Ferree 1995a). Under the Christian Democrat and Liberal party coalition, the ministry was a weak player, and was not able to turn its own in-house measures against sexual harassment into law. As a result, 1994 German law was farthest from feminist notions of sexual harassment. In part, this reflects the fact that workplace regulation in Germany is an established policy field in which new actors (e.g., newly institutionalized women's policy machineries) have a difficult time making an impact. Sexual harassment policies are not comparable to violence-against-women laws in general, a policy field in which women's movements and policy machineries have been able to promote change effectively (Weldon 2002).

Hence, the nation-state has remained a key actor and target for feminist demands for awareness and legal change, despite supranational influences that were the impetus for national-level policies, despite global links of advocates, activists, and policy-makers, and despite trans-national windows of opportunity. Nonetheless, in the EU, movements can create political opportunities by shaping institutional arrangements and creating laws, which help other advocates in turn to promote changes at various policy levels.

The politics of sexual harassment also demonstrate how social movements can change political opportunity structures and contribute to building institutions that aid future policy reforms. Offices and institutional arrangements established in response to the US civil rights and women's movements and EU women's movements now in turn shape approaches to sexual harassment.

Lessons for women's policy machineries

The relationship between women's movements and supranational and state institutions was important in all cases, but sexual harassment policies also demonstrate how heterogeneous institutions can be in advancing gendered interests. These institutions were important allies in legitimizing the issue, creating expertise, and developing laws and regulations. But state agencies do not have to be gender-specific to make an impact. Weldon (2002) has argued that interaction of women's policy machineries and autonomous women's movements is crucial in explaining anti-violence policies, but policy machineries do not seem to be necessary for the development of sexual harassment laws. The European Commission's women's unit and the German Federal Ministry of Women, as well as German gender equality advocates throughout the public sector, have been crucial actors. However, in the United States, the EEOC was more influential than the Women's Bureau. The EEOC, under Norton, brought feminist visions into the political/legal realm. Hence, not women's policy machinery but offices charged with anti-discrimination enforcement shaped the US approach.

The irony is that the policy outcomes look strikingly different. German women's offices were founded on the assumption of sexual difference, but the legal text of "violation of dignity" does not explicitly refer to gender inequality. Neither do German employer policies refer to gender differences; anti-mobbing policies subsume sexual harassment under general fairness. By contrast, the EEOC, though responsible for all anti-discrimination law, created gender-specific notions of sexual harassment as sex discrimination. The US example shows the importance of an agency empowered to implement, monitor, and enforce laws. Policy-makers will need to design effective implementation and enforcement mechanisms in the EU member states.

Neither country has adopted a coherent gender sameness or difference approach. The US women's movement most successfully framed gender equality issues as gender sameness in analogy to racial equality (Ferree 1987). The analogy supported taking down barriers for women in male-dominated jobs. The frame of sexual harassment as discrimination fits into the dominant liberal orientation of the women's movement toward ensuring equal opportunities (O'Connor, Orloff, and Shaver 1999). Gender sameness is powerful because women gain a sense of entitlement to fair and professional treatment. The simple message is that everyone should have the same playing field.

But in the courts feminist activists and legal experts have also made arguments about gender differences, for example in how women and men perceive sexual harassment and how they act when harassed. Feminists also strategically reproduced the discourse of sexuality in which women are passive and men are active aggressors (Baker 2001). The US "reasonable women's standard" is an example of embedding the recognition of gender difference in a law oriented toward gender sameness.

Hence, US courts have been willing to conceptualize sexual harassment explicitly as rooted in gender inequality, which allows those implementing the laws to address power differentials. In line with traditional notions of gender difference, the German law refers to the duty of employers to "protect" employees from sexual advances; there is no mention of women's specific vulnerability to male sexual aggression, or of the possibility that interpretations of harassment might be gendered. Neither the law nor court rulings explicitly embrace or validate a woman's perspective on sexual harassment. The law does not even point to gender inequalities as a source of sexual harassment. The concept of "violation of dignity" does not refer to gender power.

Future research could compare more thoroughly the "gendered" nature of state institutions by examining the role of the public sector in creating sexual harassment policies and laws. While some state agencies can be promoters of gender equality, a useful comparison for the effectiveness of sexual harassment laws is the public sector. Sexual harassment is such a striking example, because the state agencies can be employers themselves, and hence sexual harassment policies reveal how states themselves both set standards and enforce laws for employees. In particular, the military and police forces will remain crucial sites for examining how serious states are about including women in male-dominated organizations in changing gendered notions of work, and in transforming the gender culture in the workplace to be more inclusive of women.

The future of sexual harassment politics

In Europe, critics have argued that laws are the wrong way to effect cultural changes. Hence, we need to ask what difference the laws have made in the United States. Despite feminist concerns over laws as "tools of patriarchy" (Pateman 1988), sexual harassment laws seem to serve as instruments for challenging gender and sexual norms in the workplace. MacKinnon (2004) today celebrates the revolution in sexual harassment law as an example of successfully deploying law to incorporate women's experiences. US law has enabled individuals to challenge employers' practices more than have laws in EU member states. But there are several drawbacks of a legal-centric approach.

The challenge for both the United States and Europe is to prevent harassment from occurring. Certainly, as feminists have pointed out, there are multiple causes of sexual harassment, and the issue is inseparable from larger issues of gender and sexuality, gender inequality, hierarchical structure, and women's subordinate position. Laws by themselves do not prevent harassment from occurring or ensure that the needs of victims are met if it occurs. Most important, employers have to implement the laws. But, in the end, combating harassment means finding ways to stop men from harassing women.

The German law has helped businesses more than victims. The majority of court cases have involved conflicts between employers and perpetrators, not employees against their employers. Courts have thus applied the law more often *for or against* perpetrators than *for* victims. The law has empowered employers to intervene and sanction perpetrators, which is certainly important to ensure action against harassers, but in practice it has not yet empowered harassed women to hold employers responsible in court. However, sexual harassment laws have the potential to be tools of empowerment, giving women a language to talk about what used to be unspeakable and to signal that they no longer have to put up with it, because sexual harassment is not just a nuisance but also an injustice and illegal. We should not underestimate this symbolic power of laws. In addition, advocates and workplace activists can mobilize around laws for increased power in demanding changes in employers' practices.

Europeans can learn several lessons from the US approach. First, it is worthwhile examining the US model and its effects carefully. Popular myths exaggerate the extent to which US employers have enforced policies. Given the consistently high numbers of women who report that they have encountered sexual harassment, if it were true that employers dismiss every man at the slightest accusation, we would no longer be discussing the need for proactive approaches to hiring more women.

When asked what changes the law on sexual harassment has made, an attorney who represents employers in court believes that sexual harassment continues, but that "men who harass have become more careful *who* they harass" (interview attorney 2001). An important question for future research is therefore how employers enforce the laws. Schultz (2003) argues that sexual harassment law is used against sexual minority women and men. Certainly managers may use complaints as an excuse to dismiss employees they want to fire for other reasons. By contrast, if harassers are powerful and seen as making valuable contributions, employers might be willing to keep the perpetrators happy and try to appease the victims by promoting them up and away or paying generous severance packages. Hence, the social status of both harasser and victim is likely to influence the ways employers handle complaints.

Europeans can also learn from the US model that laws need to hold employers responsible. These laws can provide incentives to change practices of handling complaints, setting expectations for employees, and creating awareness. In addition, EU member states need to think about incentives to establish working cultures free of sexual harassment and strategies for taking complaints seriously. Because several EU countries have long-standing traditions of union participation in workplace regulations, unions need to be on the side of any effort to combat harassment. The US example shows that unions themselves can be held accountable for discriminatory practices within the unions and between union members. Several unions in EU countries have begun to recognize conflicts between union members, for example by appointing separate representatives for the complainant and the alleged perpetrator.

Once unions in the power structure are on board, they will be able to play a more important role in devising policies that will not just reflect employers' interests in protecting companies from lawsuits but also create inclusive workplace cultures. Unions need to recognize what they can gain from representing women's interests and involving more women on the shop floor. Unions can press for collective rights and demand that employers take action for employees as groups.

We see in the United States that the impetus for social change and enforcement of the laws relies on individuals coming forth with complaints, which puts an undue burden on those already most affected. In addition, the politics of fear has pitted women against men. The German and EU models are useful in gaining men as allies in this transformation process. The European approach to mobbing and bullying has the advantage that men in the majority group can identify with a potential victim. Still, this approach is limited by the absence of an explicit gender analysis.

Dignity and equality

The problem with conceptualizing sexual harassment merely as the violation of dignity is that gender inequality disappears. It has been an easy concept for unions to embrace, because it takes the politically charged underlying gender conflict out of sexual harassment. But when sexual harassment becomes subsumed under mobbing without a discussion of the power differentials between men and women, the question of who has the say in how the problem is defined and whose perspective counts drops out of the equation. Furthermore, by avoiding gender relations, these policies do not challenge the cultural assumptions that men can view women as desirous of sexual advances.

This does not mean that "dignity" has no redeeming qualities. Indeed, it overcomes some limitations of the "sameness" approach to fair, respectful, and equal treatment. The US concept's analogy to racial segregation does not translate well into the German context, because it assumes a comparable standard and flies in the face of any notion of gender difference.

The idea of safeguarding the dignity of all workers has two important advantages. First, if a lesbian is harassed because she does not conform to standards of gender performance, she does not have to argue that a man in her situation would have been treated differently (Elman 1996). Women from minority groups no longer have to decide whether they were racially or sexually harassed, because the intersectionality of experiences based on membership in minority groups is included. Women who are harassed because they belong to a racial/ethnic group may file claims for redress. Second, the concept of dignity resonates better than sex discrimination with individual women's understandings of the experience of sexual harassment, particularly in Europe, where treating men and women the same goes against strongly cherished notions of "gender difference." Violated human dignity, sexual autonomy, and integrity capture what happens to women when they feel that someone has overstepped a boundary or intruded into their emotional or physical space (see Hirshman and Larson 1998).

Third, while the US approach might be most suited to addressing harassment between an employee and a supervisor, the German approach might better deal with other harassment situations. The German model can capture group dynamics, for example when men direct hostility and sexual harassment against women in atypical jobs such as construction, police, and the military. Fourth, the European approach to the mobbing and bullying of everyone, not just protected groups, has the advantage that men who belong to the majority group can identify with victims. It is important to realize that sexual harassment is a *gender issue*, it is not merely a problem that women encounter, but instead it is a problem of masculinity in a normative heterosexist culture. Most discussions are surprisingly uninformed about how gender shapes sexual harassment, including why men harass and how men treat each other. Studies of normative heterosexual masculinity have investigated how sexual harassment serves to establish hierarchies among men (Gruber and Morgan 2005; Connell 2005). Men use words and actions to sexualize women and gay men to prove that they themselves are not only masculine but straight. These practices and norms reinforce gendered structures of sexuality in organizations (Hearn and Parkin 2001).

Hence, instead of teaching men how to avoid false accusations by untrustworthy, vengeful women, we need to find ways to mobilize men to take the lead in creating fair and equal working relations. Men need to be involved in social control of other men. Some German interviewees described men "fining" each other for sexist comments or behavior; the "fines" go into a "Macho-kasse" or "macho 'kitty'." It is not enough to say, "I am a good guy because I do not harass women"; it is crucial to be actively involved in creating equal relations with women and other men.

If the political project is to create more equal gender cultures at work, gender analysis also needs to assess working relationships among men in the context of constructions of masculinity. If we demand only that men treat women the same as men, the project will fail, because it is founded on the misleading assumption that men treat each other as equals. Minority men are often victimized through bullying or mobbing, but so are heterosexual and gay men who do not conform to gender-normative expectations. Their experience of being harassed is a gendered one, too. Because men ultimately listen to other men, it is crucial to create a political agenda in which men are allies for change in workplace cultures. Men need to actively reconfigure not only norms and expectations for femininity but also, and most importantly, norms of masculinity.

This study has demonstrated how important it is to use a gender analysis to examine the politics of sexual harassment. It is crucial to advocate for the perspective of victims, not only in legislation but in workplace policies and enforcement. Not just sensitivity to gender but a thorough analysis of *gender relations* is needed in organizations consider-ing procedures for handling complaints. Institutional arrangements, including works councils, women's offices, and EEO offices, not only shape paths for individual complaints but carry meanings and cultural understandings of injustice that shape the expectations of individuals.

Activists and individuals perceive these organizations as "gendered." US employees were able to file complaints with the EEO and EEOC. By contrast, German women perceived works councils and labor courts as too male-dominated to be sympathetic. Only with the establishment of public-sector women's offices did the issue become visible, though iron-ically most of these offices did not have the power works councils had to investigate complaints. Finally, gender does not mean "women." Women tend to feel more comfortable filing complaints with women because they expect them to be more sympathetic to their experiences, but my interviews revealed that untrained women are more likely than trained men to reproduce stereotypes and myths, for example by focusing on the behavior of victims.

When institutions take over an issue as complicated as sexual harass-ment, the challenge is to insist that gender matters and equality and empowerment are not sacrificed. Defining sexual harassment as *both* sex discrimination *and* violation of dignity is a promising move in the EU 2002 directive, as is the explicit definition of both gender and sex-ual harassment. However, advocates need to support these definitions in national legislation in member states. Creating more equal workplace cultures means that women and men need to have equal status and power in workplace hierarchies. I agree here with Schultz (2003) that we need to link sexual harassment to sex segregation and empowering women to have a say in establishing cultural norms. Otherwise, we spend our time worrying about "inappropriate" behavior and witness the continued trivializing of the problem, especially in management discourses that reduce women's experiences to questions of individual personal comfort. Sexual harassment keeps women from entering male-dominated and better-paying jobs. By engaging in it as colleagues and supervisors, men signal to women that they can choose to erotize situ-ations whenever they feel like it – which means that women are sexual objects, after all.

For both continents, creating gender equality in the workplace and eradicating sexual harassment will go hand in hand with eliminating *gender harassment*. EU member states have begun to construct stronger definitions of sexual harassment as sex discrimination. Moreover, laws on the books have the potential to effect changes, but they need to be applied, and for most European member states this means coming up with meaningful ways to institutionalize enforcement mechanisms.

The EU directive offers women the hope that sexual harassment will no longer be just a menace but also a crime. Women need to participate in policy-makers' and employers' struggle over tools for combating it. As one union woman said: "No higher being will rescue us." Finally, such important change should not depend on the risks individuals take in sticking out their necks; instead state agencies, courts, employers, unions, and everyone in the workplace need to participate to bring the promise of these laws to life and create more equal gender cultures.

Appendix A: List of cited interviews

I conducted ninety-one semi-structured interviews between 1994 and 2005 (see Appendix B). In order to protect the confidentiality of the interviewees, I am listing here only the names of those whom I quoted and who were comfortable, to be referred to by name.

Augstein, Renate, *femocrat*, Federal Ministry of Women, unit for violence against women, interview, Bonn, April 27, 1999.

Baer, Susanne, Professor, Humboldt University, Berlin, legal scholar on sexual harassment, interview, Berlin, February 14, 2004.

Bertelsmann, Klaus, labor lawyer, pro-feminist sexual harassment expert, interview, Hamburg, 1999.

Degen, Barbara Dr., feminist legal scholar and attorney, interview, Bonn, April 28, 1999.

Garcia, Ada, Professor, Université catholique de Louvain, Director of the Centre Femmes et Sociétés Belgium, interview, Paris, January 14, 2005.

Hagemann-White, Carole, Professor, University of Osnabrück, researcher on violence against women, interview, Gelnhausen, June 15, 1999.

Helfferich, Barbara, Cabinet Member of European Commissioner Anna Diamantopoulou, Employment and Social Affairs, phone interview, June 10, 2003.

Huber, Agnes, former Head of the Equal Opportunity Unit on the European Commission, interview, Athens, June 17, 2003.

Kathmann, Maria, IG Metall union, interview, Frankfurt, April 22, 1999.

Le Magueresse, Catherine, President of AVFT, interview, Paris, January 15, 2005.

Maenz, Heike, sexual harassment consultant, interview, Düsseldorf, April 19, 1999.

Meschkutat, Bärbel, researcher, trainer, sexual harassment and mobbing expert, interview, Dortmund, 2003.

Mueller, Ursula, Professor, University of Bielefeld, Germany, researcher on sexual harassment, interview, Gelnhausen, June 15, 1999.

Nussbaum, Karen, Director of the AFL-CIO's Working Women's Department, interview, Washington, D.C., June 15, 2002.

Plogstedt, Sibylle, feminist journalist and sociologist, interview, Bonn, April 28, 1999.

Rubenstein, Michael, pro-feminist, labor expert on sexual harassment, phone interview, January 6, 2005.

Wellner, Ute, lawyer and sexual harassment consultant, interview, Düsseldorf, April 19, 1999.

Wolf, Hanna, SPD parliamentarian, phone interview, July 7, 1999.

Appendix B: Data collection

This study is based on multiple data sources, collected between 1994 and 2005 in fieldwork and from extensive archival research in the United States, in Germany and at the European University Institute in Florence. Among the libraries and archives visited in Germany were the library of the German Bundestag, Bonn, the German Archive for the Press, Bonn, and the Archive for the Press at the Free University of Berlin. I visited the feminist archives of the Zentrale Einrichtung für Frauenforschung und Frauenstudien Berlin (ZE), Freie Universität Berlin, the FrauenMediaTurm, Das Feministische Archiv und Dokumentationszentrum, Köln, and at the University of Bielefeld the Interdisziplinäres Frauenforschungs/Zentrum (IFF), Information und Dokumentation. The most helpful archives for information on the German legal system were the private archive of Dr. Barbara Degen, Bonn and the library of the German Federal Labor Court in Kassel. In addition, I collected important information on the European developments in the Weibsblick Frauenarchiv Wien and in the library of the European University Institute, in Florence, Italy. Finally, the women's offices of German political parties were extremely helpful in locating official documents, reports, and communications between political actors, feminist and legal expert witnesses, and EU officials.

I conducted altogether ninety-one formal interviews and many more informal ones between 1994 and 2005. Most interviews ranged between thirty minutes and two hours. To study the emergence of sexual harassment and to locate important policy and legal documents, I conducted interviews with German, US and EU politicians, state officials and other policy-makers, as well as legal experts, feminist activists, trade unionists, and representatives from employers' associations. In addition, I analyzed parliamentary, policy, and legal documents. For example, I conducted extensive searches on the EU databases and collected and analyzed all official documents regarding the violation of "dignity" and "sexual harassment" in the workplace. To study the emergence of sexual harassment as a political issue in Germany, German policy documents, including earlier drafts of proposals that were debated in the parliament and discussed in expert hearings, allowed me to identify diverging and contested approaches to the legal definitions of sexual harassment. In addition, publications and statements of political parties, women's organizations, and trade unions allowed me to trace the timing of policy development and the framing of sexual harassment in the context of other issues of gender equality. Interviews with political and administrative actors who were involved in the process were helpful in identifying additional sources.

To study the diffusion and implementation of sexual harassment in the German public sector, I compiled information on the federal, state, and local level. For federal employers, I draw on the unpublished results of a survey by the Federal Ministry of Family, Women, Youth, and Seniors from 1999. This study asked all Federal Ministries and other Federal employers about the implementation of the 1994 law. Findings include the numbers of complaints and sanctions imposed on perpetrators of sexual harassment, and educational awareness programs. I compare these results with the survey of Federal employees by the US Merit Systems Board (1983, 1988, and 1995).

For the role of states in the implementation process, I conducted a telephone survey of all sixteen state offices for gender equality to gain information about the current state of implementation of sexual harassment policies; for example, I asked for information on state regulations or recommendations for the implementation of these laws both for their own employees and for the private sector. In addition, I located information on the extent to which educational awareness programs have been organized through these or other state offices.

Finally, for the initiation and implementation of policies on the local, communal level in the public sector, I conducted face-to-face interviews with twenty-five women's advocates using a standardized questionnaire. There are more than 1465 women's advocates throughout German cities, and towns, administrations (see BMFSFJ 1998 for 1996 figures). I chose the interviewees through a snowball sampling procedure at a nationwide Women's Fair, the *Top '99,* in Düsseldorf in April 1999. I am confident that my sample of women's advocates is diverse in respect of representation of a variety of political, geographical, and town or city sizes. The officers were from four different states (Hesse, Saxony, North Rhine Westphalia, and Baden-Württemberg), representing various German states, states known to be progressive on gender politics and those with more traditional (family) policy approaches. Since these women's advocates attended the Fair, I assume that these officers, generally speaking, were more actively engaged in gender political issues than other officers. I asked questions about whether collective agreements on grievance procedures for sexual harassment and other types of equality policies existed, and who initiated these policies. I explicitly asked about the role of the women's advocates and works councils in the complaint process and in the frequency of complaints filed in regard to sexual harassment as well as in efforts to conduct training and awareness programs.

For the private sector, I gathered information on larger corporations. In addition to finding company brochures, surveys, and policies of a number of companies, I conducted eight face-to-face interviews with gender equality officers. The sample of companies included corporations in the service industry, in manufacturing, and transportation. Consequently, the composition of the workforce varies by sex. Because of the sensitivity of the issue and the disinterest in issues relating to sexual harassment, I found it difficult to solicit interviews from personnel managers. I was usually referred to the equality officers (most German companies call women's advocates "equality" officers) and sometimes to works council members. To study the possible diffusion of policy ideas from the United

States, I chose corporations that have businesses in the United States and in Germany. In addition, I purposefully included information on companies known for progressive policies toward women, which they showed by appearing at the Fair.

To study legal developments, I conducted an extensive comparison of court rulings involving claims and allegations of sexual harassment. I interviewed ten German legal experts. In addition, I have collected legal documents, and carried out extensive searches of court rulings of sexual harassment and newspaper accounts of cases. I have been surprised by the difficulties involved in conducting legal research in Germany. Identifying lawsuits regarding sexual harassment proved very difficult. I used all available legal databases, for example JURIS, the database of the Federal Labor Court, and searched extensively through legal journals. However, these legal databases are reputed to be far from complete collections of trials. Therefore, I was fortunate to gain access to the private collections of court rulings of a prominent legal scholar and lawyer, Dr. Barbara Degen, and to the collection of cases of the only state office which specifically handles sexual harassment complaints, the *Arbeitsstelle gegen sexuelle Diskriminierung und Gewalt am Ausbildungs- und Erwerbsplatz* (Office against Sexual Discrimination and Violence in Educational Settings and Workplaces) in Bremen.

In addition to collecting statistical data on court rulings, I conducted a written survey of all nineteen German higher labor courts (state level), asking for information on court trials involving sexual harassment between 1980 and 1999 in their courts or in labor courts of the first level. Seventeen of the nineteen higher courts responded with information on a total of seventy-five cases of sexual harassment. Yet, the data have some weaknesses. Most higher courts do not keep statistics on cases of sexual harassment, thus it is likely that the answers underreported the number of cases. Even though the trials are open to the public, and court records are public documents, the courts do not keep easily accessible records (Holzbecher et al. 1990: 293). Because there was no law explicitly on "sexual harassment" before 1994, information on lawsuits concerning sexual harassment in the workplace is difficult to find through existing legal databases. The labor courts heard sexual harassment cases as unfair dismissal lawsuits but did not catalogue these rulings under "sexual harassment." Thus, it was necessary to gather information on court trials directly through the courts, from lawyers who specialize in cases of labor law and sexual harassment, and from legal journals. I am confident my collection of legal cases is as comprehensive as possible. Pflüger and Baer (2005) replicated this survey method and included all lower-level labor courts.

Their comprehensive study, commissioned by the Ministry of Women, surveyed a representative sample of 1,000 employers. They conducted in-depth interviews with judges, attorneys, gender equality advocates, personnel managers, and union officials involved in the implementation process of the 1994 sexual harassment law. Comparing my findings with theirs, I am confident they are generalizable.

For the US case, the emergence of sexual harassment is well documented. I was able to draw mostly on secondary sources regarding the development of sexual harassment policies and laws. I also collected and analyzed primary government reports and documents, documentations of hearings, and research commissioned by government agencies. For the study on the enforcement and the implementation of sexual harassment policies, I conducted extensive searches for materials of the EEOC office in Washington D.C., the administrative office of the Federal courts. For the implementation on the company level, I interviewed EEO officers in universities, attorneys representing both victims and employers, consultants, unionists, and feminist activists. I also observed several sexual harassment awareness programs. In addition, I collected materials from unions and women's organizations including NOW and 9 to 5.

References

Abrahms, Kathryn. 1998. "The New Jurisprudence of Sexual Harassment." *Cornell Law Review* 83: 1169.

Abramson, Joan. 1979. *Old Boys, New Women: The Politics of Sex Discrimination.* New York, NY: Praeger.

Acker, Joan. 1990. "Hierarchies, Jobs, Bodies: A Theory of Gendered Organizations." *Gender and Society* 4 (2): 139–58.

al Yafai, Faisal. 2004. "Royal Secretary Tells of Clique." *Guardian* November 20 p. 15.

Alliance Against Sexual Coercion. 1981. *Fighting Sexual Harassment: An Advocacy Handbook.* Boston, MA: Alyson Publications.

Alter, Karen, and Jeannette Vargas. 2000. "Explaining Variation in the Use of European Litigation Strategies: European Community Law and British Gender Equality Policy." *Comparative Political Studies* 33: 452–82.

AVFT (Association européenne contre Les Violences faites aux Femmes au Travail). 2004. "Le Droit Une Arme Pour les Violeurs." Communiqué de Presse, December 7.

Bacchi, Carol L. 1999. *Women, Policy, and Politics: The Construction of Policy Problems.* London; Thousand Oaks, CA: Sage.

Bacchi, Carol L. and Jim Jose. 1994. "Historicizing Sexual Harassment." *Women's History Review* 3 (2): 263–70.

Backhouse, Constance and Leah Cohen. 1981. *Sexual Harassment on the Job: How to Avoid the Working Woman's Nightmare.* Englewood Cliffs, NJ: Prentice-Hall.

Baer, Susanne. 2004. "Dignity or Equality? Responses to Workplace Harassment in European, German, and U.S. Law." Pp. 581–601 in *Directions in Sexual Harassment Law,* edited by Catharine A. MacKinnon and Reva B. Siegel. New Haven, CT: Yale University Press.

1996. "Pornography and Sexual Harassment in the EU." Pp. 51–66 in *Sexual Politics and the European Union: The New Feminist Challenge,* edited by Amy R. Elman. Providence, RI: Berghahn Books.

1995. *Würde oder Gleichheit? Zur Angemessenen Grundrechtlichen Konzeption von Recht gegen Diskriminierung am Beispiel Sexueller Belästigung am Arbeitsplatz in der Bundesrepublik Deutschland und den USA.* Baden-Baden: Nomos Verlagsgesellschaft.

Baker, Carrie. 2001. "Sex, Power, and Politics: The Origins of Sexual Harassment Policy in the United States." Ph.D. dissertation, Institute of Women's Studies, Emory University.

Banaszak, Lee Ann, Karen Beckwith, and Dieter Rucht. 2003. "When Power Relocates: Interactive Changes in Women's Movements and States." pp. 1–29 in *Women's Movements Facing the Reconfigured State*, edited by Lee Ann Banaszak, Karen Beckwith, and Dieter Rucht. Cambridge: Cambridge University Press.

Baur, Christine. 2002. "Harassment in Professional Life." Paper presented at the 3rd European Women's Lawyers Association (EWLA) Congress in Paris, September 20–1 *http://www.ewla.org/wf_dl/baur.doc*

Bergamaschi, Myriam. 2000. "The Gender Perspective in the Policies of European Trade Unions." Pp. 159–75 in *Gender Policies in the European Union*, edited by Mariagrazia Rossilli. New York, NY: Peter Lang.

Berghahn, Sabine. 1995. "Gender in the Legal Discourse in Post-Unification Germany: Old and New Lines of Conflict." *Social Politics: International Studies in Gender, State & Society* 2: 37–50.

Berkovitch, Nitza. 2002. *From Motherhood to Citizenship: Women's Rights and International Organizations.* Baltimore, MD: Johns Hopkins University Press.

Bernstein, Anita. 1994. "Law, Culture, and Harassment." *University of Pennsylvania Law Review* 142 (4): 1227–311.

Bertelsmann, Klaus. 1987. "Frauendiskriminierung. Sexuelle Beeinträchtigung im Betrieb." *Arbeitsrecht im Betrieb* 6: 123–37.

Bevan, Stephen, 2004. "Sex Case Woman Wins Damages." *Nottingham Evening Post* August 17 p. 12.

Bingham, Clara and Laura Leedy Gansler. 2002. *Class Action. The Story of Lois Jenson and the Landmark Case that Changed Sexual Harassment Law.* New York, NY: Random House.

Bravo, Ellen and Ellen Cassedy. 1992. *The 9 to 5 Guide to Combating Sexual Harassment: Candid Advice from 9 to 5, the National Association of Working Women.* New York, NY: John Wiley.

Brodsky, Carroll M. 1976. *The Harassed Worker.* Lexington, MA: DC Heath.

Brownmiller, Susan. 1999. *In Our Time: Memoir of a Revolution.* New York, NY: Dial Press.

——— 1975. *Against Our Will: Men, Women, and Rape.* New York: Simon and Schuster.

Brownmiller, Susan and Dolores Alexander. 1992. "How We Got Here: From Carmita Wood to Anita Hill." *Ms. Magazine* (January/February): 70–1.

Brush, Lisa D. 2003. *Gender and Governance.* Walnut Creek, CA: AltaMira Press.

——— 2002. "Changing the Subject: Gender and Welfare Regime Studies." *Social Politics: International Studies in Gender, State & Society* 9 (2): 161–86.

Buechler, Steven M. 1990. *Women's Movements in the United States.* New Brunswick, NJ: Rutgers University Press.

Buhr, Kornelia and Sabine Klein-Schonnefeld. 1996. "Kommentierung des Beschäftigtenschutzgesetzes und ähnlicher Vorschriften in Landesgesetzen." In *Frauengleichstellungsgesetze des Bundes und der Länder*, edited by Dagmar Schiek. Köln: Bund-Verlag.

Bundesministerium für Familie, Senioren, Frauen und Jugend (BMFSFJ). 2000. "Die Umsetzung des Bundesbeschäftigtenschutzgesetzes in Bundesministerien." Unpublished.

1998. *Frauen in der Bundesrepublik Deutschland.* Bonn: BMFSFJ.

1994. *Das Gleichberechtigungsgesetz des Bundes: Ein Gesetz für Frauen und Männer.* Bonn: BMFSFJ.

1993. *(K)ein Kavaliersdelikt? Sexuelle Belästigung im Arbeitsleben.* Bonn: Bundesministerium für Frauen und Jugend.

Burstein, Paul. 1999. "Social Movements and Public Policy." Pp. 3–21 in *How Social Movements Matter,* edited by Marco Guigni, Doug McAdam, and Charles Tilly. Minneapolis, MN: University of Minneapolis Press.

1998. *Discrimination, Jobs and Politics: The Struggle for Equal Opportunity Employment in the United States Since the New Deal.* Chicago, IL: University of Chicago Press.

1991. "Legal Mobilization as Social Movement Tactic: The Struggle for Equal Employment Opportunity." *American Journal of Sociology* 96 (5): 1201–25.

Cahill, Mia. 2001. *The Social Construction of Sexual Harassment Law: National and Organizational Effects.* Burlington, VT: Ashgate.

Canning, Kathleen. 1996. *Languages of Labor and Gender: Female Factory Work in Germany, 1850–1914.* Ithaca, NY: Cornell University Press.

Capell, Kerry. 2004. "Sex-Bias Suits: The Fight Gets Ugly." *Business Week.* September 6: 24–6.

Carter, Victoria A. 1992. "Working on Dignity: EC Initiatives on Sexual Harassment in the Workplace." *Northwestern Journal of International Law and Business* 12: 431–53.

Chamallas, Martha. 2004. "Title VII's Midlife Crisis: The Case of Constructive Discharge." *Southern California Law Review* 77: 307–95.

Cichowski, Rachel. 2002. "No Discrimination Whatsoever: Women's Transnational Activism and the Evolution of EU Sex Equality Policy." Pp. 220–39 in *Women's Activism and Globalization: Linking Local Struggles and Transnational Politics,* edited by Nancy A. Naples and Manisha Desai. New York, NY: Routledge.

Clemens, Elisabeth S. 1993. "Organizational Repertoires and Institutional Change: Women's Groups and the Transformation of US Politics." *American Journal of Sociology* 98 (4): 755–98.

Clinton, Bill. 2004. *My Life.* New York, NY: Knopf.

Cockburn, Cynthia. 1991. *In the Way of Women: Men's Resistance to Sex Equality in Organizations.* Ithaca, NY: ILR Press.

Collins, Evelyn. 1996. "European Union Sexual Harassment Policy." Pp. 23–34 in *Sexual Politics and the European Union: The New Feminist Challenge,* edited by R. A. Elman. Providence, RI: Berghahn Books.

Connell, R. W. 1990. "The State, Gender, and Sexual Politics: Theory and Appraisal?" *Theory and Society* 19: 507–44.

1987. *Gender and Power.* Stanford, CA: Stanford University Press.

2005. *Masculinities.* Crows Nest, NSW: Allen & Unwin.

Costain, Anne. 1992. *Inviting Women's Rebellion: A Political Process Interpretation of the Women's Movement.* Baltimore, MD: Johns Hopkins University Press.

Crenshaw, Kimberle. 1988. "Race, Reform, and Retrenchment: Transformation, and Legitimation in Anti-Discrimination Law." *Harvard Law Review* 101 (7): 1331–87.

Degen, Barbara. 2002. *Selbstbewusste Frauen – Souveräne Männer. Recht, Geschlechterdialog und -mediation zur Prävention gegen sexualisierte Machtausübung in Betrieben und Unternehmen.* Abschlussbericht zum oben genannten Projekt an der Universität/Gesamthochschule Essen. Berlin: Bundesministerium für Familie, Senioren, Frauen und Jugend.

———. 1999. "Neue Rechtsprechung zu sexueller Belästigung am Arbeitsplatz." *Der Personalrat* 1: 8–13.

———. 1991. "Sexuelle Gewalt am Arbeitsplatz." *Streit* 4: 139–46.

DeSacco, Dena. 1996. *Sexual Harassment in the European Union: A Post-Maastricht Analysis.* Brussels: European Interuniversity Press and College of Europe.

Deutscher Gewerkschaftsbund. 1987. *Sexuelle Belästigung am Arbeitsplatz: Frauen wehren sich.* Bochum: Berg-Verlag.

Dobbin, Frank. 1998. "The Strength of a Weak State: The Rights Revolution and the Rise of Human Resources Management Divisions." *American Journal of Sociology* 104 (2): 441–76.

Dobbin, Frank and Erin Kelly. 2005. "How to Stop Harassment: A Tale of Two Professions, a Tale of Two Sectors." Unpublished paper. *http://www.wjh. harvard.edu/~dobbin/.*

Dobbin, Frank and Erin Kelly. 2004. "Case Law and Corporate Politics: The Spread of Harassment Policies." Unpublished paper. *http://www.wjh. harvard.edu/~dobbin/*

Dobbin, Frank and John R. Sutton. 1998. "The Strength of a Weak State: The Rights Revolution and the Rise of Human Resource Management Divisions." *American Journal of Sociology* 104 (2): 441–76.

Drucksache 12/5468. July 21, 1993. *Entwurf eines Gesetzes zur Durchsetzung der Gleichberechtigung von Frauen und Männern (Zweites Gleichberechtigungsgesetz - 2. GleiBG).* Gesetzentwurf der Bundesregierung. 12. Wahlperiode.

Drucksache. Protokoll. November 11, 1993; 12. Wahlperiode. *Stenographischer Bericht von der öffentlichen Anhörung. 57. und 58. Sitzung.* Ausschuss für Frauen und Jugend, Deutscher Bundestag.

Drucksache 12/2096. February 14, 1992. *Sexuelle Belästigung am Arbeitsplatz.* Antrag der SPD.

Duggan, Lisa and Nan D. Hunter. 1995. *Sex Wars: Sexual Dissent and Political Culture.* New York: Routledge.

Edelman, Lauren B. 2004. "Rivers of Law and Contested Terrain: A Law and Society Approach to Economic Rationality." *Law and Society Review* 38 (2): 181–97.

———. 1992. "Legal Ambiguity and Symbolic Structures: Organizational Mediation of Civil Rights Law." *American Journal of Sociology* 97 (6): 1531–76.

———. 1990. "Legal Environments and Organizational Governance: The Expansion of Due Process in the American Workplace." *American Journal of Sociology* 95 (6): 1401–40.

Edelman, Lauren B., Sally Riggs Fuller, and Iona Mara-Drita. 2001. "Diversity Rhetoric and the Managerialization of Law." *American Journal of Sociology* 106 (6): 1589–641.

Edelman, Lauren B., Howard S. Erlanger, and John Lande. 1993. "Internal Dispute Resolution: The Transformation of Civil-Rights in the Workplace." *Law & Society Review* 27 (3): 497–534.

Edelman, Lauren B. and Mark Suchmann. 1999. "When the 'Haves' Hold Court: Speculations on the Organizational Internalization of Law." *Law & Society Review* 33 (4): 941–91.

Edelman, Lauren B., Christopher Uggen, and Howard S. Erlanger. 1999. "The Endogeneity of Legal Regulation: Grievance Procedures as a Rational Myth." *American Journal of Sociology* 105 (2): 406–54.

Ehrenreich, Rosa. 1999. "Dignity and Discrimination: Toward a Pluralistic Understanding of Workplace Harassment." *Georgetown Law Journal* 88: 1.

Eisenstein, Hester. 1995. *Inside Agitators: Australian Femocrats and the State*. Philadelphia, PA: Temple University Press.

Elman, R. Amy. 2000. "Sexual Harassment Policy: Sweden in European Context." Paper presented at the Twelfth International Conference of Europeanists, Chicago, March 30–April 1.

   1996. *Sexual Subordination and State Intervention: Comparing Sweden and the United States*. Oxford: Berghahn Books.

Equal Employment Opportunity Commission (EEOC). 1995. "Guidelines on Discrimination Because of Sex." 29 Code of Federal Regulations 1604.11. *http://www.eeoc.gov/*

   1990. "Guidelines on Sexual Favoritism." Federal Regulations N-915.048. December 1. *http://www.eeoc.gov/*

   1980. "Guidelines on Sexual Harassment." Section 1604.11 of the Guidelines on Discrimination Because of Sex, 29 C. F. R. § 1604.11. *http://www.eeoc.gov/*

Equal Opportunity Commission (EOC). 2003. "Analysis of Tribunal Cases." *www.eoc.org.uk*

Esping-Andersen, Gøsta. 1990. *The Three Worlds of Welfare Capitalism*. Cambridge: Polity Press.

European Commission. 1996. "Consultation of Management and Labour on the Prevention of Sexual Harassment at Work." Com (96) 373, 24.7.96.

European Commission. 1999. *Sexual Harassment at the Workplace in the European Union*. Luxembourg: Office for Official Publications of the European Communities.

Evans-Pritchard, Ambrose. 2002. "Eu Sex Law Puts Firms in the Dock." *The Daily Telegraph* April 19, p. 35.

Eyerman, Ron and Andrew Jamison. 1991. *Social Movements: A Cognitive Approach*. University Park, PA: Pennsylvania State University Press.

Faludi, Susan. 1991. *Backlash: The Undeclared War Against Women*. New York, NY: Crown.

Farley, Lin. 1978. *Sexual Shakedown: The Sexual Harassment of Women on the Job*. New York, NY: McGraw-Hill.

Ferguson, Kathy. 1984. *The Feminist Case Against Bureaucracy*. Philadelphia, PA: Temple University Press.

Ferree, Myra M. 2003. "Resonance and Radicalism: Feminist Framing in the Abortion Debates of the United States and Germany." *American Journal of Sociology* 109 (2): 304–44.

   1995a. "Making Equality: The Women's Affairs Offices in the Federal Republic of Germany." Pp. 95–113 in *Comparative State Feminism*, edited by Dorothy M. Stetson and Amy G. Mazur. Thousand Oaks, CA: Sage.

1995b. "Patriarchies and Feminisms: The Two Women's Movements of Post-Unification Germany." *Social Politics: International Studies in Gender, State, & Society* 1 (2): 10–25.

1987. "Equality and Autonomy: Feminist Politics in the United States and West Germany." Pp. 172–95 in *The Women's Movement of the United States and Western Europe*, edited by Mary Katzenstein and Carol M. Mueller. Philadelphia, PA: Temple University Press.

Ferree, Myra M., William A. Gamson, Jürgen Gerhards, and Dieter Rucht. 2002. *Shaping Abortion Discourse: Democracy and the Public Sphere in Germany and the United States*. Cambridge: Cambridge University Press.

Ferree, Myra Marx and Carol Mueller. 2004. "Feminism and the Women's Movement: A Global Perspective." Pp. 576–607 in *The Blackwell Companion to Social Movements*, edited by David A. Snow, Sarah A. Soule, and Hanspeter Kriesi. Cambridge: Blackwell.

Ferree, Myra M. and Silke Roth. 1998. "Gender, Class, and the Interaction Between Social Movements: A Strike of West Berlin Day Care Workers." *Gender & Society* 12: 626–48.

Fitzgerald, Louise F. 2004. "Who Says? Legal and Psychological Constructions of Women's Resistance to Sexual Harassment." Pp. 94–110 in *Direction in Sexual Harassment Law*, edited by Catharine A. MacKinnon and Reva B. Siegel. New Haven, CT: Yale University Press.

Franzway, Suzanne, Dianne Court, and R. W. Connell. 1989. *Staking a Claim: Feminism, Bureaucracy and the State*. Sydney, Boston: Allen & Unwin.

Fraser, Nancy. 1997. *Justice Interruptus: Critical Reflections on the "Postsocialist" Condition*. New York, NY: Routledge.

Friedman, Gabrielle and James Whitman. 2003. "The European Transformation of Harassment Law: Discrimination Versus Dignity." *Columbia Journal of European Law* 9: 241.

Gamson, William. 1992. *Talking Politics*. New York: Cambridge University Press.

Gardiner, Frances. 1997. "Introduction: Welfare and Sex Equality Policy Regimes." Pp. 1–24 in *Sex Equality Policy in Western Europe*, edited by Frances Gardiner. London: Routledge.

Gelb, Joyce. 1989. *Feminism and Politics: A Comparative Perspective*. Berkeley, CA: University of California Press.

Gelb, Joyce and Marian Lief Palley. 1982. *Women and Public Policies*. Princeton, NJ: Princeton University Press.

Gerhart, Ulrike, Anita Heiliger, and Annette Stehr, eds. 1992. *Tatort Arbeitsplatz: Sexuelle Belästigung von Frauen*. München: Frauenoffensive.

Gillespie, Dair and Ann Leffler. 1987. "The Politics of Research Methodology in Claims-Making Activities." *Social Problems* 34: 301–31.

Glendon, Mary A., Michael W. Gordon, and Christopher Osakwe. 1994. *Comparative Legal Traditions. Text, Materials and Cases on the Civil and Common Law Traditions, with Special Reference to French, German, English, and European Law*. St. Paul, MN: West Publishing.

Goodwin, Jeff and James M. Jasper. 2004. "Caught in a Winding, Snarling Vine: The Structural Bias of Political Process Theory." Pp. 3–31 in *Rethinking Social Movements: Structure, Meaning, and Emotion*, edited by Jeff Goodwin and James M. Jasper. Lanham, MD: Rowman and Littlefield.

Gordon, Linda. 1981. "The Politics of Sexual Harassment." *Radical America* 15 (4): 714.

Gottfried, Heidi and Jacqueline O'Reilly. 2002. "Reregulating Breadwinner Models in Socially Conservative Welfare Systems: Comparing Germany and Japan." *Social Politics* 9 (1): 29–59.

Government of Ireland. Department of Justice, Equality and Law Reform. 2004. *Report on Sexual Harassment in the Workplace in EU Member States.* The Irish Presidency of the European Union in association with FGS Consulting and Professor Aileen McGolgan. *www.justice.ie*

Goy, Alexandra. 1996. "The Victim-Plaintiff in Criminal Trials and Civil Law Responses to Sexual Violence." *Cardozo Women's Law Journal* 3: 335.

———. 1986. "Die Inszenierung des Freispruchs durch das Gericht." *Streit* 4 (2): 48.

Gregory, Jeanne. 2000. "Sexual Harassment: The Impact of EU Law in the Member States." Pp. 175–92 in *Gender Policies in the European Union*, edited by Mariagrazia Rossilli. New York, NY: Peter Lang.

———. 1995. "Making the Best Use of European Law." *European Journal of Women's Studies* 2: 421–40.

Gruber, James E. and Phoebe Morgan. 2005. *In the Company of Men: Male Dominance and Sexual Harassment.* Boston, MA: Northeastern University Press.

Gutek, Barbara A. 1985. *Sex and the Workplace: The Impact of Sexual Behavior and Harassment on Women, Men, and Organizations.* San Francisco, CA: Jossey-Bass.

Hagemann-White, Carol. 1998. "Violence Without End? Some Reflections on Achievements, Contradictions, and Perspectives of the Feminist Movement in Germany." Pp. 176–94 in *Multidisciplinary Perspectives on Family Violence*, edited by Renate C. A. Klein. London: Routledge.

Hall, Peter and David Soskice, eds. 2001. *Varieties of Capitalism: The Institutional Foundations of Comparative Advantage.* Oxford: Oxford University Press.

Hamacher, Gudrun. 1993. "Es passiert nicht jeder Frau jeden Tag, aber jeden Tag irgendwo. Warum zögern Gewerkschaftler, das Problem zu benennen?" Pp. 81–6 in *Grenzverletzungen. Sexuelle Belästigung im Arbeitsalltag*, edited by Renate Sadrozinski. Frankfurt am Main: Fischer.

Handler, Joel F. 1978. *Social Movements and the Legal System.* New York, NY: Academic Press.

Haney, Lynne. 1996. "Homeboys, Babies, Men in Suits: The State and the Reproduction of Dominance." *American Sociological Review* 61 (5): 759–78.

Harsch, Donna. Forthcoming. *The Revenge of the Domestic: Women and the Evolution of State Socialism in the German Democratic Republic, 1945–1971.* Princeton University Press.

Hart, Stephen. 1996. "The Cultural Dimension of Social Movements: A Theoretical Reassessment and Literature Review." *Sociology of Religion* 57 (1): 87–100.

Hauserman, Nancy R. 1999. "Comparing Conversations about Sexual Harassment in the United States and Sweden: Print Media Coverage of the Case Against Astra USA." *Wisconsin Women's Law Journal* 14 (1): 45–68.

———. 2002. "Sexual Harassment as an Economic Concern: Swedish and American Coverage of Astra." Pp. 88–99 in *Sex and Money, Feminism and Political*

Economy in the Media, edited by Eileen R. Meehan and Ellen Riordan. Minneapolis, MI: University of Minnesota Press.

Hawkesworth, Mary. 1997. "Challenging the Received Wisdom and the Status Quo: Creating and Implementing Sexual Harassment Policy." *NWSA Journal* 9 (2): 94–102.

Hearn, Jeff and Wendy Parkin. 2001. *Gender, Sexuality and Violence in Organizations*. Thousand Oaks, CA: Sage.

Heclo, Hugh. 1974. *Modern Social Politics in Britain and Sweden: From Relief to Income Maintenance*. New Haven, CT: Yale University Press.

Helfferich, Barbara and Felix Kolb. 2001. "Multilevel Action Coordination in European Contentious Politics: The Case of the European Women's Lobby." Pp. 143–62 in *Contentious Europeans: Protest and Politics in an Emerging Polity*, edited by Doug Imig and Sidney Tarrow. Lanham, MD: Rowman and Littlefield.

Hernes, Helga. 1987. *Welfare State and Woman Power*. Oslo: Norwegian University Press.

Hill, Anita. 1997. *Speaking Truth to Power*. New York, NY: Anchor Books.

Hill, Anita F. and Emma C. Jordan, eds. 1995. *Race, Gender and Power in America: The Legacy of the Hill-Thomas Hearing*. New York, NY: Oxford University Press.

Hirshman, Linda and Jane Larson. 1998. *Hard Bargains: The Politics of Sex*. New York: Oxford University Press.

Hobson, Barbara, ed. 2003. *Recognition Struggles and Social Movements: Contested Identities, Agency and Power*. Cambridge, NY: Cambridge University Press.

Hodges, Jane A. 1996. "Sexual Harassment in Employment: Recent Judicial and Arbitral Trends." *International Labour Review* 135 (5): 499–533.

Holzbecher, Monika, Anne Braszeit, Ursula Mueller, and Sibylle Plogstedt. 1990. *Sexuelle Belästigung am Arbeitsplatz*. Schriftenreihe des Bundesministeriums für Familie, Senioren, Frauen und Jugend. Stuttgart: Kohlhammer.

Holzbecher, Monika and Bärbel Meschkutat. 1999. *Mobbing am Arbeitsplatz*. Dortmund: Bundesanstalt für Arbeitsschutz und Arbeitsmedizin.

Hooven, Martha and Freada Klein. 1978. "Is Sexual Harassment Legal?" *Aegis* (September/October): 28–30.

Hoskyns, Catherine. 2000. "A Study of Four Action Programmes on Equal Opportunities." Pp. 43–60 in *Gender Policies in the European Union*, edited by Mariagrazia Rossilli. New York, NY: Peter Lang.

———. 1996. *Integrating Gender, Women, Law and Politics in the European Union*. London: Verso.

Husbands, Robert. 1992. "Sexual Harassment Law in Employment: An International Perspective." *International Labour Review* 131 (6): 535–59.

Imig, Doug and Sidney Tarrow, eds. 2001. *Contentious Europeans: Protest and Politics in an Emerging Polity*. Lanham, MD: Rowman and Littlefield.

Inglehart, Ronald and Pippa Norris. 2003. *Rising Tide: Gender Equality and Cultural Change Around the World*. Cambridge: Cambridge University Press.

International Labour Organisation (ILO). 1992. *Combating Sexual Harassment at Work*. Geneva: International Labour Office.

Jansen, Sarah. 1984. "Inside Out." Pp. 135–40 in *Übergriffe: Sexuelle Belästigung in Büros und Betrieben: Eine Dokumentation der Gruenen Frauen im Bundestag*, edited by Sibylle Plogstedt and Kathleen Bode. Reinbeck: Rowohlt.

Jenson, Jane. 1987. "Changing Discourse, Changing Ideas: Political Rights and Reproductive Policies in France." Pp. 64–88 in *The Women's Movement of the United States and Western Europe*, edited by Mary F. Katzenstein and Carol M. Mueller. Philadelphia, PA: Temple University Press.

Jenson, Jane and Mariette Sineau. 1995. *Mitterand et les Françaises: Un rendez-vous manqué*. Paris: Presses de la Fondation Nationale des Sciences Politiques.

Juliano, Ann and Stewart Schwab. 2001. "The Sweep of Sexual Harassment Cases." *Cornell Law Review* 86 (3): 548–602.

Kaplan, Gisela. 1992. *Contemporary Western European Feminism*. New York, NY: New York University Press.

Kathmann, Maria. 1993. "Sexuelle Belästigung am Arbeitsplatz: Anspruch und Wirklichkeit der gewerkschaftlichen Gegenstrategie." *Pro Familia Magazin* 2: 5–6.

Katzenstein, Mary F. 1998. *Faithful and Fearless. Moving Feminist Protest Inside the Church and Military*. Princeton, NJ: Princeton University Press.

Katzenstein, Mary F. and Carol M. Mueller, eds. 1987. *The Women's Movement of the United States and Western Europe*. Philadelphia, PA: Temple University Press.

Keck, Margaret and Kathryn Sikkink. 1998. *Activists Beyond Borders: Advocacy Networks in International Politics*. Ithaca, NY: Cornell University Press.

Kelly, Erin and Frank Dobbin. 1999. "Civil Rights Law at Work: Sex Discrimination and the Rise of Maternity Leave Policies." *American Journal of Sociology* 105:455–92.

Kelly, Erin and Frank Dobbin. 1998. "How Affirmative Action Became Diversity Management." *American Behavioral Scientist* 41 (7): 960–84.

Kelly, Rita M. and Phoebe M. Stambaugh. 1992. "Sexual Harassment in the States." Pp. 109–24 in *Women and Men of the States: Public Administrators at the State Level*, edited by Mary E. Guy. Armonk, NY: M. E. Sharpe.

Kenney, Sally. 1992. *For Whose Protection? Reproductive Hazards and Exclusionary Policies in the United States and Britain*. Ann Arbor, MI: University of Michigan Press.

Kingdon, John W. 1984. *Agendas, Alternatives, and Public Policies*. Boston, MA: Little, Brown.

Klandermans, Bert, Hanspeter Kriesi, and Sidney Tarrow. 1988. *From Structure to Action: Comparing Social Movement Research Across Cultures*. Greenwich, CT: JAI Press.

Kodre, Petra and Henrike Müller. 2003. "Shifting Policy Frames: EU Equal Treatment Norms and Domestic Discourses in Germany." Pp. 83–116 in *Gendering Europeanisation*, edited by Ulrike Liebert. Brussels: Peter Lang .

Kolinsky, Eva and Hildegard Maria Nickel, eds. 2003. *Reinventing Gender: Women in Eastern Germany since Unification*. London, Portland: Frank Cass.

Koopmans, Ruud and Susan Olzak. 2004. "Discursive Opportunities and the Evolution of Right-wing Violence in Germany." *American Journal of Sociology* 110 (1): 198–230.

Kriesi, Hanspeter, Ruud Koopmans, Jan W. Duyvendak, and Marco G. Giugni. 1995. *New Social Movements in Western Europe: A Comparative Analysis.* Minneapolis, MN: University of Minnesota Press.

Kuhlmann, Ellen. 1996. *Gegen die sexuelle Belästigung am Arbeitsplatz. Juristische Praxis und Handlungsperspektiven.* Pfaffenweiler.

Kuiper, Alie. 2002. *Seksuele intimidatie op het werk aangepakt.* Rotterdam: Ingeborg Luitwieler.

Lähner, Carola. 1993. Drucksache, Protokoll, November 11, p. 32, 12. Wahlperiode. *Stenographischer Bericht von der Öffentlichen Anhörung. 57 und 58. Sitzung.* Ausschuss Nr. 14, Frauen und Jugend, Deutscher Bundestag.

Lewis, Jane. 1997. "Gender and Welfare Regimes: Further Thoughts." *Social Politics: International Studies in Gender, State & Society* 4: 160–77.

———. 1992. "Gender and the Development of Welfare Regimes." *Journal of European Social Policy* 2 (3): 159–73.

Liebert, Ulrike. 2003. "Between Diversity and Equality: Analysing Europeanisation." Pp. 11–46 in *Gendering Europeanisation*, edited by Ulrike Liebert. Brussels: Peter Lang.

Liebert, Ulrike, ed. 2003. *Gendering Europeanisation.* Brussels: Peter Lang.

Lootens, Tricia. 1986. "Sex Harasser under Fire." *Off Our Backs.* 26 (11): 13.

Lorber, Judith. 2001. *Gender Inequality. Feminist Theories and Politics.* Los Angeles, CA: Roxbury Publishing Company.

Louis, Marie-Victoire. 1994. "Sexual Harassment at Work in France: What Stakes for Feminists?" Pp. 85–96 in *Women and Violence*, edited by Miranda Davies. London: Zed Books.

MacKinnon, Catharine A. 2004. "Afterword." Pp. 672–704 in *Directions in Sexual Harassment Law*, edited by Catharine A. MacKinnon and Reva B. Siegel. New Haven, CT: Yale University Press.

———. 2002. "The Logic of Experience: Reflections on the Development of Sexual Harassment Law." *Georgetown Law Journal* 90: 813–33.

———. 1989. *Toward a Feminist Theory of the State.* Cambridge, MA: Harvard University Press.

———. 1983. "Feminism, Marxism, Method and the State: Toward Feminist Jurisprudence." *Signs* 8: 635–58.

———. 1979. *Sexual Harassment of Working Women: A Case of Sex Discrimination.* New Haven, CT: Yale University Press.

MacKinnon, Catharine A. and Reva B. Siegel, eds. 2004. *Directions in Sexual Harassment Law.* New Haven, CT: Yale University Press.

Maenz, Heike. 1994. ". . . *und kaum eine traut sich, darüber zu sprechen": Sexuelle Belästigung am Arbeitsplatz; eine Umfrage bei Thyssen-Stahl Hamborn/ Beeckerwerth.* Bochum: Beratungsgesellschaft für ISA-Consult GmbH, Innovation.

Mahon, Rianne. 2002. "Child Care: Toward What Kind of 'Social Europe'?" *Social Politics: International Studies in Gender, State & Society* 9: 343–79.

Marks, Gary and Doug McAdam. 1998. "Social Movements and the Changing Structure of Political Opportunity in the European Union." Pp. 95–120 in *Governance in the European Union*, edited by Gary Marks, Fritz Scharpf, Phillip Schmitter, and Wolfgang Streek. London: Sage Publications.

Marshall, Anna-Maria. 2001. "A Spectrum in Oppositional Consciousness: Sexual Harassment Plaintiffs and Their Lawyers." Pp. 99–145 in *Oppositional Consciousness: The Subjective Roots of Social Protest*, edited by Jane Mansbridge and Aldon Morris. Chicago, IL: The University of Chicago Press.

Martin, Patricia Y. 2003. " 'Said and Done' Versus 'Saying and Doing' – Gendering Practices, Practicing Gender at Work." *Gender and Society* 17 (3): 342–66.

Mazey, Sonia. 1998. "The European Union and Women's Rights: From the Europeanization of National Agendas to the Nationalization of a European Agenda?" Pp. 134–55 in *Beyond the Market: The EU and National Social Policy*, edited by David Hine and Hussein Kassim. London: Routledge.

Mazur, Amy G. 2003. "Drawing Comparative Lessons from France and Germany." *Review of Policy Research* 20 (3): 493–523.

——— 2002. *Theorizing Feminist Policy*. Oxford: Oxford University Press.

——— 1996. The Interplay: The Formation of Sexual Harassment Legislation in France and EU Policy Initiatives." Pp. 35–49 in *Sexual Politics and the European Union: The New Feminist Challenge*, edited by R. A. Elman. Providence, RI: Berghahn Books.

——— 1994. "The Formation of Sexual Harassment Policies in France: Another Case of French Exceptionalism?" *French Politics and Society* 11 (2): 11–32.

Mazur, Amy G., ed. 2001. *State Feminism, Women's Movements, and Job Training: Making Democracies Work in the Global Economy*. New York and London: Routledge.

Mazur, Amy G. and Dorothy M. Stetson. 1995. "Conclusion: The Case for State Feminism." Pp. 272–91 in *Comparative State Feminism*, edited by Dorothy M. Stetson and Amy G. Mazur. Thousand Oaks, CA: Sage.

McAdam, Doug. 1982. *Political Process and the Development of Black Insurgency, 1930–1970*. Chicago, IL: University of Chicago Press.

McAdam, Doug and Dieter Rucht. 1993. "The Cross-National Diffusion of Movement Ideas." *Annals of the American Academy of Political and Social Science*, 528: 56–74.

McAdam, Doug, John D. McCarthy, and Mayer N. Zald. 1996. *Comparative Perspectives on Social Movements*. Cambridge: Cambridge University Press.

McAdam, Doug, Sidney Tarrow and Charles Tilly. 2001. *Dynamics of Contention*. New York, NY: Cambridge University Press.

McCann, Michael W. 1994. *Rights at Work: Pay Equity Reform and the Politics of Legal Mobilization*. Chicago, JL: University of Chicago Press.

Meehan, Elizabeth. 1985. *Women's Rights at Work: Campaigns and Policy in Britain and the United States*. New York, NY: St. Martin's Press.

Meschkutat, Bärbel, Monika Holzbecher, and Gudrun Richter. 1993. *Strategien gegen sexuelle Belästigung am Arbeitsplatz*. Köln: Bund-Verlag.

Meschkutat, Bärbel, Martina Stackelbeck and Georg Langenhoff. 2002. *Der Mobbing-Report. Eine Repräsentativstudie für die Bundesrepublik Deutschland*. Schriftenreihe der Bundesanstalt für Arbeitsschutz und Arbeitsmedizin. Dortmund: Wirtschaftsverlag NW.

Milkman, Ruth, ed. 1985. *Women, Work, and Protest: A Century of US Women's Labor History*. Boston, MA: Routledge & Kegan Paul.

Mink, Gwendolyn. 2000. *Hostile Environment: the Political Betrayal of Sexually Harassed Women*. Ithaca, NY: Cornell University Press.

Moeller, Robert G. 1993. *Protecting Motherhood: Women and the Family in the Politics of Postwar West Germany*. Berkeley, CA: University of California Press.

Möller, Simon. 1999. *Sexual Correctness: Die Modernisierung antifeministischer Debatten in den Medien*. Opladen: Leske & Budrich.

Morgan, Kimberly and Kathrin Zippel. 2003. "Paid to Care: The Origins and Effects of Care Leave Policies in Western Europe." *Social Politics: International Studies in Gender, State, & Society*, 10 (1): 49–85.

Morris, Aldon. 1984. *The Origins of the Civil Rights Movement*. New York, NY: Free Press.

Morrison, Toni, ed. 1992. *Race-Ing Justice, En-Gendering Power: Essays on Anita Hill, Clarence Thomas, and the Construction of Social Reality*. New York: Pantheon.

Musall, Bettina and Andreas Ulrich. 1999. "Ganz ungeniert." *Der Spiegel*, August, *http://www.spiegel.de/*

Mushaben, Joyce M. 2001. "Challenging the Maternalistic Presumption: The Gender Politics of Welfare Reform in Germany and the United States." Pp. 193–215 in *Women and Welfare: Theory and Practice in the United States and Europe*, edited by Nancy J. Hirschmann and Ulrike Liebert. New Brunswick, NJ: Rutgers University Press.

1989. "Feminism in Four Acts: The Changing Political Identity of Women in the Federal Republic of Germany." Pp. 76–110 in *The Federal Republic of Germany at Forty*, edited by Peter Merkl. New York, NY: New York University Press.

Naples, Nancy A. and Manisha Desai, eds. 2002. *Women's Activism and Globalization: Linking Local Struggles and Transnational Politics*. New York, NY: Routledge.

Norton, Eleanor Holmes. 1981. "Prepared Statement." Pp. 92–8 in *Oversight Hearings on Equal Employment Opportunity and Affirmative Action. Part 1*. Hearings before the Subcommittee on Employment Opportunities of the Committee on Education and Labor. House of Representatives. Ninety-Seventh Congress. First Session. Hearings held in Washington, D.C. on July 15, September 23, 24, and October 7, 1981.

O'Connor, Julia, Ann Orloff, and Sheila Shaver. 1999. *States, Markets, Families: Gender, Liberalism and Social Policy in Australia, Canada, Great Britain and the United States*. Cambridge: Cambridge University Press.

O'Connor, Karen. 1980. *Women's Organizations' Use of the Courts*. Lexington, MA: Lexington Books.

Oliver, Pamela and Hank Johnston. 2000. "What a Good Idea! Ideologies and Frames in Social Movement Research," *Mobilization* 5: 37–54.

Orloff, Ann S. 1996a. "Gender and the Welfare State." *Annual Review of Sociology* 22: 51–70.

1996b. "Gender in the Liberal Welfare States: Australia, Canada, the United Kingdom and the United States." In *State/Culture. State formation after the Cultural Turn*, edited by George Steinmetz. Ithaca, NY: Cornell University Press.

1993. "Gender and the Social Rights of Citizenship: The Comparative Analysis of Gender Relations and Welfare States." *American Sociological Review* 58 (3): 303–28.

Ostner, Ilona. 1994. "Back to the Fifties: Gender and Welfare in Unified Germany." *Social Politics: International Studies in Gender, State & Society* 1 (1): 32–59.

1993. "Slow Motion: Women, Work, and the Family in Germany." Pp. 92–115 in *Women and Social Policies in Europe: Work, Family, and the State*, edited by Jane Lewis. Aldershot: Edward Elgar.

Ostner, Ilona and Jane Lewis. 1995. "Gender and the Evolution of European Social Policies." Pp. 159–93 in *European Social Policies Between Fragmentation and Integration*, edited by Stephan Leibfried and Paul Pierson. Washington, DC: Brookings Institution.

Outshoorn, Joyce, ed. 2004. *The Politics of Prostitution: Women's Movements, Democratic States and the Globalisation of Sex Commerce*. Cambridge: Cambridge University Press.

Pateman, Carol. 1988. *The Sexual Contract*. Stanford, CA: Stanford University Press.

Pedriana, Nicholas and Robin Stryker. 2004. "The Strength of a Weak Agency: Early Enforcement of Title VII of the 1964 Civil Rights Act and the Transformation of State Capacity, 1965–71." *American Journal of Sociology* 110 (3): 709–60.

1997. "Political Culture Wars 1960s Style: Equal Employment Opportunity-Affirmative Action Law and the Philadelphia Plan." *American Journal of Sociology* 103 (3): 633–91.

Pflüger, Almut and Susanne Baer. 2005. *Beschäftigtenschutzgesetz in der Praxis. Bericht*. Bundesministerium für Familie, Senioren, Frauen und Jugend. *www.bmfsfj.de*

Pierce, Jennifer L. 1995. *Gender Trials: Emotional Lives in Contemporary Law Firms*. Berkeley, CA: University of California Press.

Plogstedt, Sibylle. 1987. "Belästigung: Sex als Crime." Pp. 62–6 in *Alltägliche Gewalt gegen Frauen*, edited by Halina Bendkowski and Irene Rotalsky. Berlin: Elefanten Press.

Plogstedt, Sibylle and Klaus Bertelsmann. 1987. *Sexuelle Belästigung am Arbeitsplatz: Frauen wehren sich*. Bochum: Berg-Verlag.

Plogstedt, Sibylle and Kathleen Bode. 1984. *Übergriffe: Sexuelle Belästigung in Büros und Betrieben: Eine Dokumentation der Gruenen Frauen im Bundestag*. Reinbeck: Rowohlt.

Plogstedt, Sibylle and Barbara Degen. 1992. *Nein Heisst Nein! DGB-Ratgeber Gegen Sexuelle Belästigung am Arbeitsplatz*. München: Piper.

Prieto, Maggie. 1983. "Women Coal Miners Fight Sexual Harassment." *Off Our Backs* 13 (8): 17.

Pringle, Rosemary. 1988. *Secretaries Talk: Sexuality, Power and Work*. London: Verso.

Quadagno, Jill. 1992. "Social Movements and State Transformation: Labor Unions and Racial Conflict in the War on Poverty." *American Sociological Review* 57 (5): 616–34.

Ragin, Charles C. 1994. *Introduction to Qualitative Comparative Analysis*. Cambridge: Cambridge University Press.

Ray, Raka. 1999. *Fields of Protest: Women's Movements in India*. Minneapolis, MN: University of Minnesota Press.

Rees, Teresa L. 1998. *Mainstreaming Equality in the European Union: Education, Training and Labour Market Policies*. New York, NY: Routledge.

Reese, Laura A. and Karen E. Lindenberg. 1999. *Implementing Sexual Harassment Policy: Challenges for the Public Sector Workplace*. Thousand Oaks, CA: Sage.

Risse-Kappen, Thomas. 1995. *Bringing Transnational Relations Back in: Non-State Actors, Domestic Structures, and International Institutions*. Cambridge: Cambridge University Press.

Rochon, Thomas R. 1998. *Culture Moves: Ideas, Activism and Changing Values*. Princeton, NY: Princeton University Press.

Roggeband, Conny and Mieke Verloo. 1999. "Global Sisterhood and Political Change: The Unhappy 'Marriage' of Women's Movements and Nation States." Pp. 177–94 in *Expansion and Fragmentation: Internationalization, Political Change and the Transformation of the Nation State*, edited by Kees van Kersbergen, Robert H. Lieshout, and Grahame Lock. Amsterdam: Amsterdam University Press.

Rosenfeld, Rachel, Heike Trappe and Janet Gornick. 2004. "Gender and Work in Germany: Before and after Reunification." *Annual Review of Sociology* 30: 103–24.

Rossilli, Mariagrazia, ed. 2000. *Gender Policies in the European Union*. New York, NY: Peter Lang.

Roth, Silke. 2003. *Building Movement Bridges: The Coalition of Labor Union Women*. Contributions to Sociology Series. Westport, CT: Praeger.

Rubenstein, Michael. 1987. *The Dignity of Women at Work: A Report on the Problem of Sexual Harassment in the Member States of the European Communities*. Brussels: Office for Official Publications of the European Communities.

Ruggie, Mary. 1984. *The State and Working Women: A Comparative Study of Britain and Sweden*. Princeton, NJ: Princeton University Press.

Runge, Annelie. 1984. "Obzöne Anrufe, viele Monate lang." Pp. 131–5 in *Übergriffe: Sexuelle Belästigung in Büros und Betrieben: Eine Dokumentation der Gruenen Frauen im Bundestag*, edited by Sibylle Plogstedt and Kathleen Bode. Reinbeck: Rowohlt.

Sabatier, Paul A. 1999. *Theories of the Policy Process*. Boulder, CO: Westview Press.

Sadrozinski, Renate, ed. 1993. *Grenzverletzungen: Sexuelle Belästigung im Arbeitsalltag*. Frankfurt am Main: Fischer.

———. 1991. "'Wer muss sich den nun ändern . . .?' Fortbildung zum Thema 'Sexuelle Belästigung am Arbeitsplatz.'" Ein Bericht im Auftrag der Leitstelle Gleichstellung der Frau der Freien und Hansestadt Hamburg. Hamburg: Freie und Hansestadt Hamburg.

Saguy, Abigail. 2003. *What is Sexual Harassment? From Capitol Hill to the Sorbonne*. Berkeley, CA: University of California Press.

———. 2002. "International Crossways: Traffic in Sexual Harassment Policy." *European Journal of Women's Studies* 9: 249–67.

Sainsbury, Diane. 1996. *Gender, Equality and Welfare States*. Cambridge: Cambridge University Press.

Sainsbury, Diane, ed. 1994. *Gendering Welfare States*. London: Sage.

Samuels, Harriet. 2003. "Sexual Harassment in the Workplace: a Feminist Analysis of Recent Developments in the UK." *Women's Studies International Forum* 26 (5): 467–82.

Sawer, Marian. 1990. *Sisters in Suits: Women and Public Policy in Australia*. Sydney: Unwin Hyman.

———. 1995. " 'Femocrats in Glass Towers?' The Office of the Status of Women in Australia." Pp. 22–39 in *Comparative State Feminism*, edited by Dorothy McBride Stetson and Amy Mazur. Thousand Oaks: Sage Publications.

Schenk, Herrad. 1981. *Die Feministische Herausforderung. 150 Jahre Frauenbewegung in Deutschland*. München: Beck.

Schiek, Dagmar. 1997. "Sexuelle Belästigung am Arbeitsplatz." *Arbeitsrecht im Betrieb* (8): 441–51.

———. 1995. *Zweites Gleichberechtigungsgesetz für die Privatwirtschaft: Textausgabe mit Kurzkommentierung*. Köln: Bund-Verlag.

Schmidt, Vivien A. 2002. *The Futures of European Capitalism*. Oxford: Oxford University Press.

Schmidt, Vivien A. and Claudio Radaelli. 2004. "Conceptual and Methodological Issues in Policy Change in Europe." *West European Politics* 27 (4): 1–28.

Schmitt, Sabine. 1995. *Der Arbeiterinnenschutz im Deutschen Kaiserreich: Zur Konstruktion der schutzbedürftigen Arbeiterin*. Stuttgart: J.B. Metzler.

Schneble, Andrea and Michel Domsch. 1990. *Sexuelle Belästigung von Frauen am Arbeitsplatz: Eine Bestandsaufnahme im Hamburger Öffentlichen Dienst*. München: Hampp.

Schultz, Dagmar and Angela Mueller. 1984. "Sexualität zwischen Lehrenden und Lernenden an der Hochschule – Sexuelle Belästigung oder Sexuelle Befreiung?" Pp. 561–76 in *Wollen wir immer noch alles? Frauenpolitik zwischen Traum und Trauma*, Dokumentation der 7. Sommeruniversität für Frauen, Berlin.

Schultz, Vicki. 2003. "The Sanitized Workplace." *Yale Law Journal* 112 (8): 2061–93.

Scott, Joan. 1988. "Deconstructing Equality-Versus-Difference: Or, the Use of Poststructuralist Theory of Feminism." *Feminist Studies* 14 (1) 33–50.

Segrave, Kerry. 1994. *The Sexual Harassment of Women in the Workplace, 1600 to 1993*. Jefferson, NC: McFarland.

Shaw, Jo. 2000. "Importing Gender: the Challenge of Feminism and the Analysis of the EU Legal Order." *Journal of European Public Policy* 7: 406–31.

Skaine, Rosemarie. 1996. *Power and Gender: Issues in Sexual Dominance and Harassment*. Jefferson, NC: McFarland.

Skocpol, Theda. 1992. *Protecting Soldiers and Mothers*. Cambridge, MA: Harvard University Press.

———. ed. 1984. *Vision and Method in Historical Sociology*. Cambridge: Cambridge University Press.

Skretny, John David. 1998. "State Capacity, Policy Feedback and Affirmative Action for Blacks, Women and Latinos." *Research in Political Sociology* 8: 270–310.

Smart, Carol. 1995. *Law, Crime and Sexuality: Essays in Feminism*. London: Sage.

Smith, Jackie. 2004. "Transnational Processes and Movements." Pp. 294–310 in *The Blackwell Companion to Social Movements*, edited by David A. Snow, Sarah A. Soule, and Hanspeter Kriesi. Oxford: Blackwell.

Snow, David A. 2004. "Framing Processes, Ideology, and Discursive Fields." Pp. 380–412 in *The Blackwell Companion to Social Movements*, edited by David A. Snow, Sarah A. Soule, and Hanspeter Kriesi. Oxford: Blackwell.

Snow, David A. and Robert D. Benford. 1992. "Master Frames and Cycles of Protest." Pp. 135–55 in *Frontiers of Social Movement Theory*, edited by Aldon Morris and Carol McClurg-Mueller. New Haven, CT: Yale University Press.

Snow, David A., Burke E. Rochford, Steven K. Worden, and Robert D. Benford. 1986. "Frame Alignment Processes, Micromobilization, and Movement Participation." *American Sociological Review* 51 (4): 464–81.

Soule, Sarah A. 2004. "Diffusion Processes Within and Across Movements." Pp. 294–310 in *The Blackwell Companion to Social Movements*, edited by David A. Snow, Sarah A. Soule, and Hanspeter Kriesi. Oxford: Blackwell.

Sperling, Liz and Charlotte Bretherton. 1996. "Women's Policy Networks and the European Union." *Women's Studies International Forum* 19 (3): 303–14.

Stein, Laura W. 1999. *Sexual Harassment in America: A Documentary History*. Westport, CT: Greenwood Press.

Steinberg, Ronnie Ratner. 1980. "The Policy and the Problem: Overview over Seven Countries." Pp. 1–25 in *Equal Employment Policy for Women: Strategies for Implementation in the United States, Canada and Western Europe*. Philadelphia: Temple University Press.

Steinmetz, George. 2004. "Odious Comparisons: Incommensurability, the Case Study, and "Small N's" in Sociology." *Sociological Theory* 22 (3): 371–400.

1993. *Regulating the Social: The Welfare State and Local Politics in Imperial Germany*. Princeton, NY: Princeton University Press.

Stetson, Dorothy McBride, ed. 2001. *Abortion Politics, Women's Movements and the Democratic State: A Comparative Study of State Feminism*. Oxford: Oxford University Press.

Stetson, Dorothy McBride. 1995. "The Oldest Women's Policy Agency: The Women's Bureau in the United States." Pp. 245–71 in *Comparative State Feminism*, edited by Dorothy M. Stetson and Amy G. Mazur. Thousand Oaks, CA: Sage.

Stetson, Dorothy McBride and Amy G. Mazur, eds. 1995. *Comparative State Feminism*. Thousand Oaks, CA: Sage.

Stone, Deborah A. 1997. *Policy Paradox: The Art of Political Decision Making*. New York, NY: W. W. Norton.

1988. *Policy Paradox and Political Reason*. Philadelphia, PA: Temple University Press.

Stratigaki, Maria. 2004. The Cooptation of Gender Concepts in EU Policies: The Case of Reconciliation of Work and Family." *Social Politics: International Studies in Gender, State & Society* 11 (1): 30–56.

2000. "The European Union and the Equal Opportunities Process." Pp. 27–48 in *Gendered Policies in Europe: Reconciling Employment and Family Life*, edited by Linda Hantrais. London: Macmillan.

Stryker, Robin. 1994. "Rules, Resources, and Legitimacy Processes: Some Implications for Social Conflict, Order, and Change." *American Journal of Sociology* 99 (4): 847–910.

    1989. "Limits on the Technocratization of Law: The Elimination of the National Labor Relations Board's Division of Economic Research." *American Sociological Review* 54 (3): 341–58.

Subhan, Andrea and Nadine Boujan. 1994. *Measures to Combat Sexual Harassment at the Workplace: Action Taken in the Member States of the EC.* Luxembourg: European Parliament.

Sunstein, Cass R. and Judy M. Shih. 2004. "Damages in Sexual Harassment Cases." Pp. 324–44 in *Directions in Sexual Harassment Law*, edited by Catharine A. MacKinnon and Reva B. Siegel. New Haven, CT: Yale University Press.

Tarrow, Sidney. 1994. *Power in Movement: Social Movements, Collective Action, and Politics.* Cambridge: Cambridge University Press.

    2005. *The New Transnational Activism.* Cambridge, New York: Cambridge University Press.

Taylor, Verta. 1999. "Gender and Social Movements: Gender Processes in Women's Self-Help Movements." *Gender & Society* 13 (1): 8–33.

Tilly, Charles. 1984. *Big Structures, Large Processes, Huge Comparisons.* New York, NY: Basic Books.

Timmerman, Greetje and Cristien Bajema. 1999. "Sexual Harassment in Northwest Europe." *European Journal of Women's Studies* 6: 419–39.

Trappe, Heike. 1996. "Work and Family in Women's Lives in the German Democratic Republic." *Work and Occupation* 23 (4): 354–77.

    1995. *Emanzipation oder Zwang? Frauen in der DDR zwischen Beruf, Familie und Sozialpolitik.* Berlin: Akademie Verlag.

UNICE. 2002. Position Paper. October 5, *www.unice.org*

US Merit Systems Protection Board. (U.S.M.S.P.B.) 1995. *Sexual Harassment in the Federal Government: Trends, Progress, Continuing Challenges.* Washington, DC: US Merit Systems Protection Board.

    1988. *Sexual Harassment in the Federal Government: An Update.* Washington, DC: US Merit Systems Protection Board.

    1981. *Sexual Harassment in the Federal Government: Is It a Problem?* Washington, DC: US Merit Systems Protection Board.

Valiente, Celia. 2000. "Left or Right: Does It Make Any Difference Regarding Gender Equality? The Case of Sexual Harassment Policies in Spain." Paper presented at the 12th International Conference of Europeanists, Chicago, March 30–April 2.

    1998. "Sexual Harassment in the Workplace: Equality Politics in Post-authoritarian Spain." Pp. 169–79 in *Politics of Sexuality: Identity, Gender and Citizenship*, edited by Terrell Carver and Véronique Mottier. London: Routledge.

Vogel-Polsky, Eliane. 2000. "Parity Democracy, Law and Europe." Pp. 61–86 in *Gender Policies in the European Union*, edited by Mariagrazia Rossilli. New York, NY: Peter Lang.

von Wahl, Angelika. 1999. *Gleichstellungsregime: Berufliche Gleichstellung von Frauen in den USA und in der Bundesrepublik Deutschland.* Opladen: Leske und Budrich.

Walby, Sylvia. 2004. "The European Union and Gender Equality: Emergent Varieties of Gender Regime." *Social Politics: International Studies in Gender, State & Society* 11 (1): 4–29.

Watson, Sophie, ed. 1990. *Playing the State: Australian Feminist Interventions.* London, New York, NY: Verso.

Weeks, Elaine L., Jacqueline M. Boles, Albeno P. Garbin, and John Blount. 1986. "The Transformation of Sexual Harassment from a Private Trouble into a Public Issue." *Sociological Inquiry* 56 (4): 432–55.

Weldon, S. Laurel. 2002. *Protest, Policy, and the Problem of Violence Against Women: A Cross-National Comparison.* Pittsburgh: University of Pittsburgh Press.

Welsh, Sandy. 1999. "Gender and Sexual Harassment." *Annual Review of Sociology* 25: 169–90.

Whitman, James. 2003. "From Fascist 'Honour' to European 'Dignity'." Pp. 243–66 in *The Darker Legacy of European Law: Perceptions of Europe and Perspectives on a European Order in Legal Scholarship During the Era of Fascism and National Socialism,* edited by Christian Joerges and Navraj Singh Ghaleigh. Cambridge: Hart.

Williams, Christine, Patti A. Giuffre, and Kirsten Dellinger. 1999. "Sexuality in the Workplace: Organizational Control, Sexual Harassment, and the Pursuit of Pleasure." *Annual Review of Sociology* 25: 73–93.

Wise, Sue and Liz Stanley. 1987. *Georgie Porgie: Sexual Harassment in Everyday Life.* London and New York: Pandora.

Women's Bureau. 1994. *Sexual Harassment: Know Your Rights.* Washington, DC: US Department of Labor.

Wright, Ben. 2004. "Discrimination Cases May Do More Harm Than Good." *The Business* September 5 p. 12.

Young, Brigitte. 1999. *Triumph of the Fatherland: German Unification and the Marginalization of Women.* Ann Arbor, MI: University of Michigan Press.

Zippel, Kathrin. 2004. "Transnational Advocacy Networks and Policy Cycles in the European Union: The Case of Sexual Harassment." *Social Politics: International Studies in Gender, State, & Society* 11 (1): 57–85.

2003. "Practices of Implementation of Sexual Harassment Policies: Individual vs. Collective Strategies." *Review of Policy Research* 20 (1): 175–97.

1999a. "Country Report for Austria." Pp. 47–55 in *Sexual Harassment at the Workplace in the European Union.* European Commission. Luxembourg: Office for Official Publications of the European Communities.

1999b. "Country Report for Germany." Pp. 78–89 in *Sexual Harassment at the Workplace in the European Union.* European Commission. Luxembourg: Office for Official Publications of the European Communities.

1996. "Nichts mehr als sexuelle und politische Korrektheit? Sexuelle Belästigungsrichtlinien an amerikanischen Hochschulen." In *Peinlich Berührt: Sexuelle Belästigung an Hochschulen,* edited by Hadumod Bussmann and Katrin Lange. Munich: Frauenoffensive.

1994. "'Die Realität sieht in den USA nicht viel besser aus, aber es ist wenigstens ein Thema!' Sexuelle Belästigung an US-amerikanischen und bundesdeutschen Hochschulen im Vergleich." Pp. 82–96 in *Feministische Erbschaften-Feministische Erblasten,* edited by Heike Kahlert and Elke Kleinau. Hamburg: IZHD – Universität Hamburg.

Index

NOTE: Page numbers in *italic type* refer to tables.